I0760192

Praise for

JUDGING MARIA DE MACEDO

"*Judging Maria de Macedo* should be required reading for anyone interested in millenarianism, messianism, Sebastianism, and the role of elite and popular culture in early modern Portugal. As an extra bonus, this study is a most important contribution to better understanding the workings of the Portuguese Inquisition in the mid-seventeenth century. Highly recommended."

—FRANCIS A. DUTRA,
author of *Military Orders in the Early Modern Portuguese World: The Orders of Christ, Santiago, and Avis*

ON FEBRUARY 20, 1665, the Inquisition of Lisbon arrested Maria de Macedo, the wife of a midlevel official of the Portuguese Treasury, after she revealed during a deposition that, since she was ten years old, an enchanted Moor had frequently "taken" her to a magical castle in the legendary land of wonders known as the Hidden Isle. The island paradise was also the home of Sebastian, the former king of Portugal (1557–1578), who had died in battle in Morocco while on crusade in 1578. His body remained undiscovered, however, and many people in seventeenth-century Portugal—including Maria—eagerly awaited his return in glory. In *Judging Maria de Macedo*, Bryan Givens offers a microhistorical examination of Maria's trial before the Inquisition in Lisbon in 1665–1666, providing an intriguing glimpse into Portuguese culture at the time.

Maria's trial record includes a unique piece of evidence: a pamphlet she dictated to her husband fifteen years before her arrest. In the pamphlet, reproduced in its entirety in the book, Maria recounts in considerable detail her "journeys" to the Hidden Isle and her discussions with the people there, King Sebastian in particular. Not all of the components of Maria's vision were messianic in nature or even Christian in origin; her beliefs therefore represent a unique synthesis of disparate cultural elements in play in seventeenth-century Portugal.

Because the pamphlet antedates the Inquisition's involvement in Maria's case, it offers a rare example of a non-elite voice preserved without any mediation from an elite institution such as the Inquisition, as is the case with most early modern judicial records. In addition to analyzing Maria de Macedo's vision, Givens also uses the trial record to gain insight into the values, concerns, and motives of the Inquisitors in their judgment of her unusual case. He thus not only examines separately two important subcultures in early modern Portugal, but also analyzes how they interacted with each other.

Introducing a unique feminine voice from the early modern period, *Judging Maria de Macedo* opens a singular window onto seventeenth-century Portuguese culture.

Stephen Davis, Pepperdine University

BRYAN GIVENS is an assistant professor of history at Pepperdine University in Malibu, California.

Judging Maria de Macedo

Judging Maria de Macedo

A Female Visionary and the Inquisition in Early Modern Portugal

Bryan Givens

Louisiana State University Press
Baton Rouge

Published by Louisiana State University Press

Manufactured in the United States of America
First printing

Designer: Michelle A. Neustrom
Typeface: Quadraat
Typesetter: Thomson Digital
Printer: McNaughton & Gunn, Inc.
Binder: John H. Dekker & Sons

Portions of chapters 1, 2, and 6 first appeared, in somewhat different form, as "The St. Paul of Sebastianism: Tracing the Millenarian Legacy of Dom João de Castro," *Portuguese Studies Review* 17:1 (2009–10): 1–20, and are reprinted by permission. Portions of chapters 1 and 2 first appeared, in somewhat different form, in "Sebastianism in Theory and in Practice in Early Modern Portugal," in *Braudel Revisited: The Mediterranean World, 1600–1800*, ed. Gabriel Piterberg, Teófilo F. Ruiz, and Geoffrey Symcox (Toronto: University of Toronto Press, 2010) and are reprinted by permission.

Library of Congress Cataloging-in-Publication Data

Givens, Bryan, 1971–
Judging Maria de Macedo : a female visionary and the Inquisition in early modern Portugal / Bryan Givens.
p. cm.
Includes bibliographical references and index.
ISBN 978-0-8071-3702-4 (cloth : alk. paper)
1. De Macedo, Maria, b. ca. 1623–1625. 2. Inquisition—Portugal—History. 3. Sebastião, King of Portugal, 1554–1578—Influence. 4. Portugal—Church history. 5. Sebastianism. I. Title.
BX4705.D29435G58 2010
272'.2092—dc22
[B]

2010019457

The paper in this book meets the guidelines for permanence and durability of the Committee on Production Guidelines for Book Longevity of the Council on Library Resources. ♾

CONTENTS

PREFACE

As you know, Your Holiness, little in this life turns out as we expect.
—Cardinal Altamirano to the Pope, in *The Mission* (1986)

As is, I suppose, the case with many manuscripts, this project began as something quite different. When I first arrived in Lisbon in September 2001, I would never have guessed that my research would lead me to microhistory. I had originally intended to seek an answer to a fairly basic sociopolitical question: During the period of Hapsburg control of Portugal, had the Portuguese Inquisition prosecuted the nationalistic (if I may use that term loosely) believers in the lost king Sebastian? All the indicators—the Inquisition's general suspicion of messianic movements and visionaries, its suspicion of anything with *converso* roots, and its generally favorable attitude toward the continued union with Spain—seemed to favor a policy of prosecution. I had hoped that, once I had examined the specific cases of this seemingly inevitable campaign against the *sebastianistas*, I would be able to use those records to create a preliminary sketch of the social composition of the *sebastianista* movement, an issue that has yet to be addressed in a systematic manner.

It was at this point, though, that the original project broke down because, after I reviewed many pages of inquisitorial correspondence and many case files, it seemed clear that the Inquisition had not conducted an organized campaign of prosecution against the *sebastianistas* during the Hapsburg period. Since I could find no evidence explaining the Inquisition's lack of interest in the *sebastianistas*, I was faced with the prospect of trying to salvage some project that was possible to complete in the remaining time of my Fulbright grant. While reading Jacqueline Hermann's *No reino do desejado*, I ran across the case of Maria de Macedo. Although I now take issue with certain aspects of Hermann's understanding of the case, I was intrigued by the brief summary she gave of it and decided to read the original case for myself. I was immediately struck by the level of detail and elaboration in Maria de Macedo's story and thought the pamphlet she had dictated to her husband about her experiences was ripe for examination by someone using microhistorical techniques. It did not take me long to decide to take on that project. I have continued to wrestle with the issues ever since, in the intervening time refining my analysis and revising my work in the hope of making it what a study of this subject should be.

I think the study that follows, for all its imperfections, does shed real light on the messianic phenomenon of Sebastianism, and popular beliefs more generally, in early modern Portugal. Ironically, Maria de Macedo's case also provided some clues related to the question of why the Portuguese Inquisition did not systematically prosecute the *sebastianistas*. This study is an attempt to understand the mental world of Maria de Macedo, and the mental world of her inquisitorial judges, through a close examination of her vision and her trial; it will be up to the reader to decide whether that attempt has been successful.

There are many people who deserve thanks for their help and support in the long years it has taken to bring this project to fruition. First, I want to thank Geoffrey Symcox, Carlo Ginzburg, John Dagenais, and especially Teo Ruiz, whose continued support for and interest in this project I deeply appreciate.

Second, I wish to express my appreciation both to the Fulbright Program and to the Commissão Cultural Luso-Americana in Lisbon, which provided funding for the initial phase of my research for this book. I am also grateful to the Office of the Dean of Research at Pepperdine University for funding that made possible the second round of research in Lisbon in the summer of 2006.

I would be remiss if I did not thank the staff members at the Arquivo Nacional da Torre do Tombo and at the Biblioteca Nacional de Lisboa for the very practical aid they provided that allowed me to conduct research in their institutions. And I am grateful to the University of Toronto Press and the *Portuguese Studies Review* for their cooperation in allowing me to reprint previously published material that appears in chapters 1, 2, and 6 in this book.

Finally, I would like to thank my friends and family, who have supported me through this long process.

Judging Maria de Macedo

INTRODUCTION
A Journey to Another World

On February 20, 1665, Maria de Macedo, the wife of a midlevel official of the Portuguese Treasury, was arrested by the Inquisition of Lisbon, having just given what was to become the first of many depositions before the Holy Office. In that deposition, she did not hesitate to reveal that, from the age of ten, she had had a series of visions or, more properly, visitations from inhabitants of a "Hidden Isle." Eventually, she had traveled to the island, where she met such illustrious figures as King Arthur, the prophet Elijah, and St. John the Evangelist. More important, she claimed to have met Sebastian, the crusading Portuguese king who had been lost in Morocco in 1578 and whose return in glory was eagerly awaited by many in seventeenth-century Portugal.

The deposition that took place on February 20 was not the first time the Inquisition had heard about the claims of Maria de Macedo. The testimony of six previous witnesses, mostly Jesuits from the Chiado area of Lisbon, had already convinced the inquisitors of Lisbon that Maria de Macedo's activities needed to be investigated more fully in order to prevent a scandal among the faithful. More than the testimony of the witnesses, it was the evidence provided by a small pamphlet dictated by Maria and written down by her husband, Feliciano Machado, that confirmed to the inquisitors that they might have a problem on their hands. By the time it came to the attention of the Holy Office, the pamphlet, which recounted in detail Maria de Macedo's travels to the Hidden Isle in her own words, was already being copied by sympathetic Jesuits and was being "commonly spoken about" in Lisbon, according to one witness.[1]

It is the fact that this pamphlet tells Maria's story in such detail and in her own words that makes it such a valuable artifact of a particular strain of Portuguese popular culture in the seventeenth century. In recent years, the appreciation of the potential of inquisitorial records as historical sources has grown dramatically, and many notable scholars, such as Carlo Ginzburg in *The Cheese and the Worms* and *The Night Battles*, Emmanuel LeRoy Ladurie in *Montaillou*, and Jaime Contreras in *Sotos contra Riquelmes*, have used inquisitorial sources as evidential bases for deeper understandings of often overlooked historical questions, whether popular beliefs, cultural practices, or the antagonisms of local clan networks.[2] In all these examples, the authors used the information collected by the inquisitors as evidence for their studies, but they also asked questions beyond those solicited by the officials of the Holy Office in order to gain the understanding they sought. As these studies demonstrate, it is only when the information gathered by the inquisitors is used to answer questions they never asked that inquisitorial records reach their true potential as historical sources.

A word of caution is always in order when using documents from the Inquisition as sources. While it has been shown that inquisitorial records are often the only documentary sources of information for many non-elite individuals in the past, there remains the concern that, by using inquisitorial records of these subaltern figures, we only perpetuate the inquisitors' views of them. Thus, inquisitorial bias could become the prism through which we understand popular figures, simply because those records are the only sources available with which to document their lives at all. However, in the case of the prosecution of Maria de Macedo we have a unique resource that minimizes the problems of inquisitorial bias: the pamphlet. Because the pamphlet was dictated by Maria to her husband (who added some comments of his own), it provides a unique opportunity to hear the voice of a non-elite figure without having to worry about mediation of the message by the Inquisition or its officials.

The pamphlet has another important characteristic besides its authenticity, and that is its level of elaboration. The pamphlet, which is reproduced in its entirety in the body of this study, recounts in considerable detail Maria de Macedo's journeys to the Hidden Isle and her discussions with the people there and, in particular, with King Sebastian. However, much in the same way that orthodox Sebastianism—the belief that Sebastian would one day return to Portugal and lead it to worldwide dominance—used elements from several apocalyptic traditions, so Maria de Macedo's vision of the Hidden Isle drew on elements from several different legendary traditions. Not all of these ingredients were messianic in nature or even Christian in origin, and so her vision represents a unique synthesis of disparate cultural elements in play in seventeenth-century Portugal. Religion, economics, and politics are discussed, or perhaps I should say revealed, in the course of her visions, and so they provide us with a series of snapshots of the cultural values of her day.

So, given that we have a source, which because of its unusual origins and nature provides us with some exceptional possibilities for interpretation, what shall we do with it? The case has been studied by scholars before—João Lúcio de Azevedo mentions it with a brief paragraph in his 1918 classic, *A evolução do sebastianismo*; Jacqueline Hermann spends around twenty pages on the case in *No reino do desejado* (1998); and, more recently, Mark Emerson Cooper dedicated two chapters of his dissertation, "Messianic Expectation and Collective Myth Formation: Prophecy, Society, and Imagination in Early Modern Portugal" (2004), to an examination of the case of Maria de Macedo.[3] None of these studies are systematic microhistories of the trial or vision, however; this study will provide that kind of detailed analysis of the case.

Therefore, this study will approach the pamphlet dictated by Maria de Macedo, along with her testimony and the testimony of others recorded by the Inquisition in her case file (*processo* in Portuguese), as artifacts—relics, if you will—which will provide us with unique windows on the popular, or better, non-elite, culture of seventeenth-century Portugal. As will be shown later, Maria de Macedo did not come from the lower levels of society, but neither did she come from the upper echelons. Her background was that of a prosperous artisan family, and she married a midlevel government functionary; all the indicators are that she was from the middling sorts of early modern Portugal. She was neither pristinely popular nor elite, and as we will see, she was influenced by cultural imperatives from both above and below. Given this fact, Maria de Macedo's visions are a crossroads of differing, and even opposing, cultural trends, and it is this intersection that makes her visions so valuable to historians today. They represent points of contact, or perhaps even fields of battle, between these trends, and we can see how the resulting conflicts were worked out in practice, at least in this single, very concrete case.

Since I have decided to approach the pamphlet and the *processo* as artifacts of cultural values, I will study them in a manner analogous to that used by appraisers of antiquities or artwork. This will entail a careful examination of minute details to determine, as far as is possible, the origin, nature, and function of the features that appear in the vision, and we will seek answers in these documents to questions her inquisitorial interrogators never asked and were not interested in. For example, why were certain elements of the traditions available to her included in her narrative, why were others excluded, and what do those choices tell us about the meaning of her story as a whole? What were the sources of the elements that she had at her disposal to create her portrait of an idealized land and an idealized king? The range of her sources was greater than might first be guessed. But answering these questions will require careful investigation, first of the origins of the elements within her vision and, once they have been ascertained, then of the ways in which those elements are integrated into a coherent (though not always intellectually rational) whole.

In many ways, this approach of determined sleuth work is similar to that undertaken by Carlo Ginzburg in *The Cheese and the Worms*, though the similarities are methodological rather than substantive. Tracing the origins and connections of the protagonists' beliefs is the core of both studies, but where Menocchio's sources were literary and philosophical texts that he had read and misread, the sources for Maria de Macedo's beliefs about the Hidden Isle and King Sebastian were largely oral or were at least received by Maria via oral transmission. Menocchio's suspect views were abstract and philosophical in nature and proceeded from a conscious working and reworking of the beliefs he had read about into a more or less coherent cosmological system. In contrast, Maria de Macedo's thoughts on the Hidden Isle and its Hidden King were concrete and imagistic in nature and came about because of a subconscious elaboration of elements from various legends and traditions she had heard during the course of her life. The results were not systematic, and at times they were even self-contradictory, as the inquisitors were keen to notice. It should be kept in mind that Maria never claimed that what she saw were visions in the classical sense; she believed that she actually traveled to the Hidden Isle—without knowing exactly how—and *lived* what she told others about. Reasoning from specific propositions was the basis of Menocchio's conclusions; experience (albeit perceived experience in this case) was the source of Maria's claims.

Another important difference between the two studies is that Menocchio's cosmology was virtually unique, given his time and place; the fact that Maria de Macedo believed that Sebastian was alive on the Hidden Isle and would one day return to Portugal was not exceptional at all. Some additional comments on this issue need to be made. If it were the case that Maria de Macedo's visions were only another example of popular *sebastianismo*, they would retain some degree of historical interest but would probably not merit a study of this scope. However, her visions did not merely tap into the common millenarian legends of her day; they drew—consciously or unconsciously—on many other legendary sources and cultural imperatives. The inquisitors prove this point by stating, in their final decision of the case, that "if it were simply a matter of the prisoner affirming what the *sebastianistas* affirm, then this matter would not fall under the jurisdiction of the Holy Office."[4] It was the other elements of her message that were to eventually lead to her conviction. Against a background of Sebastianism, many of her other core values are revealed; her faith in Sebastian's return was deeply held, but it also provided a framework within which she could express her thoughts on other issues. It is this combination of elements that gives her trial such potential as a window on seventeenth-century Portuguese culture.

Many scholars of the early modern period in Europe have come to the conclusion that, largely impelled by the ideological conflict between Catholics and Protestants, ecclesiastical authorities of all confessions took it upon themselves to bring the populations under their care much closer to the religious norms defined by those same elites.[5] In the Iberian Peninsula, this process had actually begun before Luther's critique of the papacy, though for reasons that were parallel to those given above: the Iberian kingdoms' struggle against the peninsula's religious minorities, first the Jews and the Muslims, and then their nominally converted analogues, the *conversos* and *moriscos*. Wherever and whenever this process took place, the results were largely the same. The proactive attempt to impose elite religious values on the other segments of the population was not confined only to the relatively narrow matter of the doctrines that divided the various confessional polities but encompassed an attempt to regularize faith, morals, and practice more generally.

This leads us to the question of the broader historical significance of Maria de Macedo's trial. Put bluntly, what can we learn from her case? Certainly, her trial can serve as an example of social disciplining in action and thus form part of a series of focused case studies as advocated by scholars such as Carlo Ginzburg and Wolfgang Reinhard as a means to assess the efficacy of social disciplining in the early modern period.[6] Along those lines, there have been a number of excellent focused studies produced in recent years on the related issues of social disciplining and popular culture in the early modern period, such as Kagan's *Lucretia's Dreams* (1990), Nalle's *Mad for God* (2001), Schutte's *Aspiring Saints* (2001), and, more recently, Keitt's *Inventing the Sacred* (2005), just to name a few that have influenced my own thinking. I hope that this work will find its place among these studies and others in adding to our comprehension of how these realities were understood and experienced by those who actually lived in baroque Europe.

Even beyond being one of a series of case studies that, cumulatively, add to our understanding of early modern culture, the examination of a single, non-elite individual such as Maria can give us insight into the broader historical realities of her day. Edoardo Grendi, in his defense of microhistory as a valid historical methodology, highlighted the statistical concept of the "normal exception." Generally speaking, only those non-elite individuals who became enmeshed in the machinery of early modern justice—criminals, heretics, witches—left enough traces of their beliefs and practices to become the subjects of microhistorical analysis, but the beliefs and practices of such individuals were, by definition, exceptional.[7]

However, Ginzburg and Carlo Poni build on this concept by noting that behavior considered exceptional or even deviant by ecclesiastical or judicial authorities might have been quite representative of the behaviors and the beliefs of the defendant's own social milieu.[8] I believe that this was true in the case of Maria de Macedo. While she was ultimately punished by the Holy Office for her visions, it is doubtful that any of the elements found in her account would have been considered unique by the people with whom she normally associated. Of the witnesses who testified in her case, it was only those who were closely associated with the Inquisition who rejected her claims outright; the other witnesses, while some had questions about her visions, did not find their content fundamentally strange or beyond their understanding. Thus, Maria de Macedo was a normal exception in the sense that she failed to meet the standards of her inquisitorial judges but was quite representative of the beliefs of many of her contemporaries.

The very fact that other legends and popular traditions were incorporated into her narrative leads to another reason that Maria de Macedo's case is worthy of study. Because her narrative was a meeting place of so many different cultural trends—both popular and elite—it is an excellent case study not only of cultural imposition (as stated above) but also of cultural interaction, thus giving us some insight into how each of those trends was accepted, rejected, or modified by at least one of its intended recipients. While the evidence of the attempt by the inquisitorial elites to bring Maria de Macedo back to the norms of institutional Catholicism will be clear for all to see, one should not let the obviousness of that attempt blind one to fact that Maria did retain some degree of agency in the matter. As I will demonstrate, she had access to a variety of popular and elite traditions, and she chose some elements, while rejecting others, from those traditions to construct her vision of an idealized world. The principal significance of this fact is that those choices were made and were made by Maria herself, even if only at a subconscious level. It should also be noted, in connection to concept of normal exception given above, that the syncretistic approach followed by Maria in the construction of her vision was *highly typical* of the approach followed by the *sebastianistas* generally, as even a cursory examination of their rather eclectic collections of prophetic texts proves.

The trial of Maria de Macedo is not merely a case study of cultural interaction and conflict in general, however; it is a case study that provides us with clues for a greater understanding of a very specific belief system in early modern Portugal: Sebastianism. Sebastianism is itself intimately connected to the broader Western tradition of messianism. In his classic work *The Pursuit of the Millennium*, Norman Cohn describes the careers of two messianic pretenders: the pseudo-Baldwin and the pseudo-Frederick, of Flanders and the German Empire, respectively, during the thirteenth century. There are remarkable structural similarities in the two stories: a succession crisis leading to domination by a foreign power or internal instability; the appearance of a penitential hermit; the revelation that the hermit was a ruler lost while on crusade or in the performance of God's work; the spreading rumor and his proclamation as king; his exposure as an impostor; the inevitable execution; and his unquestioning support by the poor, especially among urban workers.[9] In this study, I will demonstrate that all these features also appear in the history of the Prisoner of Venice, who was widely accepted as Sebastian, four centuries later in Portugal. It strains credulity to think that the similarities found in the stories were simply the result of coincidence. The common tropes found in these accounts are surely evidence of a deeper pattern, an underlying set of cultural expectations that were well diffused in western Europe, over a period of centuries and across a wide geographic area.

What were these underlying expectations? The best way to answer that question is to go back to what was almost certainly the original pattern for all these stories: the Byzantine legend of the Last World Emperor derived from the fourth-century prophecies of the Tiburtine Sybil. According to those prophecies, the emperor Constans would reappear after he was presumed to be dead, rescuing the harried Roman Empire from the barbarian hordes and ruling justly until the advent of the Antichrist. This tradition was decisively modified by the Muslim invasions of Byzantium's eastern provinces, and from the seventh century onward, all candidates for the role of the World Emperor would have to defeat the forces of Islam and retake the Holy Land.[10] The elements of exterior threat, interior corruption and injustice, and the providential hiding and then revelation of God's chosen leader appear in all the traditions and give us important clues in understanding the underlying causes of them all.

It is certainly not surprising that, during times of intense political insecurity and war, or in times when corruption and injustice are perceived to be endemic and beyond human efforts to reform, many people look to a supernatural remedy for society's ills in the form of a divinely chosen leader. This is political messianism in its classic form. The fact that the core of the would-be messiahs' support came from the popular classes, especially poor, urban artisans, indicates that there was a class element to these movements, though this should not be construed in an overly doctrinaire sense. Of course, it is hardly novel to say that messianism largely has its roots in and draws its strength from social, political, and economic discontents and that, since these discontents disproportionately affect the poorer classes of society, those classes will also provide the bulk of the followers for any messianic figure.[11] This observation finds a parallel in the closely related phenomenon of royal pretenders, as studied by Yves-Marie Bercé, who notes that "the demand for an impossible king is not just the explosion of fantasy, but the crystallization of a very long time of frustrations and lamentations and, above all, of an obstinate and irrational hope."[12]

This is where a case like that of Maria de Macedo can play yet another role. It should be clear that the understanding of the root causes of widespread historical phenomena can be gained only by following a comparative approach. It is an inductive approach that moves from the particulars to the general and can shed light on the underlying realities of broad historical trends that are, in reality, always circumscribed in both time and place. In the present study, an understanding of messianism in general can help us understand the particular phenomenon of Sebastianism. This is the essence of the comparative, synthetic approach to history and should be obvious and beyond dispute. However, the study of individual historical actors, such as Maria de Macedo, can provide synthetic analyses with a greater degree of nuance and specificity grounded in real cases. So if a comparative analysis of European messianism can help us understand Maria de Macedo and her visions, her visions can also help us understand *sebastianismo* and, to a lesser degree, European messianism more generally as cultural phenomena.

While the *processo* of Maria de Macedo is about her, it is not a record of her alone. It also provides us with a rare glimpse of the reception of Maria de Macedo's claims by her contemporaries. Their acceptance, rejection, or modification of Maria's stories can tell us more about the culture of seventeenth-century Portugal than what we could gain by merely looking at her vision by itself. Not only did Maria claim to have visited the Hidden Isle, but she told others about it as well. And this advance into the realm of reception opens up yet another field of study: the inquisitor's reception, or rather rejection, of Maria de Macedo's claims. I have already stated that the vision—as documented by the pamphlet and the relevant parts of the trial record—is an artifact of the cultural values of seventeenth-century Portugal, and this is certainly true. However, an inquisitorial *processo* was not simply a collection of depositions from witnesses or defendants relating to the issues being tried; it was also a collection of documents in which the inquisitors communicated among themselves about the issues involved in the case, and this is certainly true in Maria de Macedo's trial record. So Inquisição de Lisboa, Processo 4404—in which the copies of the pamphlet were kept as evidence—is not merely an artifact of the popular (or middle-class) culture of early modern Portugal; it is an artifact of the culture of the Inquisition as well. It is true that the vision narrated by Maria de Macedo embodied several conflicting cultural trends; it should be even clearer that a trial by the Inquisition is also a setting for (if not the embodiment of) conflict between different cultural systems. Following the same approach of close attention to small details, we will use the trial record to gain a deeper understanding of the values, concerns, and motives of the Inquisition in this case and during the middle decades of the seventeenth century.

Finally, we will not only examine two important subcultures in early modern Portugal on their own terms but also analyze how they interacted with each other. This study of their interaction will provide us with a number of insights into seventeenth-century Portuguese culture, the four most important of which

I will specify here. First, this examination of the vision and trial of Maria de Macedo will flesh out many of the values underlying the *sebastianista* legend in the seventeenth century and help explain its rather curious resilience and longevity as a messianic myth. Second, this longevity was due, in part, to the relative indifference of the Inquisition to Sebastianism, and the trial record provides us with some important clues about the nature of the Holy Office's attitude toward the *sebastianista* legend. Third, the trial of Maria de Macedo, while certainly an artifact of the conflict between two belief systems, also helps demonstrate the extent to which the ecclesiastical elite of baroque Portugal, as exemplified by the Inquisition, was successful in disseminating (or imposing, if you prefer) the values of the Tridentine Church among the other segments of Portuguese society in the seventeenth century. The fourth conclusion is, perhaps, the most surprising: the trial of Maria de Macedo and her mental world was not ultimately decided on the basis of raw power. While the inequality of power between the two parties in the trial should never be forgotten, this study will demonstrate that the interaction between Maria and her inquisitorial judges, including the final disposition of the case, was determined by the discrete and distinct sets of values by which each of the parties understood and identified themselves as Christians. It is important to note that the actions of both the inquisitors and Maria de Macedo, who retained more agency in her unenviable situation than one might first suppose, were determined by this self-identification. The powerful won in this situation, as they usually do, but the exercise of that power, as we will see, was not unrestrained by other, deeply held values.

I

The Millenarian Background

‹ 1 ›

THE MILLENARIAN TRADITION IN EARLY MODERN PORTUGAL

All Western prophetic traditions begin with the messianic beliefs of the Jews and the early Christians. Impelled by the despair of national disaster and the hope for national liberation, the Jewish prophets predicted the coming of an Anointed One, the Messiah, who, in a time of cosmic struggle between good and evil, would come with the power of God to defeat the enemies of the Jews and redeem them from exile. From the Babylonian Captivity through the Macabbean revolt and to the period of Roman rule, this apocalyptic worldview helped the Jews retain their distinctive identity in the midst of a hostile world. Similarly, the writings of the Old Testament prophets and the visions of Saint John recounted in the Apocalypse helped to sustain the faith of the newborn Christian movement during the waves of persecution to which it was subjected. In imagery inspired by Daniel, the Apocalypse predicted that the saints would face the severest of all persecutions before Christ returned to defeat the forces of Satan and bring a thousand-year reign of peace to the earth. Its eschatological program was so dramatic that it became the core of all later Christian speculation about the end times, though there was little agreement as to its precise interpretation.

With the institutionalization of Christianity as the official religion of the empire under Constantine and Theodosius, however, many of the factors that had driven the early hope for the end times began to fade, at least among the leaders of the church. Allegorical interpretation of scripture had long been practiced by the Christians, and methods were sought for interpreting the Apocalypse that would avoid the radical conclusions of some of the heretical groups of the day. The major figure in this allegorizing trend was Saint Augustine of Hippo. He developed a chronology of world history based on the six days of creation, which were not taken to be literal but rather as types for seven different ages in world history. He identified the age he lived in as the sixth day/age, which would be followed by a period of persecution under the Antichrist and then by the Second Advent before a seventh day of Sabbath rest in eternity. Significantly, he identified the millennium of the Apocalypse as the sixth day/age—that is, the Church Age—as well. So the time of peace and prosperity that had been prophesied was not to be hoped for literally at some future date but rather to be accepted as allegorical for the here-and-now Age of the Church.[1] It was Augustine's allegorical, amillennial interpretation of the Apocalypse that would dominate eschatological speculations in the West well into the Middle Ages.

Despite the discouragement of chiliastic interpretations at the official level, such views retained considerable discursive power among the broader mass of Christians in the Latin West. Despite the preference for allegorical interpretations among the upper levels of the clergy, the fact that dramatic eschatological narratives such as those found in the books of the Hebrew prophets and the Apocalypse were universally accepted as scripture—and therefore normative—did a great deal to nurture and sustain apocalyptic expectations among the lower clergy and their parishioners throughout the medieval period. These narratives served not only to legitimate millennial hopes in the first place but also provided many of the details of the eschatological schemata that were worked and reworked as Augustine's interpretations were more and more frequently questioned toward the end of the first millennium of the Christian Era.

It was the apocalyptic views of a late twelfth-century Calabrian abbot, Joachim of Fiore, and his disciples that were to have the most direct influence on the evolution of Portuguese millenarianism, however. As revealed in his masterwork, the *Liber concordie novi ac veteris testamenti*, Joachim developed a complex interpretation of the whole of history based on the prophetic books of the Bible. The most famous element of his eschatology was the belief that history was divided into three "Statuses," each governed by a member of the Trinity and each moving to a higher fulfillment of God's will on earth, with the final status, that of the Holy Spirit, being a time of peace, prosperity, and full-time contemplation of God, a view of history that would be transmitted to later generations only in modified form.[2]

In the middle years of the thirteenth century, Joachimite ideas were eagerly accepted by members of the newly formed Franciscan Order, especially by the Spirituals among them. The Spirituals' belief that Saint Francis was such a unique figure that he represented a decisive turning point in human history accorded well with Joachim's belief that a new status, now of the Spirit rather than the Son, was soon to come about on earth. John of Parma, who served as general of the order from 1247 to 1257, helped fuse these strands into a coherent eschatological view, and many Spirituals saw in themselves the fulfillment of Joachim's prophecy of a new mendicant order of spiritual men being founded before the consummation of the ages.[3] It was one of John of Parma's companions, Gerard de Borgo San Donnino, who provided a more revolutionary reading of Joachim's schema, though. In his *Liber introductorius*, written around 1254, he dismissed the outward church, led by a corrupt papacy, as Babylon and announced that the Third Age, the Age of the Spirit, was soon to come. During the third age, he stated, the Eternal Evangel would be proclaimed, superseding both the law (of the Father) and the gospel (of the Son) and bringing about a complete revolution of the human order on earth. The furor provoked by these claims was such that John of Parma was deposed, Gerard was condemned, and Joachim's reputation was damaged, causing him to have a heterodox reputation among some members of the clergy for centuries to come.

The hostility of the some churchmen toward Joachimism, especially as interpreted by the Spirituals, in those years did little to dampen the enthusiasm of more moderate Franciscans for Joachim's eschatology, and it was they who were to spread it far beyond its Italian homeland. One of the important early Joachimites in Iberia was Arnold of Villanueva (1238–1316), who was a zealous expositor of Joachim's thought and a close confidant of Jaume II of Aragon.[4] Manuel J. Gandra, in his study of Joachimism in Portugal, notes that Arnold also had contact with Queen Isabel of Portugal and shared his views of eschatology with her. Gandra also documents the profound influence that the Franciscans, patronized by the monarchy, had in Portugal during the fourteenth and fifteenth centuries, particularly in the dissemination of the Joachimite ideas. While he did not find evidence for any great production of Joachimite texts in Portugal during the period, he does make a convincing case for the widespread diffusion of Joachimite ideas by examining other forms of literature such as poetry, correspondence, and even iconography.[5] It is certain that Joachimism had a profound influence on the Avis dynasty after it came to power in 1385. The Avis saw in Joachimism, which was advocated first by the Franciscans and later by the Jesuits, both a prophetic incentive for and a prophetic legitimization of the crusading and empire-building policies they followed throughout the fifteenth century.[6] Taken together with the Miracle of Ourique, which will be discussed below, Joachimism led many of the Avis rulers to see themselves and their kingdom as providentially chosen to bring about the conversion of the world by conquest and evangelization.[7] This conviction was most clearly demonstrated in the aggressive policies of Manuel I in North Africa in the early decades of the sixteenth century.

The Joachimite belief in a future eschatological ruler derived largely from the Byzantine tradition of the *restitutor mundi*, an emperor who would bring justice, security, and prosperity to the harried Roman Empire, and later, who would push back the forces of an advancing Islam.[8] This figure took on some particular characteristics in the Iberian kingdoms of the late medieval period. Given Iberia's unique position (within western Europe) as a frontier with Islam and the long (and legendary) history of the Reconquest, it should not be surprising that Iberians saw the prophesied ruler's principal role as the leader of a decisive, final crusade against Islam.[9] Another element was also to make the Iberian permutation of the legend unique: an emphasis on the hidden-ness of the coming king, based on prophecies attributed to the seventh-century Iberian bishop Saint Isidore. The reasons for the inclusion of this element remain unclear, but whatever its origin, the belief that the coming king would also be hidden for a time had become standard in the Iberian kingdoms by the 1480s at the latest.

After the conquest of Granada in 1492, many saw Ferdinand the Catholic as the Hidden One (El Encubierto) of promise, a belief he did nothing to discourage. Elites were not the only ones to use eschatological discourse to further a political agenda, however. An undercurrent of Spiritual radicalism can be seen thirty years later, in the 1520s, with the outbreak of the revolutionary *germanías* in Valencia. Against the authority of Charles V, the Encubierto of Valencia—Enrique Manrique de Ribera—rose to prominence within the *agermanado* movement, and there can be no doubt that his views were radical: he preached the destruction of the nobility and the end to all distinctions of wealth.[10] This parallel use of messianism for elitist and populist purposes was to continue in Iberia throughout the sixteenth and seventeenth centuries.

Portuguese millenarianism was also profoundly influenced by the native legend of Ourique. As the story had evolved by the sixteenth century, Dom Afonso Henriques, before engaging the armies of five Moorish kings at Ourique on July 25, 1139, saw a vision of the Crucified Christ, who assured him that he would win the coming battle and go on to found a kingdom that would spread the gospel to the ends of the earth. And God's favor would never be withdrawn for this new kingdom, except for a brief period of testing during the reign of the sixteenth king. The kingdom's coat of arms was also revealed: it would be a cross of five shields, representing the five wounds of Christ, and within the shields, thirty coins symbolizing the price for which Christ had been sold. Hearing of this divine message, Afonso's men proclaimed him king before going on to defeat the "infinite thousands" of the Moorish army.[11]

Certainly, on July 25, 1139, Dom Afonso Henriques did defeat a numerically superior army of Moors at Ourique and so was proclaimed king of Portugal. Beyond those simple facts, very little else is known with any certainty. According to an excellent short study by Luís Filipe Lindley Cintra, the process of mythification had already begun by the middle of the fourteenth century, with the association between Ourique and Portugal's coat of arms by then already well established. By the early fifteenth century, the vision of the Crucified Christ had become part of the story as well. Duarte Galvão's *Crónica de D. Afonso Henriques*, which was written in 1505, became the definitive version of the legend, adding the predictions that Afonso's kingdom would spread the gospel to the ends of the earth and that there would be a time of testing during the reign of the sixteenth king.[12]

Along with the preaching of Joachimism by the Franciscans, which took place at the same time the story of Ourique was coming into its final form, the legend helped create a climate of eschatological expectation in Portugal, in which God would intervene in human history on behalf of the Portuguese. It also provided a discourse, so to speak, of national destiny: no matter how grim the situation seemed for Portugal, the promises made by Christ to Dom Afonso Henriques at Ourique provided an essential touchstone of hope to the Portuguese psyche. The story played an important role in mobilizing the Portuguese against Castile during the succession crisis of 1383–85, and throughout the sixteenth and seventeenth centuries, writers, interpreters, and apologists cited Ourique as the foundational moment by which subsequent events, especially tribulations, were to be interpreted.[13] Thus, the legend became a foundation of Portuguese national identity in the early modern period, a founding myth that gave the Portuguese proof of both the divine establishment of and divine purpose for their kingdom. As such, it is the first element in the evolution of Sebastianism that can be described as exclusively Portuguese.

All these diverse strands of messianic belief were brought together for the first time to form an independent and distinctively Portuguese eschatological tradition in the 1530s when Gonçalo Anes (better known simply as Bandarra) wrote a collection of prophetic verses known as the Trovas. In them, he predicted the coming of a Portuguese king who would convert the Jews to Christianity, destroy the Turks, and bring universal peace to the earth. Born around 1500, Bandarra was a moderately prosperous shoemaker from the village of Trancoso in northern Portugal; he was both literate and gifted with an amazing memory that he used to learn long passages of scripture and prophecy by heart.[14] For a time, he had access to a vernacular Bible, and the Trovas show the influence of Joachim, the pseudo-Isidore, and the legend of Ourique. Bandarra was also well known and well respected in *converso* circles in Trancoso and Lisbon, a fact that provides an important clue as to the origins of his prophetic views. The early decades of the sixteenth century were a time of particularly intense *converso* messianism in Portugal, as the New Christian community drew on its Jewish roots to find a source of hope in a time of violent persecution by the newly established Inquisition. Unsurprisingly, the Trovas circulated widely, both orally and in written form, in *converso* circles, and it is certain that both Bandarra and his prophecies were affected by the environment of prophetic expectation in which he lived.[15]

It was his proximity to the *converso* community that was eventually to lead to Bandarra's prosecution by the Inquisition. The Trovas first came to the attention of the Holy Office in 1540, while it was investigating a New Christian tailor from Setubal, Luis Dias, who began to claim that he was the Messiah sometime around 1535. His claims quickly spread through the *converso* community, which made his discovery by the Inquisition inevitable.[16] Dias came to the notice of the senior inquisitor of the Lisbon tribunal, Dr. João de Melo, and in 1540, after a long and thorough investigation, Dias was burned as an impenitent Judaizer. The whole episode scandalized the Inquisition and its supporters, and the readiness with which many New Christians accepted Dias as Messiah only confirmed their suspicions about the *conversos'* lack of commitment to Catholicism. Bandarra's connection to the case is revealed in documentation dated January 14, 1538, where it states that de Melo first heard from a *converso* suspect about "verses and questions from a cobbler in Trancoso that caused great harm and tumult in this city [Lisbon]." Subsequent questioning revealed that Gonçalo Anes was well known among the *converso* community in the capital as a prophet. By May 31, 1541, de Melo had received more confirmation of Bandarra's activities while investigating the statements of some *conversos* from the area around Trancoso.[17] Perhaps fearing another New Christian messiah in the making, the zealous de Melo outdid himself that summer, and by September 18, Gonçalo Anes had been arrested, imprisoned in Lisbon, and was ready for sentencing.

According to the record of his trial, Bandarra was condemned as "being a friend of novelties and, with them, *causing tumult among the New Christians*, writing verses that, for lack of understanding, are understood in other ways and not according to his intention, by giving other interpretations of many scriptural authorities and answers to similar questions without training."[18] Essentially, the charge was stirring up the New Christians, unintentionally according to the *processo*, by means of unauthorized and ill-conceived interpretations of biblical prophecy. Given the nervousness felt by the inquisitors, and by de Melo in particular, in wrapping up the matter of the Messiah of Setubal, as well as the general suspicion of *conversos* in those tense years, it is hardly surprising that they moved quickly to deal with what threatened to be the source of fresh hopes for a New Christian messiah. With that said, Bandarra's punishment was light, merely consisting of a public abjuration of the Trovas and an oath not to write any more or discuss the ones he had written. Bandarra complied with his punishment and duly abjured his errors publicly in the auto-da-fé held in Lisbon on October 23, 1541. It was also announced then that anyone possessing a copy of the Trovas was to present them to the local inquisitor within three days of hearing of or reading the edict.[19] It is clear from this series of events that the Inquisition not only wanted to prevent any new messiahs among the *conversos* but also wished to suppress any document that could undermine its policy of *limpeza de sangue* (purity of blood) by lending prophetic legitimacy to the proposition that the widespread conversion of the Jews was favored by God. Despite the Inquisition's prohibition, the Trovas continued to be circulated, and they quickly became the most important collection of prophetic literature in Portugal during the second half of the sixteenth century.

Bandarra began his prophecies with a scathing criticism of the status quo, condemning the ignorance and moral corruption of the clergy (I–IV) and being especially critical of the influence of money in the church. He went on to level a damning indictment against the corruption of the judicial system by money as well (V–X). In his view, widespread corruption among the elites inevitably led to the oppression of the poor:

> Those who do not have anything to eat
> Make very precious clothes
> They stay poor, leprous
> To make others rich.
> (XVI)

It is clear, however, that Bandarra's intent is more restorationist than revolutionary, for he also complains in *trova* XI that "the lineage of the nobles is exchanged for money." In all, one gets the impression that Bandarra's ideal is that of a return to a precapitalist "old moral economy," when economic (and spiritual) relationships were governed by custom and personal interaction rather than by money and the mysterious workings of an impersonal market. That such a criticism should come from a small-town artisan in the very period that Portugal's Asian commercial empire was reaching its peak of prosperity should not come as a surprise because the increasing monetarization of the Portuguese economy and society threatened to sweep many of the old paternal customs away.

Bandarra's prophetic schema did not end with these criticisms, which would have been echoed by many in Portugal in the early decades of the sixteenth century; he also offered a supernatural cure for the ills of Portuguese society. Bandarra predicted the arrival of a Chief Shepherd who would defend his flock—seen as poor, Catholic, and Portuguese—against the threats of Castilian aggression, commercialization, schism and heresy, and neglect by native leaders, precisely the kinds of concerns we might expect from the kind of pious and patriotic artisan we know Bandarra to have been. The major part of the eschatological program of the Chief Shepherd, as the Hidden King, is a crusade against the forces of Islam, and throughout the Trovas, the Good King is represented as a lion attacking either a swine (the Moors) or a dog (the Turks), both epithets being commonly used in early modern Portugal to describe Muslims. The issue of a crusade against the Moors was a hot issue in Portugal at the time Bandarra was writing because in 1532 João III made the very unpopular decision to pull back from several Portuguese strongpoints in Morocco. The Trovas can only be seen as a criticism of that decision, and given the influence of the Ourique legend on Bandarra, it would probably be fair to say that he viewed the pullback as an unacceptable halt in the divine crusade against the Moors begun by Afonso Henriques. In contrast to his militancy against Islam, Bandarra predicted the peaceful conversion of the Jews to Christianity, which, given Bandarra's intimate connections with the Portuguese *conversos*, should not come as a surprise. To cast the conversion of the Jews as part of God's eschatological plan for the future was to legitimize the conversions of the Jews in the present, though—a point that was all too clear to the inquisitors who tried him and banned his work.

Bandarra's contribution to the development of Portuguese millenarianism was that he wove the disparate strands of non-Portuguese messianic traditions together in such a way that Portugal was viewed as a vehicle specially chosen by God to nurture the Desired One and to bring about God's will on earth. Even though the Trovas were highly contextualized when written (i.e., the issues of monetarization, the *conversos*, and North Africa), because they brought the other traditions together in such a way that favored Portugal, they became the foundational document for all subsequent Portuguese messianism. No future claimant or prophetic interpreter in the Portuguese cultural world, whether sympathetic to Bandarra's goals or not, could afford to ignore him or the Trovas, and each sought to reinterpret him and the Trovas in such a way as to support his favored position.

Even from the time of his birth in 1554, there were some who considered Sebastian the Desired One. According to the treaty that set the terms for the marriage of Infanta Juana Maria of Spain to Principe João of Portugal, if João III died without a direct male heir, Portugal would fall under Hapsburg rule. After the death of Principe João on January 1, 1554, the issue of his widow's impending childbirth became a source of great anxiety throughout the kingdom, and the weeks leading up to Sebastian's birth were a time of great weeping and lamentation, prayers and petitions. When he was born, on January 20, 1554, he was immediately seen as having a special destiny. After all, had he not preserved Portuguese independence just by his birth?[20]

As Sebastian grew older, his behavior tended to confirm such expectations. To many, he was the ideal Christian knight, known from an early age for his piety, his chastity (and indeed, horror of women, interpreted by some as a sign or cause of his rumored impotence), and his zeal for the faith, particularly for his desire to crusade against the Moors.[21] All of these qualities were surely signs of someone worthy to fulfill God's special purposes on earth. Perhaps, though, the most important reason some people saw him as the Hidden One is that they eagerly expected that the promised king would reign during their lifetime, thus making Sebastian the obvious choice. The nearly universal desire for the immediate revelation of the Chosen One was reinforced in Sebastian's case because he happened to be the sixteenth king of Portugal, a significant association for a culture steeped in the details of the legend of Ourique.

Did Sebastian himself believe in these traditions? It is doubtful that he was unaware of them in some form, given their ubiquity. And there is evidence that some of the beliefs were conveyed personally to Sebastian. In a work entitled *Rules for the Education of the King, Dom Sebastian*, Diogo de Teive (1513?–66?), rector of the University of Coimbra, described Sebastian as the "king who was given to us by a miracle,"[22] comparing him to Apollo and Achilles and going on to predict that he would accomplish great deeds. Similarly, António Ferreira, a well-known poet and dramaturge of the mid-sixteenth century, wrote his *Carta a El-Rei D. Sebastião* in praise of Sebastian, comparing him to the sun and the North Star. While these works, and others like them, could simply be seen as typical of the overblown praise given to all Renaissance rulers, there are elements in them that stand out from the standard encomiums of the period. The first is that these poems consistently emphasize the miraculous nature of Sebastian's birth. This claim was repeated frequently, a fact that demonstrates that, in many quarters, the unusual circumstances surrounding that event were viewed in providential terms. The second characteristic of these poems is their continual assertion of Sebastian's glorious destiny in North Africa. João III's decision in 1532 to abandon several Portuguese posts on the Moroccan littoral was not popular, and many people worked to encourage Sebastian to undo his predecessor's mistakes, as these poems demonstrate.[23]

Manuel Gandra has also found several contemporaneous iconographic representations of Sebastian that indicate a providential destiny for the young monarch. In a manuscript dated to 1554–55, the illuminations and the Latin captions refer to the miraculous nature of the birth of the newborn Sebastian. More suggestive is an illumination found in the work *Sucesso do segundo cerco de Diu* by Jerónimo Corte-Real, written in 1574. In the illumination, Sebastian is depicted as wearing a closed, or imperial, crown and is surrounded by twelve knights, perhaps making an analogy between Sebastian and King Arthur. As

Gandra points out, if this was the intent of the depiction, it was not unprecedented because in 1567 Jorge Ferreira de Vasconcelos, in his book *Memorial das proezas de segunda távola redonda*, had declared Sebastian a "New Arthur."[24] The character of Arthur was well known in early modern Portugal, with William Entwhistle demonstrating that the major elements of the Arthurian mythos were widespread in Iberia from the fourteenth century at the latest. I will demonstrate later that the archetypal Arthur influenced Maria de Macedo's vision as well.[25]

Without a doubt, though, the best known of Sebastian's contemporaries who saw a special destiny for him was Luís de Camões, the author of the epic poem *Os Lusíades*. Dedicated to Sebastian, *Os Lusíades* was written in 1572, and while the story that Camões personally declaimed it before Sebastian may be apocryphal, it is certain that the epic was presented to Sebastian and that he read it. António Quadros, following the work of Wilhelm Storck, makes a good case that *Os Lusíades* was not intended as merely an nostalgic panoply of the past glories of Portugal but as a call to war, specifically war against the Moors in North Africa. Besides the epic's obvious classical allusions, it shows a heavy dependence on the legend of Ourique, a fact that lends weight to the view that Camões was urging the young king to complete the crusade of his illustrious forefather, Afonso Henriques, a process that had been stalled by João III's decision in 1532.[26] If this analysis is correct, Camões was representative of the outlook of a significant of part of elite opinion during Sebastian's reign, opinion that saw in Sebastian the opportunity to renew the tradition of crusading expansionism that had characterized the late medieval period.

Did Sebastian himself subscribe to these views? We know he had a particularly romantic and idealistic frame of mind and that, from a very early age, he felt a deep desire to go on crusade for the faith, a desire encouraged by his Jesuit teachers, many of whom were influenced by Joachimist ideas. So it is more than likely that Sebastian was highly gratified by the praise accorded to him by the poets of the realm, and it is unlikely that many of the people who surrounded him were disposed to encourage him to think more soberly. Did Sebastian, therefore, believe himself to be the Hidden One promised by Bandarra and the prophets? Owing to a lack of explicit evidence, that question cannot be answered definitively, but in all likelihood he did. After all, in 1578, Sebastian did go to Morocco to fight the Moor and find his destiny.

Whatever the precise origin of the idea of a crusade in Morocco, we know that it had become a definite plan in Sebastian's mind by 1574. It was during that year that, against the advice of his counselors, Sebastian traveled to Morocco personally, at least to the Portuguese-held port of Tangiers. The trip was a brief one; it did not take him long to see that the forces at his disposal were completely outnumbered by the Moorish armies of Morocco. He returned to Portugal disappointed but determined to return one day with a conquering army. From that time on, the preparations for the *jornada* to Africa became the central focus of the efforts of his government.

Sebastian raised taxes as a matter of course and even got into some trouble with the Inquisition in 1576 by granting the New Christians a ten-year exemption on the confiscation of their possessions in exchange for a sizable donation to the Crown. However, such was the fiscal and demographic weakness of Portugal that Sebastian was not, by 1576, even able to raise 10,000 men for his expedition. More encouraging news came that year in the form of a call for help from Mulay Mohammed, the titular ruler of Morocco, who was then engaged in a civil war against his Turkish-backed uncle, Abd-el-Malek, the sharif of Fez. Sensing that time was of the essence, Sebastian turned to his powerful uncle, Philip II of Spain, for help. In a meeting held at Guadalupe in Spain, Sebastian laid out his plans for a crusade against the Moors in Morocco, which he cast as a necessary move to block Turkish expansion in North Africa. After trying to discourage a war against the Moroccans (who were not doing him any harm), Philip reluctantly agreed to give his nephew 5,000 veteran infantrymen and 50 ships for an expedition to take place the next year, 1577.

By all accounts, Sebastian left the meeting pleased, but Portugal's crushing debt burden and its perennially overstretched finances caused a delay in his plans. The money for the German and Italian mercenaries necessary to strengthen his native levies could not be arranged until 1578. This delay caused a change in Philip's contribution as well: since the war in the Netherlands was continuing to drag on, only 2,000 men and no ships could be sent to help in the crusade. So, after nearly four years' heavy taxation and the extensive granting of judicial and economic concessions to private interests, Sebastian could assemble only a motley army of some 14,000 infantrymen (mostly pikemen), 2,000 cavalry, and a few dozen cannon. It was inauspicious beginning.

However small the force, it truly was the maximum that the cash-strapped Portuguese could muster, and when the army left Lisbon in late June 1578, it was duly sent off with great fanfare and great, if somewhat anxious, hope. The army landed at Arzila on the coast in July, and Sebastian was there joined by

Mulay Mohammed's dubious force of some 2,500 horse and 200 harquebusiers. True to form, the impatient Sebastian had no desire to stay with his army in the relative safety of the coast and ordered his army inland to find and engage the forces of Abd-el-Malek.

In the waning sun of August 3, the two armies sighted each other just outside the small town of Alcazarquivir. It was then that Sebastian should have realized the extent of his folly, for Abd-el-Malek's army was obviously much larger than his own: more than 25,000 cavalrymen, some 3,000 infantrymen, and 1,000 mounted harquebusiers, much more than the Portuguese had at their disposal. Even more ominous, Abd-el-Malek had been able to obtain, through his Turkish patrons, more cannon than Sebastian. A prudent withdrawal to the coast at that point might have saved the army, but it would have meant the end to any hopes for the Portuguese conquest of Morocco for the foreseeable future. It would have also been a blot on the honor and the *reputação* of Portugal and its monarch, as well as a demonstrable lack of faith in the purposes of the Almighty. For Sebastian, the isolated young man who had grown up reading the lives of saints and chivalric romances, such a retreat was unacceptable.

August 4, 1578, was a characteristically hot day on the Atlantic littoral of Morocco, and as the day stretched toward noon, it became still hotter, a time, perhaps, for taking an early *sesta* under whatever shade could be found. All too characteristically as well, King Sebastian of Portugal decided to order his outnumbered army of Portuguese crusaders, German and Italian mercenaries, Spanish veterans, and Moroccan allies into battle just as the sun was beginning to turn the countryside outside Alcazarquivir into an inferno. The order was only the last in a long series of ill-starred decisions reached by the twenty-four-year-old king in his invasion of Morocco to push back the borders of Islam. It is doubtful that Sebastian was too concerned about the precarious situation in which his army found itself; whatever his precise views about himself, there is no doubt that he was convinced that he was on mission from God, a holy crusade against the infidel Moors. For such a mission, surely the normal calculus of battle would not apply.

Whatever Sebastian's shortcomings in planning or common sense, he was no coward: after being blessed by the bishops of Coimbra and Oporto, as well as the apostolic delegate, he led the attacks of his infantrymen in person. Despite some initial successes against the Moorish infantry, the disproportion between the cavalry forces foredoomed the Portuguese effort. The Christian forces were soundly defeated, and during the course of the battle King Sebastian of Portugal disappeared and was almost certainly killed. In a strange twist of fate, Sebastian was not the first monarch to die that day, since his opponent, Abd-el-Malek, had already succumbed to lingering intestinal illness—whether brought on by poison or disease is still debated—and died in his tent, a fact that was kept from his men until the battle was decided. Nor was Sebastian the last king to die: after the collapse of the Portuguese lines, Mulay Mohammed fled, only to drown in a nearby river. The Battle of the Three Kings claimed all three monarchs who had brought their armies to the field at Alcazarquivir. Or had it? No one could be found that had actually seen Sebastian die, and it was this slim uncertainty that was going to change the course of Portuguese messianism forever.[27]

‹ 2 ›

THE EVOLUTION OF SEBASTIANISM

On August 4, 1578, the Portuguese lost not only a battle but their army, their treasure, most of their nobility, and their king, in whom so much hope had been placed. They were soon to lose more, however. Sebastian had not secured the succession in case of failure, and the only other member of the Avis dynasty of any standing was Sebastian's elderly uncle, the cardinal Henry, who suffered under the double disadvantages of being a priest and of having tuberculosis. Despite the fact that Henry was proclaimed king on August 22—a sign of the regime' s acceptance of Sebastian's death—reports that Sebastian was still alive were widespread. And even though a body had been identified as his a few days after the battle, the testimony of some soldiers who had fled the Moors fed the rumor that he had escaped to the fortified town of Arzila in the company of several knights. In the climate of uncertainty created by these conflicting reports, many people opted for the more hopeful of the possibilities, though the question remained of where Sebastian was, alive or dead.[1]

When Henry died, in January 1580, an illegitimate cousin of Sebastian's, Dom António, the Prior of Crato, emerged as the popular candidate for the throne against the claims of Philip II of Spain. During Dom António's brief reign, many people hoped that he was the Hidden One prophesied by Bandarra, a hope he did his best to encourage. His cause was lost, though, in the summer of 1580 when his ill-prepared army of volunteers was crushed by the veteran *tercios* of the Duke of Alba at the Battle of Alcántara. Dom António fled to the north and then to the Azores, but in 1583 the island of Terceira was captured by the Spanish, with Dom António and his remaining supporters fleeing to exile in France and England. In the meantime, Philip II was proclaimed king of Portugal by the Cortes of Tomar in 1581 after swearing to respect the rights, laws, and privileges of the Portuguese. In 1582, Philip, a shrewd ruler, had the body that had been identified as Sebastian's ransomed from Morocco and publicly interred in the Monastery of the Hieronymites outside Lisbon in a move calculated to convince his new subjects that Sebastian was indeed dead and thereby solidify his own legitimacy. Because some witnesses disputed the identity of the body, though, the burial did little to quell the belief that Sebastian was still alive.

One of the earliest pieces of evidence testifying to the continuing belief that Sebastian was alive is the rather obscure inquisitorial trial of a blacksmith named Balthasar Gonçalves from the island of Terceira in the Azores.[2] Sometime around March 1581, Balthasar Gonçalves began to proclaim that he had received a revelation that Sebastian had escaped from Alcazarquivir and was in hiding in the Monastery of San Francisco in Lisbon. What is more, Sebastian would soon reveal himself, on a Friday, to reclaim the kingdom of Portugal.[3] It is doubtful—given that the Azores were then still holding out against Philip II's forces—that the claim that Sebastian was still alive was seen as all that remarkable; it was the fact that Gonçalves said he had received his information by a special revelation from God that was troubling to ecclesiastical authorities.

Gonçalves was duly reported to the Inquisition of Lisbon and, after considerable delays stemming from the Spanish conquest of the islands in 1583,he was transferred to Lisbon to stand trial. His first interrogation took place on May 27, 1584, and in it he revealed several details of interest. Sebastian would not, when he returned, merely reclaim Portugal from the Spanish but would also conquer all of Africa in two years and then the Holy Land. In the process, he would defeat and subjugate the Moors and Turks, and once he brought peace to the world, all would become Christians. In the meantime, the Antichrist would rise and become pope, but he would later be defeated and killed, presumably by Sebastian, although this is not completely clear in the testimony. Three days after the death of the Antichrist, the Final Judgment would occur.[4]

Inquisitor Bartolomeu de Fonseca listened to all of this very patiently before asking Gonçalves if he had ever had any communication with the devil, to which Gonçalves answered no. After more testimony in which Gonçalves said he had received all these revelations from a voice speaking from his chest, Fonseca came to the conclusion that the blacksmith was insane ("doido"), a decision later confirmed by the Conselho Geral. As a result of this ruling, Gonçalves was released from prison and merely had to receive instruction in the faith.[5]

This short and unusual case is historically important for several reasons. First, it is the earliest example of direct testimony from someone who believed that Sebastian was alive after Alcazarquivir. The chronicles of the battle (all of which were written later) make general statements along the lines of "as the people believed he was alive" or "they thought he was alive" without citing any specific individuals. Second, it is the earliest example of a *sebastianista*, in the strictest sense of the term, after Alcazarquivir. Even though his beliefs were recounted only in abbreviated form, Balthasar Gonçalves did not merely think that Sebastian was alive and thus the rightful king of Portugal; he thought he had a prophetic destiny—along lines laid down by the Last World Emperor and the Encoberto traditions—to destroy the forces of Islam, bring in a golden age of peace, and convert the world to Christianity, all before finally defeating the Antichrist. This is important because it refutes the contention that Sebastianism was invented by Dom João de Castro. *Sebastianismo*, at least in its core elements, is first seen here, six years before Dom João de Castro said he came to understand Sebastian's prophetic role for the first time in 1587. To be sure, Castro was an erudite and prolific apologist of the *sebastianista* tradition, but it was not a tradition that was original to him.[6]

Third, it also proves that the eschatological faith in Sebastian did not originate in the claims of the false Sebastians (see the next section) because it antedated all of them. Last, because of the close proximity of the date of Gonçalves's alleged revelation (March 1581) to the Battle of Alcazarquivir (August 1578), this case is perhaps the clearest proof of the eschatological expectations attached to Sebastian *before* he went to Morocco. It is unlikely that the association between Sebastian and the role of the Hidden One could have spontaneously developed in the less-than-three-year period that separated the two events. It is much more likely that the association was well established by the time of the *jornada* to Africa and then reworked by true believers to account for the defeat of the Hidden One in Morocco. In sum, this case is important because it is the oldest fossil yet found of the *sebastianista* species and thus provides crucial data about the timing of the evolution of the legend as a whole.

Besides the influence of preexisting messianic associations and the uncertain identity of the corpse, the fact that several people came forward claiming to be (or more accurately, being acclaimed as) Sebastian did much to cement the idea that he was not truly dead.[7] The stories of the anonymous king of Pernamacor in 1584; Mateus Álvares, the king of Ericeira in 1585; and Gabriel Espinosa, the Pastry Maker of Madrigal in 1595 are all proof of the continuing hope that Sebastian was the Hidden One of prophecy, a hope that, seemingly, was intensified by the tragedy of Alcazarquivir. Psychologically, such a phenomenon is not hard to understand; after the Spanish took control of Portugal in 1580, many Portuguese turned to the only kind of salvation they could really hope for, that of a supernaturally chosen national redeemer. And so, after Alcazarquivir, the Portuguese millenarian tradition was used increasingly to mobilize opinion (both foreign and domestic) against continued Spanish control over Portugal; the discourse of triumphalist expansionism was transformed into a discourse of national liberation.

It was the last of the pretenders, the so-called Prisoner of Venice, who was to have the greatest effect on subsequent events, but before we discuss the Prisoner himself, we must first discuss the man who is arguably the single most influential figure in the development of *sebastianismo*: Dom João de Castro. Dom João was the illegitimate son of Dom Álvaro de Castro and the grandson of his namesake, the great viceroy of India. Born around 1550, he entered the University of Évora in 1568 and began to study for the priesthood. Since he was a student, he did not take part in the expedition to Africa, but once the news of the disaster spread, he rallied to the cause of Dom António. He fought alongside the Prior of Crato at Alcántara, fled with him to the Azores, and later followed him into exile, first in Paris and finally in London. At first, Dom João worked to rally support for Dom António in the courts of western Europe, but by May 1587 Castro's faith in the Prior of Crato had waned, and so he left Dom António's court and went to stay with supporters in Paris.

The year 1587 was decisive in more ways than one for Castro, for it was during that year, shortly after arriving in Paris, that he first read the Trovas of Bandarra and became convinced that Sebastian was not only alive but indeed the Hidden One prophesied in those verses.[8] After that, Dom João began a crusade to spread the gospel of the living Sebastian, though with only mixed results. In 1597 he took on new role, that of apologist rather than evangelist. The result was a book entitled *Da Quinta e ultima monarchia futura*, written in Latin and never published, in which he called upon his formidable erudition in things eschatological to prove his case. Using a Joachimite schema as the foundation for his views of the future, he identified Sebastian as the coming king who would destroy the Turks, overthrow Islam, and reform the church with the help of the Angelic Pope.[9] He also cited Isidore to prove Sebastian's identity as the Hidden One, and on the basis of the Trovas and some rather obscure numerology, he predicted that Sebastian would reappear in 1598. This fact goes a long way to explain his passion when, in 1598, rumors began to spread among the Portuguese community in Venice about a mysterious Knight of the Cross imprisoned there.

Living in Paris at the time, Dom João de Castro received news in the summer of 1598 that a man in Venice was claiming to be Sebastian. He had escaped from Alcazarquivir, he said, but after many years of wandering the world in penance for his defeat, he had finally come to Venice, where he had been arrested by the authorities there under pressure from the Spanish ambassador. Castro traveled to Venice himself in the summer of 1600, and after comparing the Prisoner's appearance with a list of physical signs by which Sebastian supposedly could be identified, he became convinced that the Prisoner was, in fact, the lost king of Portugal. From that moment on, he worked tirelessly to help the Prisoner's other supporters prove his identity and thereby secure his release. The Venetian Senate was divided on the issue; some thought he was Sebastian, while some agreed with the Spanish that he was an impostor. Ultimately, a compromise was reached whereby the Prisoner was released from prison—without comment on his true identity—and told to leave Venetian territory within three days. The Portuguese expatriates in Venice decided that his best chance was to travel to France and seek the protection of Henry IV, who was always looking for ways to unsettle Spain. The Prisoner made for Florence so that he could travel to Marseilles by sea, but upon his arrival in the Tuscan capital, he was arrested by Florentine officials. His supporters again pleaded for his release, but their efforts were for naught because Spanish diplomats exerted a great deal of pressure on the Grand Duke of Tuscany. On April 23, 1601, he bowed to that pressure, and the Prisoner was handed over to Spanish authorities in the kingdom of Naples. He was questioned there by the viceroy and eventually confessed to being a Calabrian named Marco Tulio Catizone. In May 1602, he was condemned to life in the king's galleys for the crime of impersonation.

This confession caused many supporters to lose faith in the pretender, but that was not the case for Castro and other true believers. By the time of Catizone's sentencing, Castro had already returned to Paris and written the *Discurso da vida do sempre bem vindo et apparecido Rey Dom Sebastião nosso senhor o Encuberto.*

Published in Paris in 1602, "with the license of the King," and addressed to the "Nobles, Clergy, and People of Portugal," the *Discurso da vida* had two principal apologetic purposes: one, to defend Sebastian, during his reign, from the criticism of hostile writers; and two, to demonstrate that the Prisoner of Venice was, in fact, Sebastian and so to rally political support for his cause. To that end, Dom João and several other partisans returned to Portugal to try to start a rebellion among the nobility in the Prisoner's favor, but the pro-Hapsburg authorities in Lisbon moved in early 1603 to forestall any such insurrection and arrested several of the conspirators. Castro had returned to Paris by then, but several letters implicating Catizone in the plot were confiscated, so the pretender was quickly transferred to San Lucar de Barrameda in Andalusia to stand trial for treason.

While Catizone was being tried in the summer of 1603, Castro completed and published his *Paraphrase et concordançia de alguas prophecias de Bandarra, çapateiro de Trancoso*. Where the *Discurso da vida* had been a historical apologetic, the *Paraphrase*, as its title implies, was a prophetic one, based on the Trovas of Bandarra. In many ways, his gloss of the Trovas varied little from Bandarra's interpretations; in the first chapter, he said that Bandarra had predicted "the conquest of the Holy House [i.e., Jerusalem] and the whole world, the universal proclamation of the Gospel, the universal triumph of Christianity over all the enemies of the Church, the major part being promised to King Sebastian and his kingdom, Portugal," although Bandarra clearly had not had Sebastian in mind.[10] Castro also discussed the problem of corruption within the church, a subject that concerned Bandarra as well.[11] So, while Castro's paraphrase of the Trovas recapitulates many of the themes and concerns of the original, there is an important difference we must examine: their very different attitudes toward the Jews and the New Christians. Bandarra's close associations with the *converso* community of his day have already been noted, but Castro had a different view of them altogether, and he consistently ignored or reinterpreted passages favorable to the Jews in Bandarra. Dom João did not merely ignore the issue, however; in an extended digression, he stated that under the rule of Sebastian the tribulations of the "Jews and apostates" would be greater than ever before and that the "Holy Inquisition" would be extended to the entire world.[12] In perhaps the most blatant example of his bias, Dom João simply excluded the most obviously pro-*converso* passages of the Trovas from his paraphrase of the text. The exclusion of these passages and, more important, of the eschatological goal of the conversion of the Jews—so important to Bandarra—was to typify Sebastianism, and indeed Portuguese millenarianism more generally, throughout the period we are studying, with one notable exception.

One unique element of Castro's eschatological schema was his belief that, after Sebastian was crowned emperor, he would undertake his campaign of conquest as a part of a Holy League of four Christian kings.[13] This conviction was based on two stanzas in the Trovas, the first found in *trova* LXXIII, "The Kings will be in agreement/Four will be, and no more," and the second in XCV, "Of four Kings, the second/Will have all the victory." This formulation, which was not repeated by any other major millennial commentator, was to play a large part in Dom João's view of the future, and in 1617 he wrote an entire book directed (in the mirror-of-princes mode) to these future conquerors, the unpublished "Avisos divinos e humanos para os memorandos conquistadores da Terra da Promissão dos nossos tempos, que he todo o universo." In the *Paraphrase*, however, he tackled what seemed to be a problem in the cited *trovas*: Castro assumed that Sebastian was one of the four kings of the Holy League and that he would be the one gaining all the victories. According to *trova* XCV, he would therefore be the second of the four kings, which seemed inconsistent with the conclusions elsewhere that Sebastian would be the emperor. How could the emperor be the second of anything? With characteristic ingenuity (in things relating to Sebastian) Dom João provided a solution to the problem: the first of the four kings would be the Angelic Pope, who, as the Vicar of Christ, was preeminent over all secular rulers.[14] This neat solution not only resolved a potential problem in Bandarra but also gave still greater preeminence to the figure of the Angelic Pope. On the basis of the "Super Ieremiam" and other Joachimist writings (all of which Castro attributed to the Venerable Abbot), the Angelic Pope became in Castro's schema a much more important figure than in the Trovas. While Bandarra concentrated on the king who was to come, Castro concluded that the work of the Reformation of the World would be the task of both Sebastian as the Hidden King and the as-yet-unidentified Angelic Pope.[15] Keep this formulation of four kings, including the figure of the Angelic Pope, in mind because it will appear, in a slightly modified form, later in this study.

All Dom João de Castro's efforts, literary and otherwise, were to fail in their immediate goal, however, because on September 23, 1603, Marco Tulio Catizone was executed by hanging in San Lucar. Unsurprisingly, this turn of events did not dampen Dom João de Castro's faith when he heard of it in the late fall of

1603. The man executed by the Spanish had been, in fact, Catizone, Castro admitted, but he was not the same man who had been imprisoned in Venice. Catizone had been switched with Sebastian by the Spanish so that they could quell the growing support for Sebastian without having the guilt of royal blood on their hands, Dom João claimed, in one of his more ingenious rationalizations. From that point on, Castro always maintained that Sebastian was still alive and would return to fulfill his destiny.[16]

In the end, the execution of Catizone spurred Dom João on to new efforts in his defense of Sebastian, and in 1604 he began what he later considered to be his masterwork, the "Aurora." Weighing in at more than eleven hundred folios, it represents the most comprehensive treatment of Castro's apocalyptic views, even though it was never published. In the "Aurora," he brought the full weight of his learning to bear to prove Sebastian's providential destiny, citing prophecies from Methodius, Bandarra, Joachim, Isidore, Saint Brigitte, the Sybils, Merlin, the German astrologer Lichtenberg, Nostradamus, and the legend of Ourique, among many others, to prove that Sebastian was destined to rule the world. Although he repeats (and even extends) the anti-Semitic comments found in his earlier works, it becomes quite clear in the "Aurora" that, in Dom João's mind, the principal enemy of Christendom was Islam, headed by the Turks. Consequently, the major part of this long work is dedicated to explaining the details of Sebastian's victorious campaign against the forces of Islam, culminating in the recapturing of Jerusalem and the destruction of Mecca. Going into vastly more detail than in this brief summary, the "Aurora" is the most complete eschatological schema ever written in the Portuguese language. It is also the most extensive elaboration in existence of the virulently racist and militantly Catholic strain of Portuguese millenarianism that Dom João de Castro represented. Dom João de Castro did not cease writing when he could not raise the money to have the "Aurora" published, and over the next two decades until his death in 1628, he stayed in Paris, surviving through the kindness of the old network of Portuguese exiles there and writing over twenty more books and treatises—none of which were published—on prophecy and Sebastian's return. He never lost his faith that Sebastian would, one day soon, return and fulfill all that had been prophesied about him.

Beyond the unpublished works of Castro, very few books on the subject were written in the first decades of the seventeenth century, making it difficult to trace the precise evolution of *sebastianismo* during that period. One important exception to this rule was the dissemination of three documents purported to be papal bulls (dated 1598, 1617, and 1630) identifying the Prisoner of Venice as Sebastian. Since none of the originals of these bulls can be found in the Vatican, they are certainly forgeries, though in a rather barren period they are evidence of the continuing belief that Sebastian, in the person of the Prisoner of Venice, was alive.

The trail of evidence improves somewhat in the 1620s and 1630s, though details remain sparse, and the nature and specific content of the belief during this crucial period are still quite unclear. These two decades were a period of increasing economic frustration and political tension in Portugal as many Portuguese resisted the centralizing policies of the Olivares regime in Spain. Unsurprisingly, the evidence suggests that these decades saw a marked upswing in the spread and militancy of millenarian ideas in Portugal. One of the rare examples of a published work from this period is a book by the New Christian alchemist, astrologer, and physician Manuel Bocarro Frances. In 1624, he published the first part of a four-part poem entitled the *Anacephaleosis da monarchia lusitania*. Though the work was dedicated to Philip IV of Spain, a careful reading of the poem makes clear that Bocarro thought the messianic prophecies he cited applied to Dom Teodósio, the powerful Duke of Braganza, significantly described as "the principal Hero of this Monarchy."[17]

This, at least, was the way the Hapsburg authorities read the poem, and Bocarro was arrested. After a brief imprisonment, and after being denounced to the Inquisition by his brother as a Judaizer, he fled to Rome. Safe there, he actually did convert to Judaism, changing his name to Manuel Bocarro Frances Rosales, in honor of his Jewish forebears.[18] His conversion did not end his interest in Portuguese messianism, however, and in 1626 he completed the "Luz pequena lunar," in which he stated that the Avis had been rejected by God because of their oppression of the innocent, specifically innocent *conversos*, thereby excluding the possibility that Sebastian was the Hidden One.[19] In another section, he stated clearly that his intention was to educate the "mistaken sebastianists," the first known use of that term. With the Avis rejected, the Braganzas became the focus of Bocarro's attention, and he ultimately concluded that the Sovereign Prince by Dom Teodósio's side, his son and heir, the future João II of Braganza (and João IV of Portugal) would be the Desired One.[20] His work is important because it is the first clear example of what would become an intense debate between the supporters of the Braganzas and the supporters of Sebastian regarding the identity of the Encoberto. "Luz pequena lunar" is also a testament to the cross-religious nature of the millenarian beliefs then circulating in western Europe. Even after Bocarro became a Jew, he remained a Portuguese patriot and continued to look to the Catholic Duke of Braganza as the messianic savior promised by the prophets and on the basis of the same sources that Dom João de Castro had used to promote his anti-Jewish agenda.

While Bocarro's contributions are important in an otherwise historically barren period, the clearest evidence of the influence of millenarian ideas in Portugal comes from the accounts of the widespread, though ultimately unsuccessful, anti-Castilian revolt known as the Alterações de Évora. In the summer of 1637, the rebellion began as an antitax revolt in response to fiscal pressure from Madrid, but under the guidance of some Jesuit professors at the University of Évora, it quickly took on radical and millenarian overtones. Dom Francisco Manuel de Melo, the principal chronicler of the rebellion, recounts that four such Jesuit fathers—among whom at least two, Sebastião de Couto and Gaspar Correia, were supporters of João of Braganza as the Desired One[21]—were leaders of the rebellion and almost certainly were part of the body ruling Évora under the aegis of the popular prophet Manuelinho. The messianic tendencies of Manuelinho can be seen in a decree written in his name at the beginning of the disorders in Évora that used radical language influenced by Molinist theories on tyrannicide to reject the Spanish king completely, stating that his rule was illegitimate because the Portuguese already had a true king.[22] One should not conclude, however, that the rebellion was, therefore, simply a pro-Braganza revolt with messianic overtones; de Melo (generally a careful historian) states that the *sebastianistas* were crucial participants in the rebellion,[23] so the most likely conclusion is that Portuguese millenarians of all stripes came together in Évora to fight for the common goal of expelling the hated king of Spain. The issue of the Hidden King's identity could wait until after Portugal was liberated, as indeed it did.

The period of repression that followed the end of the Alterações de Évora did nothing to quell the desire among the Portuguese masses for an end to Spanish rule, and by 1640 virtually all support for the continued union with Spain among the elites had evaporated as well. So on December 1, 1640, Duke João II of Braganza was proclaimed King João IV of Portugal by the nobles and people of Lisbon, a proclamation quickly accepted by the rest of the kingdom. Indeed, so complete was the support for João within Portugal that he was able to expel all the Spanish garrisons almost bloodlessly within three months of the proclamation, although the war for independence continued until 1668. Without a doubt, the efforts of those who had laid a foundation of prophetic expectation by identifying the House of Braganza with the figure of the Encoberto helped João mobilize support for the cause of Portuguese independence. The initial enthusiasm following the proclamation of João IV was accompanied by his widespread acceptance as the Hidden One, and many of his supporters and advisers were quick to use his perceived prophetic role to bolster support for the new regime, both at home and abroad.

For example, in 1643, Panteleão Rodrigues Pacheco, one of João IV's closest advisers, wrote the *Manifesto do reyno de Portugal*, using legal, genealogical, and prophetic arguments to try to persuade Pope Urban VIII to accept the Braganza ruler as the legitimate king of Portugal.[24] Another important contribution to the *joanista* cause was made by the Conde da Vidigueira, João IV's ambassador to Paris, when he redacted the first complete printed edition of Bandarra's Trovas in 1644. The text varied from the incomplete edition produced by Dom João de Castro in 1603 in several key passages, and in such a way that clearly favored João IV as the Hidden One of prophecy. Easily the most influential of the pro-Braganza apologies, though, was *Restauração de Portugal prodigiosa*, written in 1643 by the Jesuit Fr. João de Vasconcelos (under the name Grégorio de Almeida), who used the book's two enormous volumes to vigorously defend the proposition that the Restoration of Portugal (and João IV's role therein) was the work of God.[25] António de Sousa de Macedo was also well connected to the Braganza regime and served in various diplomatic and governmental positions under João IV and Afonso VI.[26] In 1645, while in London, Sousa de Macedo published an erudite defense of João's claims to the throne of Portugal, *Lusitana liberata*, which used both legal and eschatological proof to show that João was the rightful king of Portugal.[27] Written in Latin, it was clearly intended for a well-educated, international audience. Many other treatises of the 1640s, such as the *Ressurreição de Portugal, e morte fatal de Castela* (1645) by the Dominican diplomat Fr. Manoel Homen and the *Vox tuturis* (1649) of Dr. Nicolai Monteiro, echoed these themes (and most of the same arguments) in favor of João IV being the legitimate king of Portugal and the Hidden King who had been prophesied.

By far the best known of the *joanistas*, however, was the Jesuit priest António Vieira, and because of his unique role, both in the regime and as an interpreter of prophecy, he merits a discussion of his own. Born in 1608 in Lisbon, he grew up in Brazil, where he eventually became a Jesuit missionary among the Indians around Maranhão, working not only to evangelize them but to protect them from Portuguese slavers. He was also well known for his homiletic skill and is still widely considered among the best orators of the European baroque.[28] He eventually became the most eloquent of the João's apologists; ironically, however, Vieira was a *sebastianista* while in Brazil.[29]

That was all to change with the acclamation of João IV in December 1640. In early 1641, Vieira was part of a delegation sent to Lisbon to declare the loyalty of Brazil to the new dynasty. He immediately made a favorable impression on João IV, and the Jesuit missionary soon became one of João's closest confidants and most vocal partisans, as the messianic tone of his New Year's Day, 1642, sermon demonstrates. In the sermon, he chastised those who waited for Sebastian's return by arguing that João was the ruler who had been predicted by the prophets.[30] João's confidence in him was such that in 1644 he appointed him royal preacher and he often sent him abroad on important diplomatic missions to garner support for the cause of Portuguese independence.[31]

Even with royal support, Vieira was not without his critics, and in one case, he picked a fight with a very powerful enemy indeed: the Inquisition. Vieira was unsparing in his criticism of the Holy Office and its persecution of the New Christians.[32] In 1644, he advocated the return of all Portuguese *conversos* who had fled to other countries and even their return to Portugal as open Jews, a policy so radical that the generally pro-*converso* Portuguese Jesuits refused to support it, and it the plan was dropped. Vieira's greatest victory on the *conversos'* behalf came on February 6, 1649, when João IV issued a decree suspending the ability of the Inquisition to impose confiscations on those convicted of Judaizing. Such confiscations, the king reasoned, only served to disrupt the Portuguese economy and hamper his ability to raise the moneys he needed in order to defend the kingdom God had given him.[33] None of this sat well with the Holy Office, but still feeling the effects of the inquisitor general's participation in the August 1641 plot to overthrow João IV and return Portugal to Spanish rule, it was too weak to act against Vieira. While he was protected by the king, the Holy Office had to bide its time and wait for a more opportune moment to strike back, which is what it did.

In 1652, the Jesuit priest returned to his mission work in Brazil, and while in Maranhão, he received the news he never thought he would hear, that João IV had died on November 8, 1656. João's death, however, did not shake Vieira's faith that he was the Prophesied One, as can most clearly be seen in a letter, dated April 29, 1659, from Vieira to his fellow Jesuit André Fernandes, confessor to the queen regent and bishop-elect of Japan. Ostensibly intended as a means to comfort the still-grieving queen, in reality it was Vieira's attempt to arrest a resurgent Sebastianism in the wake of João's death. Similarly, though Vieira claimed that it was intended to be a secret letter, it was widely disseminated in Portugal by figures sympathetic to him.[34] Even the term "letter" is a misnomer; in reality, it was a treatise dealing with the prophecies of Bandarra and arrived with a title in place, "Esperanças de Portugal, quinto império do mundo."[35] From the very beginning of the work, Vieira made his intention clear: "although all refer to the coming of Sebastian," he would demonstrate "the future resurrection of our good lord and master, João IV."[36] He would prove his case, he claimed, by proving the truth of the following syllogism: "1. Bandarra was a true prophet; 2. Bandarra prophesied that João would accomplish many deeds he has not accomplished, nor could he accomplish unless he were resurrected; 3. Therefore, João will be resurrected."[37] The rest of the letter is Vieira's attempt to prove the major and minor premises so that the desired conclusion would inevitably follow.

In the course of trying to prove these points, Vieira also demonstrated that his support of the New Christians (and the Jews) was not pragmatically based on their potential support in the struggle for Portuguese independence; their protection was an essential part of Vieira's eschatological vision. Citing the same corpus of prophecy that had been used by Dom João de Castro, and by including the pro-Jewish parts of the Trovas that Castro had excluded, Vieira tried to prove that João would peacefully convert all the Jews to Christianity once the ten lost tribes of Israel were found, a prospect that Castro would surely have found anathema.

"Esperanças de Portugal" was to be the principal legacy of Vieira's brand of millenarianism, and it, with its pro-*converso* claims, was to lead to his conviction by the Inquisition. In 1649, Vieira had been denounced to the Holy Office for his pro-*converso* statements, but it was not until after João's death, and during the regency of the weak Afonso VI, that the inquisitors avenged themselves on their most trenchant critic. Having to flee Brazil because of the colonists' anger at his defense of the Indians there, Vieira returned to Portugal in November 1661 and was immediately taken into custody by the Inquisition, which by that time had already obtained a copy of the "Esperanças."[38]

As the formal charges make clear, Vieira was not (officially, at least) prosecuted because of his long history of pro-*converso* activism but because his eschatology, as revealed in the "Esperanças," contained several suspect propositions, the three most important of which were that Bandarra (whose Trovas were in 1665 again placed on the Inquisition's Index of Prohibited Books) was a true prophet, that João would be raised from the dead to fulfill his destiny, and that the Jews would convert to Christianity en masse.[39] Delayed because of the missionary's ill health, the bulk of his trial took place in the summer of 1666. Vieira mounted a vigorous defense—recorded in the collection of papers known as the *Defesa perante o Tribunal do Santo Oficio*—but the end result was a foregone conclusion. In December 1667, Vieira was condemned as "heretic, a judaizer, and a *bandarrista*" and was permanently stripped of his ability to preach. Given Vieira's attitude of impenitence, it was a light sentence, but the Inquisition was constrained because Vieira still had powerful supporters, both in Portugal and in Rome.[40] In 1675, those supporters were able to persuade Pope Clement X to nullify the Inquisition's sentence and to permanently exempt Vieira from the jurisdiction of the Holy Office.[41]

After his release, Vieira went to Rome and then to Brazil, where he attempted to complete what he intended to be the definitive statements of his apocalyptic views, the seven-part *História do futuro*, and a related treatise in Latin, the *Clavis prophetarum*. Vieira was unable to complete either before he died in 1697, though he did leave an outline and the text of the first two parts of the proposed work, both of which demonstrate that his thought by then had become more millenarian than messianic; the future Fifth Kingdom, rather than the Desired King, was to be the focus of the book. Vieira is often cited as one of the premier expositors of the Portuguese prophetic tradition in the seventeenth century, but his legacy in that regard is rather doubtful. Only the "Esperanças de Portugal" was widely disseminated in his lifetime, and his sermons and his letters were available only to a select group of people, most of whom were already members of the dwindling circle of *joanistas*. The most compelling evidence for a limited view of Vieira's influence, however, is that, despite his efforts, *joanismo* essentially died out in the 1660s.

Even before João IV's death on November 8, 1656, support for him as the Hidden One had begun to wane, largely because he seemed unable to accomplish any of the goals of the Encoberto save the liberation of Portugal, and even that was not secure. Whatever sense of creeping pessimism had begun to infect the ranks of the *joanistas* by the early 1650s, it was nothing compared with the wave of disillusion that swept the supporters of the Braganzas upon João's death. However, since the prophetic legitimization of the Braganzas was one of the primary means by which the still-embattled regime garnered support, there was an attempt to recast *joanista* interpretations in such a way that they would include a providential role for João's heir, the sickly Afonso VI, though with virtually no success.[42] The dismal and disappointing reign of Afonso did nothing to bolster popular faith in the Braganzas' providential role, and the attempt by some to recast the prophecies yet again in support of Pedro II when he came to power in 1667 produced no literature worth commenting on. After the high tide of support for the Braganzas in 1640s, the *joanista* faith was in deep crisis by the 1660s, which left the field of prophetic interpretation open for a resurgent Sebastianism.

Though the 1640s were a time of widespread faith in João as the Hidden One, there were those who remained committed to Sebastian. One of the few *sebastianista* treatises of the 1640s was "O tratado da quinta monarchia" (ca. 1645) by the Trinitarian Sebastião de Paiva. De Paiva's work is one of considerable learning in which he used many scriptural and prophetic references to reassure his readers that Sebastian was still—even after the acclamation—the Desired King.[43] De Paiva's work is also another piece of evidence demonstrating the crucial influence of Dom João de Castro throughout the evolution of the legend of Sebastian. While de Paiva quotes all the standard prophets—the Erythrean Sybil, Saint Isidore, Joachim, Bandarra, Simão Gomes, and even Manuel Bocarro (selectively)—he does so in a way that almost completely mirrors Castro's use of those sources, and de Paiva's own description of the life of Sebastian is completely dependent on Castro's published works, the *Discurso da vida* and the *Paraphrase*.[44] Because of his significant role in the story of Maria de Macedo, more will be said about Sebastião de Paiva in later chapters.

While de Paiva's work represented the erudite end of the spectrum of *sebastianista* literature, the "Jardim ameno," produced sometime around 1650, is from the popular end. It was an early example of the prophetic collection, and thus it had no central argument or any text of its own. Instead, it was an anthology of the high points of other prophetic works—including all the standard eschatological references that made up the Western prophetic corpus—

summarized *Reader's Digest*–fashion and placed in a single volume. Copied and recopied through the seventeenth and eighteenth centuries, collections such as the "Jardim ameno" were well suited to their intended audience of literate, though not erudite, readers and their illiterate listeners.[45] Both of these works are proof that many held onto their *sebastianista* faith even in the heyday of pro-Braganza prophetic interpretation.

While works like these kept the cause of Sebastian alive during João IV's lifetime, the debate between the *joanistas* and the *sebastianistas* regarding the identity of the Hidden One only began in earnest after João's death in 1656. In the years immediately following the king's death, the *sebastianistas* produced several works intended to refute the conclusions of the *joanistas*. The widely copied "Livro das cousas mas notaveis que tinha lido acerca dos fundamentos dos sebastianistas" and the similarly anonymous "Resposta de certa pessoa a outra," written in 1658, are examples of this literature, and both concluded that the claims of Sousa de Macedo in *Lusitana liberata* and Vasconcelos in *Restauração de Portugal* were false, since João IV had not fulfilled the deeds prophesied of the Hidden King.[46] The author of the "Resposta" also makes reference to Dom João de Castro's *Discurso da vida*, and, indeed, it is during this period that the true extent of Castro's legacy begins to take shape, since he was increasingly cited by *sebastianista* authors during the decades of debate after the Restoration.[47] These, along with the "Ante-Vieira," the "Opinião contrária," and the "Epítome das esperades venturas de Portugal," are only some of the more important examples of the voluminous *sebastianista* counterliterature written in the 1650s and 1660s in response to the official line promulgated by the *joanistas* in the first decade of the Restoration.

It was also during the Restoration period that the idea of the Hidden Isle began to be associated with Sebastian. The idea of a hidden island of wonders has a long history going back to ancient times, though the Arthurian Island of Avalon and the Iberian myth of the Seven Cities of Cíbola were probably the most direct sources for the Portuguese Ilha Encoberta. The earliest written references clearly linking the Hidden Isle to Sebastian both date from 1648, but the ways in which they describe the belief show that it was already widely held by that date.[48] The long heroic poem "Monarchia luzitana," written around 1660 and frequently recopied in the anthologies, was heavily influenced by the legend of the Hidden Isle,[49] and only a few years later, the "Noticia da Ilha Encuberta," which claimed to be the account of two Capuchin monks' journey to the Hidden Isle, began to circulate in the collections.[50]

What conclusions can be drawn from these examples? One has already been alluded to: the proliferation of *sebastianista* texts in the late Restoration period is proof of the enduring faith of Sebastian's followers in his return, and equally, it is evidence of the waning appeal of the Braganzas, at least when speaking of them as candidates for the role of the Hidden One. Given the course of Portuguese history in the 1660s and 1670s, it not difficult to understand why a remote and semilegendary figure such as Sebastian would win out over the prosaic rulers of the period. João IV's heir, Afonso VI (r. 1656–83), had a disappointing reign, the last sixteen years of which were a regency led by his brother due to Afonso's mental incompetence. Such a situation was hardly an inspiring circumstance in which to find a great leader.

There is a deeper reason, however, that explains the triumph of Sebastian over the Braganzas besides the mediocrity of the Braganza candidates after João IV, but to grasp it requires that we pay attention to a small detail that has been heretofore ignored by scholars. I have already noted that the authors of the *joanista* apologies of the 1640s and 1650s—Vasconcelos, Pacheco, Sousa de Macedo, Vieira—were all members of the elite and that they produced the official millenarian view designed to strengthen the claims of the Braganza regime. It is also true that all their works (with the exception of Vieira's "Esperanças," thanks to the quick intervention of the Inquisition) were printed, often by royally connected publishers. It is worth bearing in mind that none of the *sebastianista* works listed above was printed; they all circulated in manuscript. In fact, besides the *Discurso da vida* and the *Paraphrase* of Dom João de Castro, which were printed only because of a uniquely favorable political circumstance in France, there is no evidence that any *sebastianista* work was printed in seventeenth-century Portugal.

This is a small detail perhaps, but one that may provide an important clue about who the readers and writers of each corpus were. The *joanista* writers were members of the elite, and they addressed educated audiences, both within and outside Portugal. The *sebastianistas* as individuals are shrouded in historical obscurity. It is unlikely that the *sebastianista* authors had either the money or the influence to have their treatises printed or that their readers had the money to purchase them; their crude, hand-copied collections of prophecies (like the pamphlet produced by Maria de Macedo) were clearly aimed at a minimally literate, domestic audience of modest economic means at best. The *joanistas* lost the struggle because, outside the period of initial enthusiasm following the acclamation of João IV, they never did command the hearts and minds of the people of Portugal. The *joanistas* were concerned about the power of the regime and targeted their resources toward those who could best strengthen it, largely ignoring the vast mass of the Portuguese in the process. The *sebastianistas* had different motivations, and when they spoke to the common people across Portugal about the return of King Sebastian, they received a favorable hearing, simply because they were speaking to themselves.

II

The Vision and the Trial

‹ 3 ›

MARIA DE MACEDO AND THE VISION IN HER OWN WORDS

The story of Maria de Macedo began in 1635 and came to an end in 1667, at least according to the extant documentation. These thirty-odd years were an interesting period in Portugal for at least two reasons: one, they comprehended the entire length of Portugal's struggle to free itself from Spanish domination; and two, they coincided with the period of the most intense debate within Portugal as to the identity of the Encoberto. Both the war and the debate were to have their effects on Maria de Macedo and her vision.

Before we proceed to her story, however, we must address the question of who Maria de Macedo was. An answer to this question is possible only because she had a story that was recorded by the Inquisition. The Great Lisbon Earthquake of 1755 destroyed virtually all the parish records from the Lisbon area before that date, and so in a somewhat ironic turn, the only genealogical information available for Maria de Macedo comes from inquisitorial records. As has been demonstrated in many other studies, only the fact that they became enmeshed in the machinery of the early modern judicial system saved many non-elite people from the cold anonymity of history, and this is certainly true in the case of Maria de Macedo.

So, who was Maria de Macedo? In her fifth deposition before the inquisitor Fernão Correa de la Cerda on March 5, 1665—a session that was dedicated to her genealogy—she stated that she was an Old Christian and that she was forty-two years old.[1] This is at odds with the testimony in her pamphlet, which gives her age as somewhere between ten and eleven as of November 1635, thus making her forty in 1665. Little should be made of this slight discrepancy, though, because in the early modern period, neither the accounting nor the recounting of ages was an exact science. In any event, she was born sometime between 1623 and 1625.

Maria was married to Feliciano Machado, styled as a senior official ("official maior") of the secretary of the Treasury, Gaspar de Abreu, although other witnesses described him as merely an official. Perhaps both were correct: It is possible that the witnesses who described him simply as an official had dated information, for in a September 4, 1663, decree Feliciano had been promoted, along with João de Costa and António Correa, to a higher position within the Treasury with an annual salary of 8,000 reis—not a princely sum, but a comfortable one for a midlevel functionary.[2] Maria went on to depose that she was a native of Lisbon and that she and her husband lived in a neighborhood of Lisbon close to the Church of the Martyrs.

Turning to her family, Maria gave her father's name as Luis Ribeiro and stated that he was still alive and was a guitar maker ("violero") for the king. Her mother, Agostinha de Macedo, was an Old Christian from Lisbon who had died many years before. According to testimony from Maria's stepmother, she had been married to Luis for thirty-three years in 1665, so Maria's natural mother must have died while she was a young child. Maria mentioned no brothers or sisters. Her paternal grandparents were both dead, both Old Christians, and were named as Diogo Ribeiro, a tailor, and Maria Luis. Both had also come from the Lisbon area. Her maternal grandparents were also deceased, had been Old Christians, and had lived in Lisbon. Her maternal grandfather was named João Delgado, a native of Carrasqueira and also a guitar maker; her grandmother was Lourença de Almeida, a native of Lisbon. To mitigate any suspicions the inquisitor might have had as to her religious ancestry, Maria made sure to point out that João Delgado had been a familiar of the Holy Office. From other documentation within her *processo*, we know that Feliciano and Maria had four children: three daughters who, in 1665, would have been between fourteen and ten years of age, as well as a boy of five.[3]

Maria went on to state her religious history. She was a Christian and had been baptized in the Church of St. Nicholas in Lisbon by the parish priest there. She did not know his name, but she did mention that Francisco de la Pinha, a chief notary in the customs service ("sellador mor da Alfandega"), had been her godfather. She had been confirmed in the same church, though her godfather for that service was Fernão Vaz, a sword sharpener, a rather less prestigious position than de la Pinha's. Since the "age of discretion" she had gone to church, heard Mass and the sermons, made confession, taken communion, and done the "other works of a Christian." She then knelt, crossed herself, and recited the

Our Father, the Hail Mary, the Salve Regina, the Creed, and the Commandments of God's Law and of the Holy Mother Church, all of which, the inquisitorial scribe noted, she recited well. She testified that she knew how to read and write, though in another deposition she was more specific and claimed to know how to read but said she could write only badly.[4] She finished the deposition by stating that she had never left Portugal or even Lisbon, and that neither she nor any of her relatives had ever been imprisoned or tried by the Inquisition.

Perhaps the first question to ask is whether this account should be taken at face value. I see no reason to doubt the information conveyed by Maria de Macedo—none of the claims seems inherently unlikely or tendentious—and indeed, as has been mentioned, there is no documentary basis on which to dispute the facts she relayed. This does not mean, however, that the document is a fully disinterested, transparent record—even in an abbreviated form—of Maria de Macedo's life to that point. Her answers had to conform to the pattern of questions asked by the inquisitor de la Cerda. Though the individual questions were not recorded, they were stereotypical and can easily be reconstructed. However, since the questions were standard, the range of possible kinds of answers available to the deponent was similarly limited. Generally speaking, it was not a good idea (nor a good strategy) to stray too far from the questions the inquisitor asked. However, within the limits imposed on her by "o estilo da Inquisição," Maria was able to point out one fact that she may have deemed helpful to her defense, namely, that her maternal grandfather had been a familiar of the Holy Office. Even within the constraints of formulaic questioning, one could cast one's answers for one's perceived benefit.

What, though, of casting by the Inquisition? While the fact that all the information recorded in a trial record was taken down by an inquisitorial scribe and for the Inquisition's purposes should always be kept in mind, in this particular section of the *processo* the dangers of inquisitorial mediation and bias are minimal. Perhaps ironically, this is true because of the highly formulaic nature of the questioning. Inquisitorial preconceptions and procedures limited the options available to the inquisitors as well as to the deponents; because the formula of the genealogical depositions was largely fixed, the inquisitors had little room to ask leading questions and, indeed, probably had less freedom than the defendants to tailor what they said. But beyond the lack of opportunity for biased questioning and recording on the inquisitor's part, there is also the issue of a lack of motive. The purposes of the genealogical deposition were imminently practical ones for the inquisitors: first, to resolve the crucial issue of whether the defendant was a *converso*, and after that, to determine whether the defendant conformed to the minimal ceremonial aspects of Catholicism and knew the core elements of Catholic dogma. To be sure, all manner of ideological assumptions underlay that quest for information, but because the procedure was so set and the questions so similar in each deposition, the inquisitors actually had very little room in which to interpose extraneous elements of their own, at least in this type of deposition. If an inquisitor wanted to entrap a defendant, there were plenty of venues better than the genealogical deposition to do so. Because the questioning was so formulaic, its biases can be anticipated and kept in mind; because the answers sought were prosaically factual rather than interpretive in nature, there was little incentive for the inquisitorial notaries to record something other than what the deponent said. Finally, it should always be remembered that inquisitorial documents were created *only for internal use*, which is evidence in favor of the view that deliberate falsification or spin was unlikely, given that the intent was to provide the officials of the Inquisition with as accurate a record as possible. These documents were never intended for public consumption.

So, given that the information provided in this deposition is probably correct, as far as it goes, what can be concluded about Maria de Macedo as a person, apart from her role as a visionary? It is clear that Maria came from artisan stock: both her father and her maternal grandfather were guitar makers, and her other grandfather was a tailor. These were professions by which one could earn a living, though hardly a fortune. Her father must have had some skill to have made guitars for the king, and the payment he received almost certainly resulted in a somewhat higher standard of living than that of other members of his profession. In her narrative of the first appearance of the visions, Maria stated that, in order to free her from her terrors, her father rented new lodgings, all the while keeping the original housing since he had his workshop there. She does admit that it caused him a great deal of distress (financial and otherwise) to keep two houses, but to paraphrase Samuel Johnson about watching a dog walk on its hind legs, one should not wonder that he does it badly, one should wonder that he does it at all. The fact that Maria's father, Luis Ribeiro, had the resources in the first place—even if only for a limited period of time—to maintain two houses demonstrates that he had a reasonably good and, more important in the seventeenth-century, stable income during Maria's childhood. The possibility that Luis made some helpful connections owing to his presence at court cannot be wholly discounted; after all, his daughter's godfather, at least at the time of her baptism, was a chief notary in the customs service, certainly not a power player among the nobility of the day but certainly not a bad position for a non-noble *letrado* to occupy. So far, the impression is one of a moderately prosperous artisan family, perhaps with some special connections due to Luis Ribeiro's work for the royal court. Economically and socially, the family of Luis Ribeiro was made up of middling sorts, though perhaps with greater chances of recognition or upward mobility than most.

Maria's choice of a husband, Feliciano Machado, tends to confirm this conclusion; he was an *oficial*, a midlevel bureaucrat serving under a nobleman such as Gaspar de Abreu. Further testimony reveals that, before taking a position in the Treasury, Feliciano was a servant in the household of Alvaro de Sousa, a nobleman who was named as the father-in-law of the chief doorman for the king. What Feliciano's duties were while in Don Alvaro's service are unknown, and the term used to describe him ("criado") was a generic one that could be used to refer to anything from a manservant to a confidential secretary. I am inclined toward the latter possibility because both his position in the Treasury and an extremely good writing hand (as revealed in one copy of the pamphlet) indicate that he received an education of some kind. Whatever his educational career, we can be quite certain that he never received a licentiate; had he received one, he certainly would have been called by that title in a status-conscious society such as seventeenth-century Portugal. Other testimony reveals that Feliciano may have been the illegitimate son of a noble clergyman in Guimarães, and midlevel positions of trust in noble families or in the government were often given to people who were educated but who suffered under the cloud of a mixed pedigree. Feliciano's job as an *oficial* in the Treasury was, in economic terms, the rough equivalent of Luis Ribero's occupation as a guitar maker for the king: both provided a steady, though certainly not luxurious, income. A government position such as Feliciano's enjoyed more prestige than that of a skilled artisan such as Luis, but probably only marginally in this case: the cloud of illegitimacy may have lowered Feliciano's social status a step or two, while Luis's connection to the court may have elevated his. Whatever the specific dynamics involved, it is clear that when Feliciano and Maria were married in September 1649, they were, socially and economically, a match, and both fit well into the Portuguese middle class of the seventeenth century, which was largely made up of non-noble government officials, skilled artisans, and medium-sized merchants.[5]

Issues of class and status are not the only ones that can be addressed on the basis of the genealogical information found in Maria's *processo*. Since it was an inquisitorial prosecution, the question of religious devotion also figures prominently. The religious self-portrait painted by Maria was one of a pious Catholic woman who described herself as, from an early age, having attended church, listened to sermons, confessed, and taken communion—"all the works of a Christian." She also knew the principal prayers of the Catholic faith and the Commandments of God and the church and recited them all well according to the scribe. Her ability to read was somewhat unusual for a woman of her background at that time in Portugal but was not so unusual that it dramatically set her apart from all her contemporaries of similar background, and it becomes less marked as a characteristic when one considers the connections and, perhaps, the ambitions of her family. Of great importance in seventeenth-century Portugal, and particularly to her personally as one appearing before the Inquisition, she was an Old Christian, and indeed an Old Christian whose family had never had difficulties with the Holy Office before. While all these claims might be dismissed as merely rhetorical ploys to aid in her defense, they largely conform to the descriptions of her given by other witnesses, and so there is little basis to call them into question. All the evidence (in the *processo* and the pamphlet) tends toward the conclusion that Maria was exactly the kind of pious Catholic woman that she described. So, in many ways, Maria de Macedo was a member of an almost stereotypical religious, middle-class family of seventeenth-century Lisbon. Her apparent predilection for intense inner spiritually was somewhat unusual, but this may be partially explained by her frequent associations with the Jesuits of the Chiado area in Lisbon. So, now that we have at least an outline of who Maria de Macedo was, aside from her visions, we will examine how she stood out from the crowd and came to the attention of the Inquisition in the first place.

Many allusions have been made to the pamphlet that Maria de Macedo had written to spread the news of her visions. Maria dictated her narrative to her husband in September 1650 in her own words, and so the resulting pamphlet was not mediated in any way by an inquisitorial scribe. It provides us with an exceptional opportunity to hear a popular voice in the way that she intended to communicate her thoughts to her contemporaries. This pamphlet is the principal source for a good deal of the analysis that follows in Part III, and because of its lack of mediation and its degree of elaboration and detail, I have decided to reproduce it in its entirety so that the reader can hear the voice of Maria de Macedo with as little mediation as possible. Of course, as the translator of the text, I have interposed myself in the process, but only, I hope, to a minimal degree. For those interested in the original text, a transcript of both versions of the pamphlet can be found in the Appendix (see below for a discussion of the two versions).

Before we look at the content of the pamphlet, a brief explanation of the nature and the source of the physical document is necessary. The pamphlet falls into a fairly precise genre, the manuscript chapbook, a type that has not been studied extensively in Portugal.[6] Without a doubt this is because a relatively limited number of exempla of this type of literature have survived, owing to the fragility of the paper on which the chapbooks were written and the fewer manuscript copies produced when compared with printed chapbooks. Although I have found no copies of it outside her *processo*, Maria's pamphlet is almost a perfect example of the type of *sebastianista* literature incorporated into the collections of the seventeenth and eighteenth centuries: it is a relatively short, coherent narrative written in accessible language and full of graphic images and dramatic claims, all geared toward literate, though non-elite, readers and illiterate hearers. R. A. Houston has drawn similar conclusions about the audiences, structure, and content of printed broadsheets and chapbooks in the early modern period,[7] and there is every reason to believe that those conclusions are true of manuscript chapbook readers (*sebastianista* or otherwise) in Portugal as well. In fact, though manuscript copies were produced in much smaller numbers than printed chapbooks, they did have two distinct advantages over their printed counterparts. First, they were even cheaper to produce than printed works, since no outlay beyond the paper and ink was needed, and second, in places like Portugal, their production did not require the prior permission of the Inquisition. They were, therefore, probably the preferred medium for writings intended for poor audiences or for works whose subjects could be deemed questionable by the authorities.

Two different versions of the pamphlet were kept as evidence in Inquisição de Lisboa, Processo 4404, and it is extremely fortunate that we know the origin of both: one is the pamphlet brought to the Inquisition on February 7, 1665, by Paulo de Faria Baracho (the portionist of the Irish Seminary); the other is a copy (or possibly the original) handed over on March 9, 1665, by Feliciano Machado, who had first taken his wife's dictation about her voyages to the Hidden Isle.[8] The two pamphlets largely follow each other word for word with the exception of minor variations in word order and orthography, which is not surprising for seventeenth-century manuscripts. The exceptions to the statement above are two extended passages in Feliciano's section of the pamphlet that give more details of Maria's voyage to the Hidden Isle, which are included only in the long version of the pamphlet.

This is somewhat odd because, by comparing the handwriting found in the *processo* (namely, signatures on depositions), we know that the shorter version was the one written by Feliciano. The short version, which is considerably more readable than the long version, has no date except for the internal one Maria gives as the date of her dictation of her story, September 29, 1650, whereas the long version includes a title page and a copy date, May 12, 1658. Because certain passages in the long version make reference to dates in 1651 as having already passed, the additional material certainly represents later additions to the original pamphlet. This should not cast doubt on the passages found only in the long version, however; their content conforms to what is found in Maria and Feliciano's later depositions before the Inquisition. These facts lend weight to the conclusion that Feliciano handed over the original pamphlet (or at least an early version of it) to the inquisitors and that the additions found in the long version were probably added at Feliciano's request while pamphlets were being copied by the Jesuits of the Irish Seminary for wider distribution. The added passages may have become part of the *textus receptus* of the pamphlet by 1658 simply because they were parts of the vision that had been revealed after the original dictation date of September 29, 1650, or because, as Maria's reputation as a visionary spread, there was a desire on the part of the pamphlet's readers for a fuller narrative of what she had seen.

The truly important item to note here is that both versions of the pamphlet were copied before the Inquisition first became aware of Maria's visions in 1658 and well before the Holy Office took an active interest in the case, beginning in February 1665. The contents of the pamphlet, therefore, have not been altered by the Inquisition in any way, and indeed, as the *processo* itself demonstrates, the inquisitors themselves used the pamphlet as a source in their interrogations.

Thus, through this pamphlet, we can hear, with exceptional clarity, the voice of Maria de Macedo, if not precisely a subaltern, then certainly a non-elite, voice. These are exactly the words Maria and Feliciano wanted to use to describe their experiences; we can be confident of this fact simply because they were the ones who chose them.

The text that follows is a translation of the composite text derived from both copies of the pamphlet:[9]

The Wonderful
Things that Happened to
Maria de Macedo
Which, from the very beginning, are given
A brief notice; &
Afterwards is given as well an
addition (although not complete) of her
Husband
Feliciano Machado

Lisbon, 12th of May in the year 1658.

In the month of November 1635, I felt myself being touched at night in bed, being at this time between ten and eleven years of age. And because of the great fear that I felt, I shouted out loud, waking up my father and the whole household, without seeing anyone, nor who had touched me. My father, considering that this was my imagination, told me to leave a candle burning at night and took me to his bed, where he was not pleased with me since there was a great disturbance in the house. Returning the next night to my bed, which was at the foot of my father's, with a burning candle [beside me], I ended up dreaming that they carried me to a field, where they showed me a great variety of flowers and trees. At the side of my bed, I saw a creature, which, by the knowledge I later gained and will refer to in the future, I discovered was a large lizard, but at the time, since I did not know what it was, it appeared to me to be the figure of a dog, although I could not see its feet. Shouting loudly, I woke up my father, who asked me what was wrong. I showed him and the rest of the people in the house that creature, but they did not see it. My father again brought me to his bed, irritated that I had woken him up and saying that life was insupportable when such things occurred at night. And he told me that he would put me out the window if I did not calm down and try to get out of my imagination whatever was causing me these fears. After retiring again that same night, and after falling asleep with his arms outside the covers, they gave him a such a big hit on his arm that he could not feel it for several days.

Later, on the following night, the same figure appeared to me. And since I again shouted because of the fear I felt, my father scolded me even more, saying that he needed to punish me. At that moment, we heard a great disturbance in the house, breaking a great number of dishes that were in it, with the effect that the candle was put out twice. In the morning, we found only one room wrecked and all the rest of the dishes scattered in a closet where they were broken and out of place.

Seeing that these terrors continued to haunt me, and the misery in which I lived, my father tried to give an account of everything to learned and religious men such as Fr. Nicolau dos Anjos, Fr. Manoel Falco, Fr. Thomas de Villanova, all of whom were of the order of Saint Augustine; and to others from Our Lady of Carmo. All of them took my confession and examined my life, and I told them the entire story. After taking my confession, they gave me many relics and exorcised the house, without anything being enough to stop the same figures from appearing to me. The pain and agony in which I lived was great, considering the variety and uncertainty of opinion with which many people spoke of the matter, each of them concluding that there was no way I could get rid of the curse of these terrors. My father tried to move from these rooms to others, close to the Lazaro, which he rented to that end, because it seemed to some people that the appearances, since they were not my fault, would cease if we moved to new lodgings. And we were [in the new house] for two months without anything appearing to me, except that I always felt and heard something walking through the house at night.

And on one occasion when I was home alone going up to the rooms above, I heard a voice that told me, "Here I take you now according to my will." Placing my hands on my chest, without seeing who [had spoken], I was pushed down the stairs, with the result that I ended up so maltreated that I could not even open the door for my father when he came, nor answer him because I was unable to speak. Since a long time had passed [without anything happening], I told him what had happened to me.

During this time, which was in the month of May 1636, it happened that an aunt of mine, by the name of Pelonia de Almeida, the sister of my mother, came from Castile to the house of my father. Since we lived together, she learned about what was happening to me from the beginning. My aunt took great pains to see if she could find out what it was, but she did not succeed. After making a number of inquiries for me, my father took me to some novenas for saints and to one that my mother had vowed when she was dying. She had not completed it and so I fulfilled it for her. [After this] my aunt told me that she did not think this could be anything else but enchanted Moors, since neither the holy things nor relics that I carried, nor the exorcisms that were performed, caused them to leave. She asked me whether one of these figures appeared with a red cap, to which I responded that, up to that time, I had not seen one. Despite that, my aunt encouraged me a great deal by telling me not to be afraid of anything and, when he appeared to me again, to ask him what he wanted of me, [my aunt] supposing that I would do so now, [since I was] protected by a crucifix. So, I continued to feel more relieved about it because my aunt had assured me that nothing harmful to the soul was appearing to me and that, being enchanted Moors, as she understood them to be, they could result in great good for me.

Later the following night, they came to me in bed at night, and they touched my hand, squeezing it. Since I was calmer in spirit because of what my aunt had told me, I did not scream as I used to when I felt great fear. Another day, my father being in his house (because he had not given up the one we were in before because he worked in it by day), thinking about the misery in which he lived having two separate houses, a voice that he heard without seeing anyone told him: "Come back to your house." So, later the same day, he brought me back, very much against my will because of the fear that I had that the appearances would come back to me in it.

During this whole period of time, which, as I said before, was two months, the clerics never ceased to attend me as before. Hearing that [the figures] might be enchanted Moors, some of them informed the Provincial of Our Lady of Grace (which was then in front of the house), who was named Aveiro and who called the chapter about the case in order to find out if there were enchanted Moors or not. As all superstitions are against our holy Catholic faith and it does not speak of such, the question was fully discussed, and almost all of them agreed, though with many doubts, that there could not be any such thing. Only one cleric brought a book that stated there could be enchantments among the Moors.

And going back to my old house in which these occurrences began, he [the Moor] came looking for me one night, touching me like before. I asked what the one touching me wanted, and he replied by asking if I wanted to be lifted from the bed, to which I responded, "Yes." And I did it, grasping his clothes, which seemed to me to be a silk camlet. Taking me to a window in the house, I saw a man with a dark complexion; coarse, blond hair; colored [lit. "pintado"] white; of good stature, dressed in the Turkish manner, with a red cap, with a scimitar and matching boots with spurs, and many other ornaments. He asked me why I was afraid, if I had not done anything wrong. And I told him that if I had known who he was, I would not have been afraid and that the blame was his because he had not revealed himself earlier. And saying that it did not matter because it was all past, he asked me if I wanted to go with him. Seeing his design and intention, I said, "Yes." Taking me then to a corner of the house, he opened a door in the wall, which I clearly saw, without there having been any door there at all. He passed through, while I remained in my house. From there he showed me a jar full of gold.—(?), he took me back by hand. This continued for next several nights, showing me each night a piece of gold, each of a different shape, without me ever leaving my father's house, since he only passed through the door that he had opened. He would hit the outside of it and show me the pieces [of gold], and, in this way, things continued for seven nights. On the last of them, he asked me what I had had for dinner. And telling him some mackerel, he scolded me because I had not saved anything for him from my supper. I told my father everything, and he told me to leave him something to eat every night, such as cookies, cheese, olives, wine, and other things one eats in one's house. But if he was looking for special items like candies or sweets or something else one does not eat in one's house, then he would get nothing to eat. The table was placed next to my father's bed, and the rest of the household heard him eat and talk with me, after my father was in bed and the house shut up for the night, but only I heard [what he was saying—trans.] and the others did not.

This continued until the Eve of St. John the Baptist of 1636 during which this same man asked me if I wanted to go with him some day to the upstairs room that my father kept empty. Since it was daytime, I said, "Yes." He told me to bring my lunch with me, which I did, since my father had given me some cake, bread, fruit, and other things that I will omit to avoid being superfluous. I was in that room, seated next to a window, waiting for the Moor to come when I saw a lizard in the house that came toward me doing flips. Reaching me, it circled me and then placed its head on my lap, looking at me, at which I, being afraid (though much less than I had been before because of the experience that I had), put my hand on its head. As soon as I placed my hand there, it was immediately transformed into the same Moor that I had seen before. And after we began to eat the lunch that I had brought, he asked me if I wanted to go to his house. Since my fear was already subsiding because of the time I had spent with him, I accepted the offer that he made, I suppose without any great fear, even though everything that had happened had taken place in the house of my father and I had no idea what would happen in his house. I attribute all my thoughts on the matter to Our Lord. Seeing that he had not sought any ways or means to take advantage in this case, nor dealt with others who tried to persuade me, I decided, my innocence being great at that time, to go with him on St. John's Day in that year of 1636.

In the room that I have referred to, there is a corner in it that is located to the right of the room below, where he opened the same door that I had seen below. The Moor taking me by the hand, I freely crossed through behind him, and after passing through the door, we were walking down a staircase, and after it came to an end, down a hallway about fifty-five feet [lit. "15 varas"] long. At the end of the hall, he entered a large, beautiful room that had seven windows, fitted with lavish arrases, three facing the sea, which was nearby, and four facing the land. The walls were of smooth, worked stone, and the grounds were paved with the same stone. From one of the windows, one could go down some stairs of large stones to a garden that had many herbs, including rosemary, marjoram, sage, roses, and a fountain where I always used to get water for fifteen years (as I will explain later). Further on, there were five rooms, not as large as the first, but worked out of the same stone and felt [i.e., the arrases]. And in the last room there was another spiral staircase with eighty-seven steps that led to a very large hall of the same stone. That room contained five tables of touchstone, a large one in the middle of the room and the other four in the corners. Beneath all these rooms, there were three long corridors, very wide and dark, where a rooster as large as a turkey walked; [it] had no comb but with very long tail feathers. Those corridors were called Alminas, and they had no light besides what came from a door that opened on the sea. Light came from that door at times, but since the corridors were long, it was difficult to see unless one had a candle, even during the day. Looking from that house, the sea was as large as from this city [Lisbon—trans.] to Almadar, and on the other side houses and land could be seen.

Coming to the first room I mentioned with the Moor, I met his wife, of good stature and beautiful with a child in her arms and another at her feet. The Moor told her, "Here I bring you our Christian; tell me what you think." And she answered him that she was glad to see me, although she scolded me for feeling such great fear, but she excused me because of my youth. And she asked me to pay attention to that man who was her husband, who did not intend any harm to me, and she asked me to promise by my Law to serve him in everything that he commanded me, even if some inconvenience were involved. And I told her that I would do so. [She said] she had come there that day just to see me, and she showed me that those children were her children, asking me if I wanted to take them with me. I responded that I could not take such great lords to my land except to serve them, since the father had told me that he was a great nobleman and that the title he had in that land was equal to that of a Duke in ours. She continued by asking if I thought she looked good and whether there were more beautiful women in my land. I told her that she was very beautiful and that in my land there were some who were beautiful. With this, she put her hand on my face and took her leave of me with great recommendations from her husband, who returned me to the house of my father by the same way we had come.

And from then on, the same husband always came to find me, sometimes at night, other times by day, in the same way as the first time. And each time I went there, I saw one more person. They multiplied until they reached the number of thirty-six people—eleven women and the rest men, all dressed in the Turkish manner. They were all together on the last day on which I finished meeting them and introducing myself, and they gave me a great, joyful feast. I remained anxious seeing so many people, so they told me not to get angry or feel sad because it was better for me that there be many people. I will not give all the names here, since they were named by families, but those I found out and heard named were the following: Fatima, Arlaxa, Gumelia, Zygres, Guazales, Bencarrages, Benamares, Murças, Amet, Dyalees, Villaron, Jazemin, Muleyneque, and Dianêa. The Zygrereal was the first Mooress, or I should say, Turk, as were the other people I have named, who came to me.

And after this had ended and they had introduced themselves, they each began to change into the shape of various creatures, such as snakes, lizards, salamanders, hippopotamuses, lions, and other kinds of animals and creatures of which I have no knowledge. These figures appeared to me in my father's house, and each day one person from the aforementioned figures would come to me until they had all come. When they had all come, another came who caused me a great deal of fear and, approaching me, was transformed into the person that I later knew. I should point out, I suppose, that in none of these figures did the eyes ever change nor did they change in form; they were always the same creature. Many times I knew the person coming in that form by their eyes before they changed back into human form.

This diversity and mystery [lit. labyrinth], which was very great and which lasted for a long time, coming to an end, they took me through the dark corridors below, which they called Alminas (as I have said before), and they made me dig up the earth from which they took great riches, such as gold and silver and jewels of all kinds and in great quantity. From the gold and silver, they forged and hammered out coins, and they made me serve with them equally in all the necessary work, besides having to go get water from the fountain that was in the garden. Two years, more or less, having passed in this task of getting water, they asked me if I wanted to see their King. And telling them yes, they took me to the last room upstairs that was the one that had three, I mean five, tables, which I mentioned before. And the one called Realmurça and the other people were all of great authority and respect, both in their clothing and in their persons. The one who appeared to me the first time was called Bencerrage the Great and his wife, Zygrereal, and they presented me to the King, I told His Highness that I was a Christian who was his servant and that I was named Maria, and the King praised me a great deal, saying that he was glad to see me and asking me if anyone had done me any harm. I told him no, although a few times they had ordered me about and kept me busy. And he told me not to shirk in anything that they told me to do and that he would see to it that I would be well satisfied with everything. After all the riches were taken from the ground where it was found, the King commanded that it be divided, setting aside what he said he thought was for me. After all this was put into order, he always looked to my service and treatment in all that those people commanded me for the length of fourteen years.

The work of these people was singing, playing, and dancing in their free time and working when it was necessary (in the way I have mentioned before). They lived in the following way regarding food, which was to eat bread, meat, a little wine, pork, and fruits. Their clothing was all Turkish. And nothing ever caused me scruple in regard to our holy Catholic faith because I saw there Our Lady, the baby Jesus, St. Joseph, and our Crucified Lord and they always spoke of God and his things, saying that they had become Christians and asking me several times if I would greet them if I saw them in my land. I told them, "Yes." And in this conformity I lived and served with this people until May of 1650, visiting them every night and many times by day without ceasing to come look for me, it not being enough that I was injured thirteen times because they took me away in that way. And while I was sick, I was not abandoned and was visited by some of those people, which only I saw in the house of my father; no one else in the household saw them. These illnesses and sicknesses were caused by the work that I had with them, the work they gave to me because I was not used to it. And thus it gave me a great deal of suffering, especially on winter nights from which I would come home so abused that many times I could not move for three or four days, and even this was not enough for them to excuse me from continuing the work.

During this time, which was in September, I married Feliciano Machado, my husband, on the twenty-seventh of that month of 1649. Fearing that he would not be able to find me in bed, I was compelled to frankly tell him everything from the beginning of this situation. (Until then he did not know of it, since no disaster had befallen me.) The greatest torment I had was telling him about it because of the incredulity he always showed to me on this matter, never believing me, and telling me that such a thing as this could not occur in life nor had he heard of it, nor seen it, nor read of it, nor has such a thing been spoken of(?). Finally, though, there were so many of these experiences that I told him [about them], so that from that point on he could speak of it as a witness of the truth of all that I have related. I sign here and in the Description of what occurred to me that my husband includes below, that it is all the truth. He wrote it only because I told him to, begging Our Lord that He be served in what I have related, so that the world will also see and know it for His Most Holy Service and Praise, and so that they will then believe that I am telling the truth. Lisbon, 29 of September of 1650.

Maria de Macedo

It would be quite superfluous (excepting mere curiosity) to have any desire to refer in detail to that which my wife, Maria de Macedo, has given me to write about the events that she has related and that she has mentioned so that Heaven (I trust) will favor her. But so that I will not fall into the fault that the curious could charge me with if I failed to make such a grave matter available to those who are wiser and more educated, I make this small work (although painful for me for the reasons I will describe below) in which I will give an account and a brief summary of my experience and of what I could find out from her about this matter, with all the work and care that I have sought to do so, from the 27th of September of 1649, when I married my wife.

Having been married a few days, she told about what has been written before, with a light so dim that the pen cannot clarify it to any intelligence, because she was afraid to tell me due to the trouble and burden involved, especially to me who gave her little credit. Out of curiosity to know what my wife was telling me, I made it easier for her to speak, and in such a way that she was encouraged not to hide anything that had happened.

Having heard from the beginning the whole of what had happened to her, I confess before Our Lord that I believed it my greatest harm and misfortune in the whole world, which I attributed several times to the Enemy of the Soul who pursued and tempted her in this way and others to lay an ambush for her. Though thousands of thoughts and ideas tormented me, I did not believe any of it. Knowing her and having experienced how she treated [me?], [I wished to see] her free and at ease from all the experiences [literally, changes] (when she had them) that could give me occasion to have a different opinion of her or to think that these were fantastic and diabolical things. [In the conversations] I did not see any sign that showed me [one way or the other—trans.] Finally, I decided to try to communicate with my confessor and other wise people, always pretending that I was happy and content, so as not to give them the occasion to force me to reveal [what was going on]. I am the first to admit that many times it seemed to me that I was losing my mind because everything she was saying to me did not seem to conform to our holy Catholic faith, and they seemed to be more superstitions than something from God.

One night, I decided to stay awake (while pretending to sleep) and I felt someone touch me lightly on the shoulders and neck, and it seemed to me that they were trying to put me back to sleep [lit. influencing sleep over my eyes.] But I remained vigilant, and an hour after this, my wife got up from bed. I had told her before to call me when they came for her, to see if she would do what she had promised me. But I saw that she paid no attention to me nor to what she had promised me, which caused me great discontent because I thought she had lost her mind. Since she had completely left the bed, I sat up in it and I clearly heard someone speaking, without seeing who, or even seeing her, since we were without light. The person with whom she was speaking asked her what I was doing, and my wife told him that I was asleep. The voice that I heard speak to her then said the following words to her in this way: "He is not asleep, nor was he asleep." After this they spoke for between a quarter and a half an hour, but I was not able to understand it because her voice was very soft, and the other voice I heard was strange, half Castilian, half Portuguese, raspy and crude, difficult to understand, in the manner of a Moor. After my wife returned to bed, I scolded her for not calling me when she came, since I had told her to do that. She responded that the person she had been speaking with was an enchanted Mooress, one of the thirty-six people that she has referred to, and that she did not consent to my wife calling me because she knew I was awake. And in truth, I was and this time she did not take her with her.

The following night, the same thing happened, and feeling my wife get up from the bed, I sat up again to see what her intention was. Concluding that she had not left yet, I waited for half an hour before I got up to see if I could find her in the house, since she only experienced this in the house. I asked her what she was doing and why she had gotten up from bed, and she replied that she was going to get water for her people from the fountain. And since she did not know whether I was awake or asleep when she left, I asked her how long it had taken her to go get [the water] after she left. She told me that it seemed to have taken three hours. From this, I realized how far from the truth, and how false, she was, since when she left, it was around midnight, and she could have been gone, at most, around a half an hour from that time. As a result, I was very doubtful and very unhappy seeing that she would not tell me the purpose or the truth about what had happened. I could not find out what I especially wanted to know: if she left the house and if she went bodily or invisibly, or if all these things she had told me about were shown to her inside the house. I told her to ask the Moors for permission for me to come along with her one time when they took her, or at the least, that they let me see her when she went. This came from my lack of confidence, seeing, by this means, a way to find some circumstance, word, or deed to come to some agreement with her on it. They told her to tell me that I should not be too curious and that it was neither convenient nor important for me to know more. This caused my mistrust in my wife to grow even more, since I thought this was a Fantastic thing, since they had shut the doors on the test I wanted to conduct. No certainty remained to me at all because of her statement. And living this way, in this misery from which only God Our Lord could liberate me, I tried to find out more, and using good words and kindness, to explain to her the doubts and scruples that I felt and that [her situation] was causing me. In this regard, I asked about the time at which she remembers having the use of reason *de vita et moribus*, telling her many times what it seemed like to me and what I had been able to figure out about it, almost as if I were her confessor. I explained to her that the knowledge and slyness of the Demon were very great, and how he could use these means to deceive her, giving her many examples of his cunning and his tricks, all with the end of making us lose ourselves. I was also confident that, because we were friends and because we had a good marriage, even besides the obligation of matrimony, she would not hide anything from me nor that she would want to lose me. And from the relation she gave of her treatment and customs, I did not find anything in her that could endanger our, I mean, her salvation. She told me that in this matter she had done nothing against our holy Catholic faith, and that her confessor had not found anything, either, but that [he had said that] this was simply her imagination, which she should try to get rid of.

{During this time, I was playing a guitar one night when my wife told me to keep playing the way I was playing because I had a good listener. I asked her who it was, and she replied that it was that Moor who had first appeared to her, whom she always called Rabam. I stopped playing, without paying attention to anything she said or believing her, [and was putting away the guitar] when I saw the figure of a small man, about an ell tall below a desk. He then left there and went down beneath the stairs quickly (?) (just as when a cloud moves with great speed through the air). I did not see the figure's face because he always had his back toward me, but his clothes (in my opinion) looked long(?) and dark green. And later the next day, my wife told me that the Moor had told her that he wanted to appear to me so that I would know the truth and not doubt anymore. However, because he chose such an ill-advised means, my doubts were growing each time, as I will explain more later. For these reasons, which did not move me to believe in him more, nor to follow the opinion, which many people followed in this case, truly believing in him, as if [he were?] God Our Lord, falling away from faith, with shallow arguments, as I later experienced. [The translation, and I may say, reconstruction, of this last sentence is tentative at best because of the illegibility of the text and awkwardness of its construction. The translation, as it stands, was the one deemed to best suit the broader context of the passage—trans.]}

{And after this, around midnight (I was with my wife in bed), there was a light that walked through the house, and the brightness it gave off was like the rays of a large diamond. I asked her what it was, and she said that the person who came to get her (as she had told me) always wore a piece of glass on his chest, which was the source of the light, and which he carried so that he could see where he was going wherever he was. I saw this light many times, without paying much attention to it and without being concerned about it, simply because it continued [occurring] so many times. However, I did continue to suffer a great deal of distress because of what my wife was telling me, without being able to make her understand that I had not been able to discover anything about this matter, nor understand the difficulties(?) of the 14 years when she walked in the land of the Moors, which my wife had told me about.}

{But, since divine mercy is never lacking to those who value it, even though I was such a great sinner, by Christ Our Lord, by his immense goodness and clemency, it took place during this very time of my greatest distress, that I expressly tried to investigate this case, pursuing it vigorously—(?) by the ways and means that I will relate later, which God supplied (with the result that I was obligated to write about it, as I am doing now), forgetting the disgrace, forgetting the—(?), and so it happened in the following manner:

Since my wife's case was known by some people in this city, who had heard that she dealt with enchanted Moors, it happened that in the month of May of 1650, a man by the name of João Penalvo came and told my father-in-law that there was a woman in the neighborhood of the Alfama named D. Maria Loba, who had a grandchild of King Sebastian, and that the Moors, with whom my wife had continued those 14 years, were the people of the very same King Sebastian, who revealed that he was hidden under the sign of election ["encoberto debayxo de signio de elleyçam"]. And that he [João Penalvo] knew this to be true because he had a sister-in-law, who was named D. Luiza de Portugal, who also visited the same King and people, just as my wife did, saying that the whole story ["façiam"] was—(true?).}

{Seeing and hearing all this Babylonian confusion and this maze of deception, I considered it the most diabolical error that there was in the world, or that there could be. I tried, with my wife, to give an account of this to Holy Office. We both went to appear [before it], as one should in a case of such importance, to give them the whole truth of the experience, with as much certainty as possible, even besides the approval of our confessor, so that with everything clarified and with all the evidence, they could resolve this as easily as possible. Since I made every effort—(?) in the investigation of the facts behind this mysterious case, I tried to meet the aforementioned João Penalvo; D. Luixa de Portugal, his sister-in-law; and D. Maria Loba, of whom I had no knowledge before, nor even the opportunity to, so that they could tell [the truth about the matter—trans.], given the contradictions and variations that these matters had caused even in those of the best judgment. And I will confess that I took great care and used many means to find these people (since all the curious will want to know if I found them), who told me clearly that what I took, and had always taken, and was still taking to be a lie and a trap, was true. They told me that the Moors that my wife had seen were the people of King Sebastian, and they said this so calmly and with such confidence that it became public among many people in this Kingdom [Portugal—trans.] that they ignorantly considered it to be true.}

{Taking all this to be an illusion of the Demon, I had an experience with my wife, and I was going to tell my wife to find out more about these Moors of hers and to ask them if what the aforementioned João Penalvo, his sister-in-law D. Maria Loba [*sic*] and D. Luiza de Portugal had said was true. She did so, and they replied and said that it was just as those three people had said. As a result of which, my wife (as she told me) complained to them and asked why they had hidden the title, and the names of the Moors, if it was something related to King Sebastian. They told her not to become angry with them that they had not revealed who they were, since it was better that they had not and that it had all been necessary. They went on to tell her more, namely, that they had all become Christians and that King Sebastian, after his defeat, had always wandered up to that time in the greatest penitence and that he now lived on the Hidden Isle. He was married to the Lady Auriana [*sic*], daughter of the King of Denmark, who had with her two brothers, one named Federico and the other Ricardo. King Sebastian had five living children, three males, and two females, because one daughter had died. The eldest son was named Dom João, who was already married to one of his cousins, daughter of the lord Ricardo, and with whom he has a daughter named Lady Joanna. The second son of King Sebastian was named Dom Fernando and the third, Dom Duarte. The daughters were called the Lady Ignacia and the Lady Ursula. The one who died was named the Lady Catherina, who is buried in Santa Maria Mayor, one of the principal churches of the island, as the description of the island below states.}

{And seeing what my wife was telling me, and how it conformed to what the three others had said, I still thought that, for reasons I will show later, it was a very subtle and cunning trap and plan of the Devil. In order to give more clarity to our confessors and to the Holy Office, I decided to continue in this matter, though only to see what happened.}

{With all this hardship (if I may so call my punishment) during the month of May and during the time this was revealed to her, I watched every night to see what they were doing and what their design was, though in the end such a fantastic and vain hope [was disappointed]. And seeing that the changes [lit. "mudanças"] that occurred every night were growing greater and greater, just as one can see in the Description that I give below, I wrote what my wife told me about the revelation of this King.}

She told me that all those people or Moors had taken Christian names and had been baptized and that when that King came, there would be great revolutions and punishments in this city [Lisbon—trans.]. {He has 323 boats, 202 warships, and many galleys by which to enter it, including 14 gilded ones with banners of scarlet satin and with awnings of scarlet velvet, which were prepared in 1651.} And it will be during his night that the sun will be reborn and that King Sebastian will bring different laws, of which there will only be five, written by his hand and confirmed by Our Lord Jesus Christ. And I was given to understand that he speaks with Our Lord {Jesus Christ} three times a week, on Mondays, Wednesdays, and Sundays. This King has in his company a Franciscan monk, who serves as his confessor, by the name of Angelico, {de Christo, and as his Chronicler, a Benedictine monk, by the name of Fr. Angelo.} The aforementioned King also has five children with him, 3 males and 2 females, namely, the oldest is D. João; the second, D. Fernando; and the third, D. Duarte; and the females, D. Ignacia and D. Ursula.

{On the morning of the 27th of May, he came in the company of two Moors, natives of the Island, one named Francisco and the other, Pedro, to where the Prince was, which they told her was in Germany, where he was in company with King Arthur of England for a few months. And to the aforementioned King, he carried one of two letters and the other one for the Prince, King Sebastian. [The letters] contained a treaty in which he suggested that he join together with him and with the King of Aragon, who was already [located in?] the Castle of this city of Lisbon. And the aforementioned King, upon arriving, also wrote a letter to King Sebastian that same night and then left from there to go to Germany. And all three of them wrote to each other, and they decided to meet on Saturday, the first of April in the year 1651 in the Church of Our Lady of Tribulations, where she saw a young girl from Oleiras named Maria de Concepção, whom she knew, in the company of D. Jaime of Aragon; she had also seen her a few times on the Island. And with King Arthur, she saw a boy named Jorge Balaguer, a Venetian. She arrived with the Lord King [Sebastian] and the other two who were waiting for him. Later, they all entered the church, the three servants remaining in the porch. Three holy prophets also came, and they gave to each one a sword, specifically, St. John the Evangelist to King Sebastian, Elijah to [D. Jaime] of Aragon, and Enoch to [King Arthur] of England, all of whom were protected by the Cross. Each one was also given a piece of paper, and each Prophet blessed his King, and then they separated, [the Prophets] staying in the church and the Kings going back to the countries from whence they had come. Afterward, my wife said that these holy prophets were guarded [lit. deposited] in a temple that would appear before the revelation of King Sebastian.}

{All this was presented to Father Fr. Luiz de Madre de Deos, a cleric of the Franciscan Order in this city and an examiner of books, and he asked her the three questions given below. She gave the following answers, which astonished the aforementioned cleric:

Q. 1 Whether the Church should follow the opinion that St. John the Evangelist is dead or that he is alive?

Q. 2 Also whether the two Prophets, Elijah and Enoch, were kept and protected to come and preach at the coming of the Antichrist, and if this is the case, whether they were coming with King Sebastian?

Q. 3 And whether the aforementioned three Prophets were in the earthly Paradise, which was to be located on the Hidden Isle?

A. 1 As to whether the Church should follow the opinion that St. John the Evangelist was dead, and thus not a saint, his death came to an end and he is alive and guarded so that he can come with King Sebastian to preach the judgment of the Reformation [of the world].

A. 2 It cannot be denied that the other two Prophets are guarded in the earthly Paradise to return to preach the coming of the Antichrist which will take place at the end of the world. But the world must first be Reformed.

A. 3 It is doubtful that the earthly Paradise is located on the Hidden Isle, because asking many sailors and others about the earthly Paradise, they say it is certain that it is confined to the land and not in the sea.}

{On that St. Michael's Day of 1619(?), it was 32 years since God hid King Sebastian on the Mount of Camposallo, which lies at the end of the kingdom of Germany toward the port of Venice. Between noon and one in the afternoon, he left, fleeing the King of Castile (who was searching for him) with Lady Auriana, his wife, and with two noble sons, one carried by the aforementioned lady in her arms and the other with Our Lord Sebastian. Being tired from traveling on the mountain, they laid down to sleep, but when they woke up they found themselves on the Hidden Isle, without knowing how.}

{Description of that Island, Given by my Wife}

Arriving at that island with Prince João, I saw three churches that were in a city, whose size I cannot comment on, since I did not see more than five streets, between which are the churches I mentioned. The names of the churches are the following: the Cathedral church, Santa Maria Mayor, which has an Archbishop and a Bishop; the second is St. Stephen; and the third is St. John. I cannot comment, either, on the interiors of the churches because I never entered the churches and only saw them from the outside. The streets coming to an end, I came to a large field in the form of a square with three fountains in the middle, so it was called the Square of the Fountains. After that, there were the fields where they get fruits from the earth. The sustenance of those people is in the following manner:

The people of that island are of great stature, corpulent, and not very white. [They speak] Portuguese, but very crudely. They celebrate all the divine offices and keep the law of God much better than we do, and in the same form and manner that the Holy Mother Church teaches us. In that land, there is abundance, since everything one could want is available without any work. Nothing is cultivated; instead each person simply carries what is necessary to his house, namely, bread, meat, fruits, and other things, the land being very full of flowers and flying birds. The fertility is so great that all live abundantly without anyone administering them, nor is there anyone who knows how to do so, because if one wants wheat, one simply goes to the fields and carries it home, threshing it with one's feet. And one grinds it between some weights of stone with a hand-crank device. For meat, there are oxen, sheep, and chicken, which one can get in the fields and bring home easily, since none of them resist. The birds are so gentle that everyone can take one without them flying away and without any being wild. The clothes they wear are made from the wool of sheep and lambs, according to whatever color—black or white—God has made them, since there is no one there who knows how to dye them or make them in colors. They regularly sew the black with the white and the white with the black.

In this island, there is a great deal of gold, but little silver, and very little of good quality, and for this reason they do not use it or pay attention to it because it is not necessary. And the abundance of gold is so great that, as I have said before, you see it in the water of the fountains, in nuggets, which, after they have been cleaned in a tank, each one takes home what he wants, but not because it is necessary.

They told her that the island was very large because my wife did not visit more than the one mentioned, nor have they shown her [all of] it even now. And they do not tell me anything else about it because they do not want it to be(?) an annoyance.

This island is found in the middle of two other, smaller, islands, which they allowed [her] to see, but she never went to them nor did they take her there.

<And she told me nothing else about the island.

At this time, I sought out the Reverend Doctor Fr. Sebastião de Payvão, a cleric of the Most Holy Trinity, because I had heard that he was a learned man and to see if he could more easily explain this case to me and alleviate the pain and torment in which I lived. Recounting everything to him, I begged him to take my wife's confession, and making him promise that if it was something diabolical, he would do all he could to stop the devil.

And after taking her confession, Doctor Fr. Sebastião de Payvão told me that I should live calmly and without concern because what she was saying may [have] come as a gift ["agolidade," ability], which God commanded to be revealed to her in whatever place or house she was in. With this, he told me not to pursue or worry about the matter any more.>

Feliciano Machado

‹4›

THE TRIAL OF MARIA DE MACEDO

All investigations undertaken by the Inquisition began with a denunciation, someone reporting suspect activity to the Holy Office, and an examination of the *who?* and *why?* of denunciations forms an essential part of the analysis of any inquisitorial prosecution. This is certainly true in the case of Maria de Macedo and the details of this denunciation merit special consideration. Testimony against Maria de Macedo was first recorded by the inquisitorial notary João Teixeira in Lisbon on May 31, 1658. Like all information not yet part of an active investigation, the testimony was recorded in the Quadernos do Promotor—the record books of the chief administrative official of the Inquisition—though once an active case against Maria de Macedo was begun in 1665, the denunciation was copied in its entirety into the newly opened file on Maria, which would become Inquisição de Lisboa, Processo 4404.[1] The principal item of interest in the denunciation is the original accuser: the first person to bring the visions of Maria de Macedo and her visits with King Sebastian to the attention of the Holy Office, Dr. António de Sousa de Macedo. As noted in chapter 2, Sousa de Macedo was a familiar of the Inquisition, a member of the Royal Treasury Council, and the prominent *joanista* who had written *Lusitania Liberata* to identify the Encoberto as João IV and to uphold the claims of the House of Braganza against its detractors.

António de Sousa de Macedo began his denunciation by informing the inquisitorial officials that he had heard a rumor from several people that there was a woman who lived in the Chiado district who claimed to have traveled several times to the Hidden Isle. He knew that she was married to Feliciano Machado of the Treasury Department but could not remember her name correctly, calling her Francisca de Macedo. He went on to name Father Manoel da Costa, S.J., as someone with whom he had spoken specifically about the matter and offered his opinion that da Costa believed in what the woman was saying. Through da Costa, who by that time was well acquainted with Maria and Feliciano, António de Sousa de Macedo arranged to meet the woman and hear for himself what she had to say.

So, on Sunday, May 26, 1658, Sousa de Macedo went to Maria's house and, along with Feliciano and Maria's stepmother, heard Maria recount her travels to the Hidden Isle from the beginning of her experiences as a child. Although at several points António de Sousa de Macedo stated that he could not remember all the details of her story, the account he gave the Inquisition of what she had said is virtually identical to what was contained in the long version of the pamphlet, which had been copied by someone in the Irish Seminary not even a month before. After hearing the story of her travels, the nobleman asked her whether she traveled to the island bodily or only by "representation." She answered that she did not know but, while there, she saw things as clearly as people did in everyday life.

Sousa de Macedo then asked Feliciano if he had ever found his wife absent from the house during those times. Feliciano told him that to resolve that issue he had stayed up watching her several nights, and at times when she was still in bed, she would wake up and tell him that she had just come from the island. One day, Feliciano went on to say, he heard the Moor come to speak to his wife. Feliciano got up and moved to where Maria was, but then felt someone place his or her hands on his shoulders, though he saw no one. He complained to his wife, and she made a signal with her head toward the area behind Feliciano, whereupon he felt the weight of the hands lift from his shoulders. He then admitted to his guest that he was the most confused man in the world, though he also told him that Maria's father could confirm everything she said about her childhood.

The story and Feliciano's testimony did not impress Sousa de Macedo, however. On the basis of her manner of speech and "other circumstances" (which he never specified), he concluded that Maria's story was false and that she was an impostor. After all, Sousa de Macedo continued, what she was saying was ridiculous. His suspicions were also raised by her reluctance to speak to him, only doing so because Feliciano had insisted. The inquisitor taking the denunciation then asked him if he had formed an opinion as to whether she was in her right mind or disturbed by some passion. Sousa de Macedo answered that he did not see any evidence that she was out of her mind or disturbed, although he did say that he thought she had "more simplicity than understanding" before reiterating his conclusion that she was faking the whole thing. With that, the denunciation came to an end.

Before proceeding to the trial itself, we should address a crucial question: Why did António de Sousa de Macedo feel the need to report what he had heard to the Inquisition of Lisbon a mere five days after he heard it? Unfortunately, there is no direct evidence to answer this question, although a number of possibilities present themselves: a political motive, a personal motive, a dogmatic motive, or some combination of the three.

Perhaps the most obvious reason would be a political motive. António de Sousa de Macedo was a prominent and published *joanista*, and Maria de Macedo was someone claiming to have visions of Sebastian as the Hidden One who was to come. As noted in chapter 2, the period after João IV's death in 1656 was a time of waning enthusiasm for the Braganzas, at least as messianic candidates. Although efforts were made to rework the interpretation of the prophetic corpus so that Afonso VI could be identified as the Encoberto, he was never to enjoy as much popular support in such a role as his father, the Restorer, did. Perhaps, given the disillusionment of the *joanista* camp after João's death and the struggles involved in transferring those expectations to Afonso, it was decided by those who continued to support the Braganzas' millenarian claims, such as Sousa de Macedo, that it was necessary to clamp down on those who still believed in Sebastian. A dramatic and, in many ways, exciting hypothesis, but one that does not accord well with the weight of the evidence, simply because there is no evidence for a crackdown on the *sebastianistas* in the records of the Inquisition, the most likely venue for such prosecutions, or among the records of the royal courts. And if a political crackdown on the *sebastianistas* was the motivation, why prosecute Maria de Macedo among all the interpreters and visionaries who favored Sebastian during that period? And why would the Inquisition have waited seven years to actually prosecute the case if she was intended, by Afonso's supporters, as an example to be avoided? The decisive evidence against this option is the fact that the trial against António de Vieira—a *joanista*'s *joanista*—was going on at virtually the same time as Maria's trial, although this could be partially accounted for by his previous antagonism toward the Holy Office. So, however intriguing the possibility of a political/ideological motive might seem, there is no evidence to support it, and several positive objections to it, and so it should be rejected.

Another possibility within the political realm is that there was some unknown disagreement, having nothing to do with messianic speculations, between António de Sousa de Macedo and Feliciano Machado, or more likely, between Sousa de Macedo and Feliciano's patron, Gaspar de Abreu. In this regard, it should be kept in mind that Sousa de Macedo and Abreu represented two different and, oftentimes, opposing wings of the royal administration. Sousa de Macedo was a prominent part of the council system, whose members were appointed directly by the king to the councils, which were policy-making bodies. Abreu was the secretary of the Treasury Department. Though department secretaries were also appointed by the king, they served not primarily as advisers but as the chief administrative officials of the permanent royal bureaucracy, a bureaucracy concerned with the day-to-day implementation of policy and running of the mechanisms of the early modern Portuguese state. This is, admittedly, a somewhat overly neat and schematic description of the two systems, and in practice, despite theoretical demarcations between the two wings of royal governance, conflicts over jurisdiction and authority were frequent between them.[2] Also, councillors were generally grandees and members of notable noble families and therefore often represented the interests, or at least the views, of the upper aristocracy. Secretaries were also nobles—Gaspar de Abreu was—but the bulk of advice the secretaries were receiving came from the non-noble *letrados* who staffed the royal bureaucracy, which had a notably more *letrado* complexion than the councils did. Perhaps either one of these areas of friction or a political quarrel of a different nature provoked hostility between the two men and, by extension, between them and their followers. Was the prosecution of Maria de Macedo a form of political payback against Gaspar de Abreu or Feliciano Machado (or both)? Again, an intriguing possibility, and again, there is no direct evidence to support it, though it cannot be discounted out of hand.

Perhaps there was personal antagonism between António de Sousa de Macedo and Feliciano Machado. In her second set of defense papers (*contradittas*), Maria de Macedo stated that there was just such an enmity between the two men. She claimed that Sousa de Macedo was not friendly ("não era affecto") to her husband because her husband had refused to implement some provisions of the Council of State that would have directly benefited Sousa de Macedo.[3] However, this statement should be viewed with a good deal of suspicion. In her first set of defense papers,[4] Maria names Dr. António de Sousa de Macedo as a defense witness, a fact that calls into question her motivations for trying to discredit him in her second set. If this personal feud between her husband and Sousa de Macedo was really so intense that his testimony should be held suspect, why had she chosen to call him as a witness in her favor less than two months earlier? It is more likely that, whereas she initially thought that Sousa de Macedo would be a helpful witness for her cause, she changed her mind when she heard the formal reading of charges (Prova da Justiça) on October 10, 1665; after figuring out that Sousa de Macedo had been the one who had first denounced her, she then tried to discredit him to save herself. While the version of events given in her *contradittas* is thus suspect, one cannot wholly dismiss the possibility that there was some kind of enmity between Sousa de Macedo and her husband.

What, then, is left? There is the possibility that the denunciation was driven by, for lack of a better term, a dogmatic motive, namely, that Dr. António de Sousa de Macedo denounced Maria because he truly thought she was guilty of a crime worthy of the Inquisition's attention. And while it is a somewhat prosaic answer, it cannot be discounted simply on that basis. Sousa de Macedo studied law at Coimbra and was well known for the erudition of his theological and patriotic works. He was also a familiar of the Inquisition and thus well acquainted with the range of suspect activities falling under the jurisdiction of the Holy Office. In his deposition, he stated that his concern was that Maria was a fraud faking her visions. In Portuguese legal terms, he thought she was guilty of *fingimento*, which, according to book 3, title 20, of the Regimento de 1640, the book of procedures still used by the Inquisition in 1658, was a punishable offense under the jurisdiction of the Holy Office.[5] Sousa de Macedo almost certainly knew the text, interested as he was in both legal and theological matters, not to mention the good order of the Inquisition. These facts are consistent with someone reporting an offense simply because he or she felt it merited investigation on its own terms. While no conclusion on this matter can, with the available evidence, be considered definitive, I tend toward this last option of a largely disinterested denunciation on the part of Dr. António de Sousa de Macedo rather than one motivated by personal or political calculations.

There is another aspect of this denunciation that remains unresolved, and unfortunately there is little evidence that is even suggestive of an answer. It is rather easy to understand why the Inquisition opened an investigation of Maria de Macedo on the basis of a single denunciation, which was somewhat atypical but hardly unprecedented. After all, testimony from a well-connected and highly regarded familiar of the Inquisition such as Sousa de Macedo would have carried great weight with any inquisitor, even without immediate corroboration.

The question remains, though, why the Inquisition decided to wait seven years before actively pursuing the case. In the certification given by Manoel da Costa de Britto, the notary who recorded the testimony of the initial witnesses in the case, on February 4, 1665, he was ordered by the Conselho Geral to reopen the case and copy the denunciation into a new case file.[6] The only reason given by the members of the Conselho Geral was that news of the matter had spread a great deal and that there was much talk about it, especially among "the fathers of the Company [of Jesus]," even to the point where some Jesuits in the Irish Seminary were copying "a paper" that told of her visits to the Hidden Isle. The fact that Maria's growing reputation, especially among clerics, was a concern to the Conselho Geral is not surprising; institutionally, the Inquisition was extremely suspicious of anything that might cause *escándalo* among the faithful. But while this explains the motive for the prosecution, it does nothing to explain the seven-year delay, for Maria's reputation was spreading and the Jesuits were copying the pamphlet in 1658, even before Sousa de Macedo's denunciation. Perhaps it was a matter of degree—perhaps knowledge of Maria's visions had, in 1658, not yet reached a critical mass sufficient to warrant the Inquisition's attention, but this remains an unsatisfying conclusion, since it was generally the Holy Office's preference to squelch such activities as quickly as possible. The issue will have to remain unresolved unless further evidence is discovered.

Before commenting on the initial witnesses, we should say a few words about the inquisitorial officials involved in the case. The principal inquisitor for the prosecution was Fernão Correa de la Cerda, who had served as an inquisitor in the tribunal of Évora before being promoted to the Inquisition of Lisbon in November 1662. His fellow inquisitors, Francisco Barreto and João de Castilho, who play larger roles in the later phases of the case, were also career officials in the Inquisition. Barreto, a doctor in canon law, was the senior inquisitor in Lisbon and had held that position since the summer of 1656. Castilho was a canon lawyer who had served as a *deputado*—second in rank to the inquisitors in judicial matters—of the Inquisition of Lisbon since 1660 before being appointed an inquisitor in Évora in 1664. His tenure there was a short one because in July 1665—after Maria's trial was well under way—he was appointed to the Lisbon tribunal to replace the recently deceased inquisitor D. Veríssimo de Lencastre. Manoel da Costa de Britto, the notary who took down the testimony of the initial witnesses in the case, had apparently been a notary with the Inquisition of Lisbon for some time, although due to gaps in the administrative records of the court, the exact date of his appointment to the post is not known. These brief descriptions should demonstrate that the officials involved in Maria de Macedo's case were all experienced and well versed in the procedures of the Holy Office.[7]

Once the decision to proceed with the investigation was taken, the Inquisition of Lisbon moved quickly, and between February 5 and February 10, 1665, six witnesses—Padre Pedro Peixoto, Padre Bento Perreira, Padre Manoel da Costa, Padre Paulo de Faria Baracho, Padre João Ribeiro, and Padre Diogo Fernandes—were summoned before the tribunal to give their testimony about Maria de Macedo. All of the men were Jesuit priests residing at either the Professing House of São Roque or the Irish Seminary, both Jesuit institutions in the Chiado area of Lisbon.[8] All six men recounted stories that generally follow the account given by Maria in her pamphlet, though there were a number of minor variations among the witnesses, which should not be surprising. Padre Peixoto, for example, had a tendency to conflate events that were separate incidents in Maria's account, and he emphasized Sebastian's prophetic role (along the lines of the Last World Emperor tradition) more than Maria had, at least in her pamphlet. Manoel da Costa's retelling was much closer to the version that appears in the pamphlet. He did include some additional material that is well corroborated by other witnesses or in the testimony of Maria herself. Like Peixoto, he makes mention of Maria's claim to have traveled to Lisbon in the company of Queen Aureliana to celebrate a novena in the Convent of Our Lady the Mother of God. He also adds an extended description of the oratory where Sebastian prayed. It was very decently ornamented, with icons of Christ, Saint John, and Saint Anthony adorning its walls, and on Wednesdays and Fridays Sebastian spent the entire day there, praying and fasting on bread and water without speaking to anyone—all details that impressed Father da Costa regarding Sebastian's piety. There was one story that da Costa recounted that Maria later denied having said: he claimed that Sebastian had asked Maria to deliver a letter of alliance to the king of Denmark. A small detail perhaps, but one that Inquisitor Fernão Correa de la Cerda thought held considerable significance.

The details of the Hidden Isle were what had captured the imagination of Diogo Fernandes, but João Ribeiro gave only a short description of what Maria had said. Bento Perreira gave a similarly brief summary of Maria's claims and admitted that he had heard them only from Pedro Peixoto, since he had never gone to hear Maria himself. Paulo de Faria Baracho was not asked what he heard about Maria; he was asked only if he had in his possession a pamphlet that dealt with the Hidden Isle. When he answered that he did, he was ordered to present a copy of the work to the Holy Office the next day. So, on February 7, 1665, Paulo de Faria Baracho duly brought in a copy and was then dismissed, never to be called back by the Inquisition regarding this case. It is one of the more curious aspects of this trial that the man the inquisitors knew was copying and distributing Maria's pamphlet was never questioned more extensively regarding his involvement with Maria de Macedo and her visions. Whatever the reason for failing to question him, by February 7, Inquisitor Fernão Correa de la Cerda had the ability to read for himself what Maria had to say about her voyages to the Hidden Isle.

The reactions of the witnesses to Maria's claims were more varied than their descriptions of those claims. Diogo Fernandes had the most favorable assessment of Maria and said unabashedly that he thought she was "truthful, and without any pretense whatever, of good judgment and great virtue." He had concluded that what she said was true and was from God. He also mentioned that the story of Maria de Macedo was "commonly spoken of in this city [Lisbon]." Father Manoel da Costa was also quite favorable toward Maria, judging her a "sincere and well-intentioned" woman and very contemplative. His testimony reveals him to be one of the principal conduits of Maria's stories to the Jesuit fathers of Lisbon. He did, however, have one question that he wished to resolve: he wanted to know why Maria de Macedo had been chosen to be a witness of the things she claimed. He said that she did not know, but that she would ask the next time she spoke with Sebastian. After a delay because the king was praying and fasting, she brought back the answer that Sebastian could admit only seven people—non-island people, presumably—who would serve as witnesses to the rest of the world when he returned to Portugal to fulfill his destiny. Maria then identified two of these other witnesses: a girl from the town of Oleiros, near Lisbon, Maria de Conceição, and an unnamed man from Genoa.[9] Da Costa was then asked the obligatory question of what judgment he had formed of Maria and of what she had said. He said his judgment was suspended and that he could not decide whether it was true, a fake, or an illusion of the devil—a claim that is rather hard to believe, given the amount of time and interest he had shown in what Maria was saying over the previous eight years. Inquisitor de la

Cerda may not have accepted this answer either, and da Costa later clarified that he tended toward the conclusion that it was true, citing the wondrous things he had read about in the works of Martin del Rio and the third-century writer Lactancius.

João Ribeiro, when asked his judgment of the situation, noted that Maria retained her reason ("juizo") and that she had a good reputation ("boa fama"), but he could not decide whether she was making it all up or whether it was an illusion from the devil, so only God knew what the truth was. Bento Perreira had the most skeptical reaction, saying that after he had heard about Maria from Pedro Peixoto, he had decided against visiting her himself because he did not believe in such things. He admitted that he had seen, but not read, a copy of the pamphlet and named Paulo de Faria Baracho as the person who had shown him the copy. He noted that the story of the lizard turning into a human was particularly disturbing to him, using the opportunity to suggest that the lizard might be the devil, since he had never heard of good angels appearing in such a way. Not coincidentally, Perreira was a *qualificador*, an expert in theology or canon law who examined suspect propositions on behalf of the Inquisition.

The most interesting reaction to Maria's story among these witnesses was that of Pedro Peixoto. He mentions that he brought a portrait ("retrato") of Sebastian and showed it to Maria, asking if this was the old man she had seen on the island. This rather original means of corroboration elicited the expected response: yes, it was the man she had seen, although she noted that his face was fuller and ruddier while his nose was thinner. She went on to say that a better portrait of Sebastian was in the possession of a Mother Ines of the Convent of St. Bridgette in Lisbon. This, of course, gives away the source of her own understanding of Sebastian's physical description, and it is a tribute to the power of her imagination that she appropriately aged the image. Whatever the nature of the portrait she had originally seen or of the one he showed her, the incident shows that the issue of royal identities was a live one in early modern Portugal.

The portrait was not the only means by which Pedro Peixoto tried to determine the validity of Maria's claims. In time-honored fashion, he asked for information that the real Sebastian would have known, that is, the name of the man leading the royal navy during the *jornada* to Africa. She replied that she did not know but would ask the king the next time she journeyed to the Hidden Isle. In a later interview with Peixoto, she told him that she had not been able to ask Sebastian that question because the day she had traveled there he was deep in prayer in his oratory and could not be disturbed. She went on to explain, though, that one of the people on the island, Dona Maria Maior, told her that the name of the man in charge of the royal galleys was Pedro Peixoto's grandfather, Pedro Peixoto da Sylva, an answer that must have been somewhat gratifying, although entirely incorrect. Peixoto also asked Feliciano about his wife's claims. Feliciano responded that when she claimed to have been to the island, he had never found her missing from their house, though when he called her and moved her to try to wake her, she would not wake up. When asked for his judgment of Maria's claims, Father Peixoto was careful to say that his judgment was suspended ("suspenso") and that he really did not incline toward any particular option. It could have been true, it could have been *fingimento*, or it could have been an illusion from the devil; he could not decide. Perhaps he really had not come to any conclusion, although his interest is clear given his admission that he had met with Maria four or five times by that point.

Who were these initial witnesses? They were all Jesuits living in the Chiado neighborhood, with four of the six being residents of the Professing House of São Roque. The role of the Jesuits as leaders within the Portuguese millenarian community has already been noted, and so it should be no surprise that these Jesuits showed a great deal of interest in Maria's claims, nor should the fact that they were also involved in spreading her message, both orally and by means of the copies of the pamphlet they were producing. Of course, not all Jesuits showed an interest in prophetic speculation, as the testimony of Bento Perreira demonstrates, but it is striking that so many did. It should be remembered that it was the fact that Maria's stories were spreading in the city, and especially among the priests of the Company of Jesus, that finally prompted the Inquisition to pursue the case actively.

Another noticeable correlation seen in the testimony of these witnesses is that they were all of a similar age: the youngest was fifty-eight, the oldest in his seventies, most in their sixties. These were not young, excitable men; rather, they were mature men of (probably) considerable theological education, a profile that also fits the demographics (as far as we can reconstruct them) of the Jesuit professors who led the anti-Castilian revolt in Évora. All of these Jesuits were of an age and a background that enabled them to provide stable leadership for a lay millenarian movement, and it seems as though that is what happened. Manoel da Costa's offhand comment that he was "speaking casually about the things of Sebastian" with Manoel Soares de Britto (who would also be called as a witness) when he first heard of Maria de Macedo is suggestive of the ubiquity of the legends about Sebastian during the period. Beyond this anecdotal description, the fact that Manoel da Costa was to become, in time, the principal conduit for the dissemination of Maria's stories also provides us with a concrete example of how her message was transmitted and received in practice. He heard it from a friend and then spread it to his fellow Jesuits, who in turn spread it, both by mouth and by pamphlet, until the story was "commonly spoken of" in Lisbon, as Diogo Fernandes's clearly exaggerated description puts it. The casual nature of da Costa's conversation with Soares de Britto is indicative of the receptivity to millenarian ideas and stories during the period, but da Costa became the crucial catalyst that allowed Maria's claims to spread, first among the Jesuits of Chiado and then more widely in Lisbon.

Returning to the case, the testimony of six witnesses and the evidence found in the pamphlet at their disposal provided the Inquisition with enough evidence to conclude that Maria de Macedo had, indeed, made the claims attributed to her. The question remained of what the Inquisition should do about it, if anything. To that end, an internal summary of the evidence presented in the case was prepared by the office of the *promotor* of the Lisbon tribunal. As the document shows, there were two areas of primary concern to the Holy Office: one was the issue of being "spiritually transported" anywhere; the second was Maria's claims to have seen Saint John the Evangelist, Enoch, and Elijah in the Church of Our Lady of Nazareth while Sebastian, Arthur, and Jaime were being commissioned by those prophets to fulfill their eschatological roles.[10] These two issues, together with the strangeness of the claims as a whole, raised the suspicions of the *promotor.* As he put it, "because the aforementioned things cannot occur, it is the easiest to conclude that this is a fraud and a trick on the part of the suspect." It also could be the result of "deceit by the Demon," he added. In order to determine its true nature, he recommended a further investigation of the matter and requested that Maria de Macedo be imprisoned until the issues were resolved. On February 13, 1665, the summary was read and endorsed by the two serving inquisitors in the tribunal of Lisbon, Fernão Correa de la Cerda and Francisco Barreto. It was also read the same day by the members of the Conselho Geral, and they approved its reasoning and conclusions. Maria de Macedo was to be brought before the Inquisition, and the investigation was to proceed.

On February 20, 1665, Maria de Macedo made her first appearance before Inquisitor Fernão Correa de la Cerda.[11] After swearing to tell the truth and maintain the secrecy of the Holy Office, she related what she claimed to have experienced in her journeys to the Hidden Isle. The account she gave the inquisitor closely matches the narrative recorded in her pamphlet, and after hearing her account of what she had seen, de la Cerda asked her about her mode of life and whether she undertook any special exercises or devotions to commend herself to God. Maria answered that she followed no special mode of life and commended herself to God by means of the prayers of the Catholic Church. He asked if she knew how to read or write and whether she had read any books or pamphlets dealing with or had spoken to anyone about the things she had told him. She replied that she could read but could write only badly and that she had never read anything about those matters (which may or may not have been true), nor had she ever spoken to anyone about them (which was certainly false).

De la Cerda then asked a series of questions that attempted to assess Maria's psychological state: Was she prone to "apprehensions and melancholies"? Was she curious about future events or in the working of miracles? Had she ever done anything to induce dreams? When she answered in the negative, the inquisitor clarified the issue by saying that people who had such experiences should do their best to free themselves from them and that the devil often appears as a good angel in order to deceive the faithful. She stated her agreement with those positions, but de la Cerda was not finished; he wanted to know what she had done to rid herself of such strange thoughts. She then recounted the prayers and exorcisms that the clerics had performed for her as a child, but she noted that nothing had stopped the visitations. Clearly unsatisfied with her answer, he asked how she could have truly taken advantage of the exorcisms and the spiritual exercises while continuing to have dealings with the people who appeared to her. She admitted that she did not know how to respond to that question.

De la Cerda pressed her on the issue, trying to develop a case that she had, wittingly or unwittingly, made a pact with the devil by interacting with the people of the island. Her response to his grilling was that she had never heard the islanders say anything against the faith and that she was especially reassured when she saw Sebastian's oratory and the images of saints it contained. The inquisitor was not impressed, and wondered, even if she had seen some things of the Christian faith, how she could possibly reconcile those items with the "horrendous and ridiculous" things she had seen, namely, that animals had been transformed into human beings. Maria conceded she did not know how to answer that question. De la Cerda then asked what she felt when she was carried away by the islanders; did she feel any distress or fear while there? Did it cause her interior "consolation or disconsolation," and after dealing with those people, did she feel more or less fervor in things relating to her spiritual well-being? The answer was more certain here: she never had negative feelings while on the island, and her experiences there had only made her feel more fervor for the things of God.

Inquisitor de la Cerda next asked a question he would follow up on extensively in later depositions: Had Maria ever found that the people who visited her had lied to her? No, she said, and she added that they spoke only of their belief in God and in the Holy Mother Church. He then asked another doctrinal question: Did she know that future contingencies were reserved in the hand of God and that humans could not know them with certainty beforehand? She knew it well, she said. If it is true that she knew that, he immediately followed up, how was it that the people of the island told her of future events? Her answer was that she did not know how or why they predicted those events. Why, then, had she felt the need to tell others about them, especially since they involved suspect propositions about the Judgment and the role of Saint John? She had been reluctant to do so, she claimed, and had told only a few people when they had implored her to tell them what she had seen. With that, the first session came to an end, though not before de la Cerda warned her of the danger to her soul because of the things she was claiming, nor before she maintained that she was telling the truth. The warning given, she was ordered into custody and placed in the prisons of the Inquisition in Lisbon.

It is clear from the report that Inquisitor de la Cerda wrote to the Conselho Geral that day that he was not pleased with what he had heard.[12] The small inconsistencies and unanswered questions bothered such a detail-minded man as he was, but de la Cerda was principally disturbed by what he saw as the "suspect propositions" embedded in Maria's account. Her insistence that Saint John was alive, contrary to the opinion of the Church, and that he would participate in the Reformation of the World, in particular, disturbed him, because how could a vision that contained such things be from God? He was worried, too, about the issue of her delivering a letter from Sebastian to the king of Denmark, a matter he had not brought up in the questioning but which he clearly remembered from

Manoel da Costa's testimony. Anything implying that she had obeyed the command or request of one of the visionary figures could be evidence of a pact with the devil, he reasoned, and so he recommended that she be kept in prison while the matter was further investigated. Fernão Correa de la Cerda was not alone in his concerns, and both his fellow inquisitor Francisco Barreto and the members of the Conselho Geral endorsed his conclusions and his recommendations.

Maria de Macedo was interrogated by Inquisitor de la Cerda three more times between February 23 and February 27, 1665.[13] Most questions in these sessions were simply new attempts to obtain answers to the issues de la Cerda had raised in the first deposition, but he opened some new lines of questioning as well. During the second deposition, for example, he made a point to find out whether Maria had received any spiritual or temporal benefit from her visits to the Hidden Isle. Her responses were the epitome of piety: she had received no temporal benefit, but it had been a spiritual blessing, since the people of the island had told her to commend herself to God and to have patience during troubles, which was the highest good of all. He then asked her a very practical question: Why had she not reported these appearances to the Holy Office so that the nature of her visions could be determined? She admitted that she had not reported them—thus contradicting Feliciano's claim in the pamphlet—but only because her confessors did not think such a step was necessary, since they attributed it all to her imagination. De la Cerda did not believe it could have all been imagination, since it involved real items such as the lunch the Enchanted Moor had eaten and the answers she brought back from the island to some of her curious listeners. She conceded that she was not really sure why her confessors had overlooked those details. De la Cerda then asked if she had heard anything before about the earthly paradise, or Saint John, or Sebastian. No, she said, she had known nothing about any of those subjects, except that Sebastian had been lost in Africa—an answer that is almost impossible to accept as truthful given the ubiquity of the legends about him in mid-seventeenth-century Portugal. De la Cerda's next question was, how did she know about them then? She replied that she had heard about them from the people on the island, and where they had learned about them she was not sure, she gratuitously added. The hour growing late, Inquisitor de la Cerda warned her again to examine her conscience regarding the truth or falsity of her testimony, and she again insisted that she was telling the truth. With that, he dismissed her, and she was taken to her cell.

It was during the third session that the inquisitor asked Maria a question that was to become a major element in the case against her. After a series of questions in which he simply requested confirmation of earlier information she had given him, he asked for clarification about the thirty-six people she had met on the island. What were their names and how were they dressed, and by what law did she think they lived? She replied that they had both Moorish names, like Zygres and Abencerraje, and Christian names, like João and Francisco, as well. Their clothes were like Portuguese clothes, and they lived according to the Law of Jesus Christ. She added (and probably soon wished she had not) that they had told her that, in the beginning, they had used Moorish names as disguises to conceal their true identity from her. The inquisitor now smelled blood, and he was relentless. How was it possible, he asked, that people claiming to be Christians would take Moorish names when such acts were forbidden to Christians, since one can determine a person's faith by his or her name? Did not those who took Moorish names prove themselves to be followers of Islam? It is clear that Maria was not prepared for that question, and all she could say was that she did not know. De la Cerda went on and asked how she could testify that the people on the island had not lied to her when she had just said that they had disguised their names? She had to admit that they had lied to her about their names and that she had forgotten about that when asked about it before. He continued to grill her on this issue, stopping only when she admitted that she did not understand these "points and subtleties," as the scribe tersely recorded.

In the third session, the inquisitor also asked how Sebastian and the other inhabitants had come to live on the island, where it was located, and whether it was in conformity with the Roman Church. Maria answered that no one had told her exactly how the king or the others had reached the island but she did know that the people of the island lived "in all conformity" with the Church of Rome. Any relief she may have felt probably evaporated when she heard the next question: How was it possible that the island lived in conformity with the Roman Church if it had no interaction with the Apostolic See in matters such as the confirmation of bishops? Again, she conceded she did not know how to answer that but that Sebastian had traveled to Rome and that there was a bishop on the island, although she had not seen him in person.

One other important line of questioning that de la Cerda opened in the third session dealt with the manner of life and government of the people on the island. Maria admitted she did not know very much about the government of the island but it seemed everyone there obeyed Sebastian. Otherwise, she knew that they lived in common, without any distinctions between them at all. The land there was so fertile and the animals so tame that no one had to work for food. This happy scene was to provoke de la Cerda to his highest level of humorlessness. How was it possible, he asked, that the islanders lived in complete harmony and without having to work when, because of Adam's sin, disharmony entered the world and man was cursed to live by the sweat of his brow? Probably completely disheartened by this latest display of inquisitorial pitilessness, Maria said she had nothing else to say about it besides what they had told her. After that, the inquisitor ended the session, telling Maria that his suspicions that she was making her entire story up, or that they were an illusion of the devil, were growing dramatically.

De la Cerda followed only three important lines of questioning during the fourth deposition on February 27. The first series of questions dealt with whether the inhabitants of the island had any religious practices that were not the "common usage" of Catholics. Maria answered that the only difference was that for Sundays they would stop work late on the Saturday before and not resume it again until the time of Mass on Monday. Almost certainly she saw this as an exemplary display of piety on the islanders' part, but the inquisitor did not interpret it that way, since his next question was how she thought it was possible that they conformed in everything with the Roman Church when they engaged in a practice outside the common usage of the Catholic faithful, the very fact of which raised the suspicion of heresy. Did she think, he pressed, that it was "good and licit" that people calling themselves Christians would engage in a practice outside the common usage of Roman Catholics? She answered that she did not think it was either good or bad because she had not come to any judgment on the subject. How was it possible, he then asked, that she had not come to a judgment on such an important issue? Maria replied that, since she was not educated and had only limited judgment, she had not undertaken any reflection on the subject.

The second line of questioning concerned whether anyone on the island had made her promise to do anything on their behalf. Maria answered that only once had anyone asked her to do anything: one of the women had asked her to hear Mass in the House of the Discalced Carmelites in Lisbon on her behalf. Hearing this, de la Cerda again harangued her: Did she not know that making promises to unknown people, whose appearances were supernatural, puts one at risk of making promises to the devil, who regularly appears in different forms thereby to deceive the faithful? Her short answer was that she knew it now. He then asked a question on a related subject: Had she ever addressed anyone on the island in terms implying her subjection to them and their dominion over her, and if so, who were they and what had she called them? Maria admitted that there was a woman on the island named Dona Maria Maior, whom she called her mistress ("Ama"), but simply because they got along so well together. The inquisitor was not impressed and asked why she had decided to call the woman her mistress, given that she could have been the devil in disguise, which would have resulted in her giving homage to him. Increasingly taciturn under de la Cerda's relentless questioning, Maria simply said she had done it out of ignorance. Had she, or anyone else on the island, he asked, ever been held to be a saint, and was the figure she said was Sebastian held to be king and Lord? No one there had ever been taken as a saint, she answered, though Sebastian was honored as both king and Lord.

The third line of questioning revolved around whether Maria had ever seen Enoch, Elijah, or Saint John the Evangelist during her visions. She recounted the story of her journey with Sebastian to the Church of Our Lady of Tribulations, where she had seen all the prophets who had been named. De la Cerda then asked a seemingly innocent question: For which saints had the three churches on the island been named? The churches were named for Santa Maria Maior, for Saint John the Evangelist, and for Saint Stephen, she reported. How was it possible, he asked, that she had seen Saint John alive on the island and that there was a church there dedicated to the same saint, when it was not the practice of the Catholic Church to worship the living or to erect churches in their honor? The trap sprung, Maria acknowledged that she had no satisfactory answer to the question. Had she then intended, he asked, to introduce false doctrines among the faithful, contrary to the opinion of the church? "No" was her only answer. If it were true that she did not want to introduce false doctrines, he went on, why had she told others about subjects like the Judgment of Reformation or that Saint John was still alive, when both were suspect propositions? She answered that she had not talked about those things to anyone besides Manoel Soares de Britto, who was a friend of her husband's. How could she say that, de la Cerda wondered, when she had already admitted that she had talked about these matters to others beside Britto? The strain of interrogation was clearly beginning to affect her, and she could answer only that she had forgotten the others. The inquisitor then lectured her. Did she not know that those who had visions, or who saw strange, hidden, or future things, put themselves at risk of becoming the means by which the devil can deceive the faithful? Beaten down, she admitted that she had not known that but she knew it now.

The questioning came to an end, but the session was not yet over. Inquisitor Fernão Correa de la Cerda had some things he wanted to tell Maria before she was taken back to her cell. Once again, he warned her that she needed to examine her conscience and confess the truth about the things she had claimed because he had sufficient evidence to prove that what she was saying either had been made up by her or came to her by means of the devil's illusions. She had already been caught in several contradictions, he said, and he reminded her that there were several questions she could not answer. Her soul was also endangered because she had spread several suspect propositions, namely, that Saint John was alive and that there would be a Judgment of Reformation before the end of the world. The former was contrary to the opinion of the church, and the latter stood condemned because it was an article of faith that there would be only one Judgment at the end of time. Added to these problems was the ridiculous and horrible nature of parts of her story, especially animals turning into human beings before her very eyes. He then warned her "with great charity" that she should confess before the Tribunal the truth of why she had claimed these things, for the "salvation of her soul," for the "unburdening of her conscience," and so that she could "gain the greatest good she could expect in her present state," the implication of such a statement being quite clear. In all likelihood exhausted by the grilling and the inquisitor's harangue, Maria de Macedo stood by her story; she had only told the truth, and she had nothing to add to it. After being warned once more, she was taken away.

Firmly convinced that he had enough evidence to convict her, de la Cerda wrote another report to the Conselho Geral, repeating all the evidence against her outlined above and then upping the ante considerably by informing the council that elements of her story—especially the transformations of the animals and the fact that she had been asked to do concrete acts by the people on the island—all carried with them the presumption of a pact with the devil.[14] He urged the strongest possible punishments in light of her refusal to confess. In what was to be the first difference of opinion about the case within the Inquisition, his fellow inquisitor Francisco Barreto agreed that she was guilty enough to merit punishment but wrote that he found no indications within her testimony that indicated she had made a pact with the devil. He pointed out that she had not sought out the appearances, as a diabolist would, but that they had come to her involuntarily. Nor were there any elements of sorcery or witchcraft in her story, so he advised that she (and her husband) be admonished that the things she was saying were "vain and without foundation" and that they should stop talking to people about them. The Conselho Geral's answer of March 3, 1665, steered a middle course between these two conclusions—probably because the councillors were, as yet, unsure as to the actual nature of her "visitations"—and opted to continue the investigation by interviewing other people who had been named as potential witnesses, especially Maria's husband, Feliciano Machado.

Feliciano, therefore, first appeared before Inquisitor de la Cerda two days later, on March 5.[15] He was not able to remember all the details of his wife's claims, but he did mention that he had a copy of the pamphlet in his house and said that if he could review it, he would be better able to answer the inquisitor's questions. The request was granted, and Feliciano was ordered to return to the Tribunal with the pamphlet to complete his testimony. So on March 9, 1665, he duly handed over the pamphlet and then retold his story, this time in much greater detail than before, following the pamphlet's account of her visitations very closely. After that, the questioning again returned to the ways in which he had tried to verify his wife's account of her experiences. He admitted that, at first, he thought she was out of her mind, but a series of events had convinced him that there was more to it than that. As an example of this, he repeated the incident found in the pamphlet in which he heard a voice speaking to her one night but saw no one. Pretending to be asleep, he waited to see where his wife went; she left the bed, he was sure, but never left the house, and she had a conversation with the disembodied voice of a woman who spoke Portuguese, though in the manner of a Moor. When Maria returned to bed, he scolded her for not waking him up as he had told her to, but she defended herself by saying that the Mooress had told her not to because he was already awake. He also retold the story recorded in the pamphlet in which he felt someone place his or her hands on his shoulders, though he could not see anyone around him.

After those incidents, Feliciano was sure that his wife's visions were "fantastic," or possibly even diabolic, in origin. When he shared his concerns with her, she reassured him that she had seen nothing in her visions that was against the Catholic faith and that her confessors had told her that they were all due to her imagination and to do her best to free herself of them. He also mentioned that Father Sebastião de Paiva had put him more at ease on the matter when he told him that he did not think that, whatever they were, the things Maria was experiencing were from the devil. Feliciano's testimony here changes subject suddenly, probably in response to a specific question that was not recorded, and he tried to make clear that the inhabitants of the island were all baptized Christians. He went on to say that when King Sebastian returned to Lisbon, there would be "great revolutions and punishments in this city." His return would occur when the sun rose in the middle of the night, and he would bring with him new laws, five in number, that he had written and that had been confirmed by Jesus Christ. Feliciano ended his testimony by saying that everything he had said was truly what his wife had told him. He was dismissed without further questions, and the inquisitor and his aides agreed that he was a truthful witness.

Two other witnesses were summoned at that time to testify in the case: Manoel Soares de Britto and Isabel de Britto.[16] Soares de Britto was a notary and a friend of Feliciano Machado's who had known for some time about Maria's visions. Some five years before, he had invited Feliciano and Maria over to his house so that she could tell her story to his sister-in-law, Dona Isabel de Britto, and Father Manoel da Costa of the Company of Jesus, since both of them had expressed interest in what she had to say. He then gave a version of Maria's story that was similar to what Maria and Feliciano had testified to, though he included one story that was a conflation of separate details in Maria's account. According to Soares de Britto, the letter Sebastian had asked Maria to deliver to the king of Denmark was an invitation for him to meet Sebastian at the Church of Our Lady of Tribulations, and a similar letter had been sent by a Genoese man to King Arthur. This was a conflation of the incident of the meeting of three kings and the account of Sebastian's letter being sent to the king of Denmark as told by Manoel de Costa, since further evidence will show that Maria never made the claim that Sebastian had given her a letter to take to the king of Denmark at all. Despite this confusion, when Soares de Britto was asked what opinion he had formed about Maria de Macedo's reason and her claims, he answered that she appeared to have her reason and to be of "good life and customs." As far as her visions went, they did not seem to be fraudulent in his opinion; he could see no reason to invent them, since she had had no material gain or other benefit from discussing them.

His sister-in-law, Dona Isabel de Britto, came to a rather different conclusion about Maria's claims, however. She told a story consistent with her brother-in-law's with a few minor differences of emphasis. But when she was asked what judgment she had formed about Maria and the things she had told her, Isabel de Britto said that she had believed it to be true until she asked Maria to ask someone on the island when her husband was going to return home. Her husband had not returned at the time Maria had told her, so de Britto had come to the conclusion that it was all a lie—an interesting example of the practical nature of prophetic verification in early modern Portugal.

The last witness to appear in the case for several months was Maria de Almeida, Maria's stepmother.[17] Her deposition was taken on March 18, 1665, and it revealed that she had been married to Maria's father, Luis Ribeiro, for thirty-three years, making her the only eyewitness in the trial to testify about the events of Maria's childhood. She confirmed Maria's stories of how the Moor first came to visit her and how she and her husband had tried to find some way to relieve their daughter of her "visitations" and "appearances." Her account is entirely consistent with Maria's version of her childhood, though Maria de Almeida adds details not found elsewhere. For example, she said that they had set out a little table near Maria's bed and laid out food for her visitors, and because some food was missing by the morning, she had come to the conclusion that the Moors had eaten it. Though this seems a bit naive on her part, she did go on to explain that they had locked all the doors and that she had hidden behind the headboard of the bed to wait and see what happened. She saw nothing that night but did hear strange voices. As she was getting up from her hiding place, she saw the lighted candle moving but saw no one moving it. She also claimed to be a witness of the later incident in which Feliciano suddenly felt hands placed on his shoulder, and she said she could not see anyone then, either. After explaining that she remembered very few details of what Maria had seen during her journeys to the island, she was asked if she had ever thought her stepdaughter was making the stories up. She answered that she had never even considered that possibility, and she was dismissed after the notary signed for her, since she did not know how to write. After she left the room, she was deemed a truthful witness worthy of credit.

After the inquisitors examined the evidence from these witnesses, the focus again returned to Maria de Macedo, and her sixth deposition took place on March 24, 1665, three weeks after her fifth session, the genealogical session.[18] Immediately after determining that she had no desire to modify her testimony or confess, Inquisitor de la Cerda asked her a series of questions dealing with an issue that had come up during the second round of witnesses he had questioned in the case. Did she believe that the Law of Jesus Christ would one day come to an end and be replaced by another law? No, she answered, she did not believe that, clearly contradicting her earlier testimony. He then asked her a series of closely related questions: Did she think it was permissible for people to disseminate stories they had made up or propositions that were suspect because they were contrary to the opinion of the church? Did she think it was permissible for anyone to spread word of future contingencies that were reserved to God? Did she think that it was permissible for people to speak of visions when they were not sure if they came from God or not? Did she think it was permissible for anyone to spread superstitions? Did she think it was permissible that those ignorant of spiritual matters speak of such matters among other ignorant people? Her answer to all the questions was the same: no, she did not think any of those things were permissible. Neither, though, did she think any of them applied to her.

De la Cerda then began a new series of questions: Did she think it was permissible for anyone to make a pact with the devil in exchange for certain promises from the devil? Did she think it was permissible for anyone to deal with the devil, to profess friendship with him, to take him as one's master, invoke him in any way, ask him questions, believe his doctrines, or make prognostications on the basis of something he had revealed? Did she think it was permissible to receive promises or material goods from the devil? Did she believe anyone could, by learning from the devil, gain certain knowledge of future contingencies, which depend on the free will of man and the decision of God? Did she think that think it was permissible to deal with enchanted people, not believing that such enchantments were either witchcraft or illusions of the devil designed to deceive the faithful? Her answers were more emphatic to these questions: no, she did not believe any of those things, nor had she ever believed them. She then was admonished once more to confess to the truth, but she again maintained that she had told the truth. De la Cerda warned her that, since she had done the things he had asked her about, there was a strong presumption that she had made a pact with the devil and that, by the mercies of Christ, she should confess the truth. She again refused and was taken back to her cell.

The seventh and eighth depositions, which took place on March 25, 1665, and April 17, 1665, respectively, were principally concerned with confirming the details of the claims that Maria had earlier made in her testimony or in the pamphlet, or claims made about her by the other witnesses.[19] They therefore covered very little material that has not been covered before in this work, and so they will not be examined in detail except to point out the few new elements that Maria confirmed or added to her story. One such element was the names of Sebastian's companions on the Hidden Isle, which had been listed by several witnesses but not confirmed by Maria herself until this point. She explained that the companions who were lost at Alcazarquivir with Sebastian and then followed him to the Hidden Isle were the Duke of Aveiro, the Count of Redondo, Dom João de Castro, Henrique Moniz, and Ruy de Tavora. When asked to confirm how Sebastian had found himself on the Hidden Isle, she said stated that while he, his family, and his followers were fleeing the persecutions of the king of Castile, they fell asleep as they crossed the mountains of Italy. They were covered by a great cloud and then woke up and found themselves on the island, which was clearly the work of God. She was also asked about how the inhabitants of the island had come to live there. They were, she clarified, the descendants of those who fled the Iberian Peninsula in the time of King Rodrigo (i.e., the time of the Moorish invasion of 711). In a later follow-up question about Sebastian's return, she stated that she had said that when Sebastian returned to Lisbon, there would be great revolutions and punishments in the city and that he would bring with him new laws. She added that she had told that to her husband, just as it appeared in the pamphlet.

Inquisitor de la Cerda also wanted more information regarding Sebastian's future activities. She answered that he would return to Portugal, reform the world, conquer the Moors and Turks, convert the heretics, put everything right ("pôr tudo em razão"), and, because he was the Encoberto, retake the Holy House of Jerusalem, where he would reign until the age of 120. He would then die and be buried in a tomb next to the Holy Sepulcher, leaving his kingdom to one of his sons, who would continue the perfection of the world. Sebastian would accomplish all these things with the help of Saint John the Evangelist.

During these sessions she was also able to clear up some misconceptions. When de la Cerda asked her where she was and to whom she had spoken about the thirty-six people who turned into animals and then back into humans, she insisted that she had only seen them transform from animals into humans and had never said otherwise. In response to the inquisitor's question about the incident in which she had delivered a letter from Sebastian to the king of Denmark, she denied that she had ever said that happened, and indeed the incident never appears in the pamphlet, in her testimony, or in the testimony of Feliciano. Despite the fact that three witnesses—Manoel da Costa, Manoel de Soares de Britto, and Isabel de Britto—recounted the story (although not always with the same details), I am inclined to believe Maria that she had not made that claim. It is possible that, due to some lack of clarity in her narrative when she told them her story (all at the same time), they all conflated elements of her story (i.e., Sebastian as the son-in-law of the king of Denmark, and the story of two islanders being sent with messages to Arthur and Jaume to summon them to Our Lady of Tribulations) in a similar way. Because of a lack of decisive evidence, this will have to remain an open question, however.

The details confirmed and clarified, the session came to an end with another series of warnings about the grave danger to her soul and her case if she continued to refuse to confess the truth about her claims. De la Cerda again repeated that she fell under the strong presumption of having made a pact with the devil, but she again said she had nothing to add to her testimony, since she had told the truth. She was then dismissed to her cell and would not appear again until June 17, 1665, when she was briefly called in to be given one final warning—the *amoestação antes do libello*—before the formal charges against her were submitted by the inquisitor to the *promotor* and her prosecution was formally begun. The charges were read against her, and she again refused to change her testimony. Her defense was about to begin.

On July 6, 1665, Licentiate Domingos Vieira de Santo was appointed defense counsel for Maria de Macedo. De Santo had had a long ecclesiastical career: he had been both an apostolic prosecutor and the prior of the Church of San Miguel de Alfama in Lisbon before being appointed a defense counsel (*procurador de presos*) attached to the Tribunal in Lisbon in January 1660. He thus had experience on both sides of an ecclesiastical prosecution.[20] He was given a copy of the charges against Maria, and they soon got to work on the defense strategy. Before proceeding to the details of that defense, I should say a word about the role of the defense counsel within an inquisitorial prosecution. A *procurador de presos* was, like an inquisitor, an official of the Holy Office, and this fact raises the issue of the defense counsel's true loyalties. Was he working on behalf of the defendant assigned to him or on behalf of the Inquisition? There is no simple answer to the general question involved because the record is mixed. In the case of Maria de Macedo, however, it seems clear that de Santo made a good-faith effort in Maria's defense to have the charges against her dropped or at least to mitigate the punishment she would receive.

Three days after being appointed to the case, on July 9, 1665, de Santo submitted the first set of defense papers (*contradittas*) on Maria de Macedo's behalf to the inquisitors of Lisbon.[21] Consisting of thirteen articles, the document deserves careful examination because it gives insight on the type of arguments an experienced inquisitorial official thought would help the case of a defendant. In the first two articles, de Santo sought to establish Maria's good character by stating that she had always been a "good, true Christian" and that she always lived in an "honest and retired" way in her parents' house, never "having illicit conversations with people of bad reputation," claims that were repeated in article 11. She was God-fearing, he went on, and very inclined toward prayer, to hearing Mass on Sundays, and toward frequent confession, "almost every month and on all the feast days," he adds. The next two articles emphasized the great efforts to which first her parents and later her husband had gone to find some way to free her of the "appearances" and characterized her as having been an unwilling participant in it all; she had been "terrified and tormented" by what she experienced, in fact. He also emphasized, in articles 6 and 9, that she had tried to find some way to escape the visions by confessing what she had seen to Father Sebastião de Paiva, Father Luis de Madre de Deos, and other clerics, all without positive result. Not only was she a reluctant participant in these experiences, but she was also a reluctant conduit of them, since in article 10 he claimed that she had voluntarily told only her parents, her confessors, and "other grave people" about her visions. She had been hesitant to tell the other people about it and did so only because they asked her what she had seen.

De Santo included a related argument in article 12, one that also provides us with a peek at the state of millenarianism in Portugal at the time. She had, he stated, heard many people, including "grave and religious people," speaking about King Sebastian and the possibility that he was alive and would one day return to Portugal. Since "she was a woman and of weak judgment," she had no idea that it was in any way illicit to speak about those subjects. In articles 7–8, de Santo also described her as "having a great deal of simplicity on these matters."[22] Sexist to be sure, but her counsel was clearly trying to emphasize her "feminine weakness" to gain some sympathy among the inquisitors.

Article 13 claimed that Maria had never received any material benefit or favor because of her visions, a crucial point in de Santo's developing defense. The tone of the fifth article is somewhat at variance with the attitude she had taken earlier in her depositions because the article states that she had never truly thought that the things she saw were real or that they had any substance; she understood that she saw them only by "representation," realizing that she was unworthy to receive any signs of favor from God. Given her previous testimony, this argument is hard to believe, but it makes clear that de Santo had opted for the strategy of convincing the inquisitors that she—a faithful Christian—had been deceived by the illusions or "representations" of the devil, a much less serious charge than that of deliberately making the stories up. Against that possibility, he raised the points that she had made many efforts to make the visions cease, that she had been reluctant to tell others about them, and that she had never benefited (or tried to benefit) from them.

Attached to these articles was a list of witnesses who, de Santo claimed, could testify to their truthfulness. Most of the witnesses who had earlier been deposed in the case were named on the list, but in the end, the inquisitors called only three of those on the list, none of whom had been called as witnesses before. In addition, the three defense witnesses were called to give testimony only regarding articles 1, 2, and 11, the articles that dealt with Maria's honesty and character, especially during the time before her marriage when she still lived with her parents. These three witnesses—Manoel Francisco, Pedro Nunes, and António Perreira—had all been neighbors of Maria's while she lived in her father's house. The three witnesses were deposed on August 28, 1665, in separate sessions, and they gave fairly similar testimony regarding their impressions of Maria.[23] All remembered that she had attended church regularly with her stepmother, with Pedro Nunes adding that he had often seen her carrying a rosary ("vela com as contas na mão"). All of them also reported, with varying degrees of detail, that they had heard a rumor that she had had an "illicit conversation" with a certain Alexandre de Sousa while she was unmarried and that once she had let de Sousa into her house while her father was not there. Pedro Nunes even claimed to have been a witness of the incident, since he lived directly across the street from her house. Manoel Francisco noted that he had also heard that she was a *sebastianista*, and António Perreira said that, while he was young, he had heard rumors that she suffered great sadness because of some strange things she had seen.

After these witnesses were dismissed, the trial record falls silent until October 10, 1665. No reason for the delay is given, though presumably the time was taken up in a review of the evidence by the inquisitors, since on that date the Prova de Justiça—a summary of the testimony given in the trial—was circulated to the inquisitorial officials. After yet another warning to confess, the document was read to Maria, though to preserve the secrecy of the tribunal, none of the sources of the testimony were named. After listening to the long recitation, she was asked if the content of the Prova was correct. She said that the things she had confessed to were true but that everything else in it was false. She refused to confess that she had done anything wrong and said she did not want to retract anything. Since she had again refused to confess "for the unburdening of her conscience and the welfare of her case," she was returned to the prisons of the Holy Office. On October 15–16, more witnesses were called to testify; the first was Joseph Ribeiro, Maria's uncle.[24] He stated that she was a good Christian and that he knew she confessed and took communion frequently. He admitted that he was not sure why she had been arrested by the Holy Office, though he did know she had spoken to some people about the "things of King Sebastian." Having nothing else to say, he was then read defense articles 3 and 4 and confirmed that Maria had begun to have visions around the age of nine or ten and that her parents and her husband had made great efforts to free her of the appearances because of the fear they caused her. Joseph Ribeiro added nothing in the way of new evidence, although he is still an important witness because he was the only direct witness, besides her stepmother, of Maria's experiences during childhood. The other two witnesses called on those days, Marçal da Rocha and António da Costa, were colleagues of Feliciano Machado's from the Treasury, but beyond confirming that they had heard that Maria often spoke about Sebastian and the Hidden Isle, they added little in the way of evidence to the case. Once they had been dismissed, Inquisitors Francisco Barreto and João de Castilho agreed that the time had come to bring the case to an end. The prosecution of Maria de Macedo was about to enter its final phase.

On October 20, 1665, Inquisitors Barreto and Castilho, along with their principal deputies, produced what they intended to be the final report on the case for review by the Conselho Geral.[25] The claims made by Maria de Macedo were very strange, they said, and could not have come about by natural means and so had merited investigation. As a result of that investigation, the inquisitors had come to the conclusion that if what she saw were visions, there was no evidence to support the possibility that they had come from God, nor was there any evidence that Maria de Macedo was of such a virtuous life that she would receive visions and special favors from God. The incident of her letting Alexandre de Sousa into her house before she was married was cited specifically in this regard. The inquisitors had not, however, found any evidence of witchcraft or superstition, and so there was no basis for presuming that she had made a pact with the devil. They made a special note of the fact that she had told religious and educated people about her visions, a fact that, as they said, was "greatly in her favor" in proving to them that she did not think the visions were from the devil, a necessary condition if she was to be found guilty of having made a pact.

Neither had they found any evidence that the visions were the illusions of the devil, which left only the possibility (for them) that she had invented the whole thing, which was punishable by the Inquisition. However, even on this point the inquisitors were inclined to be lenient because talk about "the return of Sebastian and the existence of the Hidden Isle" was so common and even after all those things had been shown to be without foundation, "no one stopped talking about them." Given these facts, the inquisitors felt the time Maria had already spent in prison would be sufficient punishment for her crimes. They added that she should pay the expenses of the trial and be forbidden to speak about her visions anymore, but that would be all provided that she finally confessed that she had made up all her stories. If she was not willing to confess, she could be put to the torment in order to compel her to tell the truth. With that final suggestion, the report was signed by both inquisitors and their deputies and then sent to the Conselho Geral for review.

In a document dated October 27, 1665, the Conselho Geral responded to the report, and the councillors were not inclined to be quite so lenient.[26] There was still the issue of the suspect propositions contained in her vision, which the inquisitors' report had not dealt with (or even mentioned) at all. So, the Conselho Geral ordered that these propositions be sent for qualification. *Qualificadores* were either theologians or canon lawyers who provided outside examinations of suspect propositions for the Inquisition. The six questions sent to the *qualificadores* in this case tell us all we need to know about the concerns of the Conselho Geral and why the councillors felt the inquisitors' proposed resolution of the case was unsatisfactory. The first proposition they wished to be examined dealt with the fact that Maria (unnamed) had seen a lizard turn into a human, and when he asked her to bring him lunch, the next day she prepared a lunch and shared it with him. The second was that Maria readily agreed to go with the man when he asked her if she wanted to come with him, with the result that he took her to a distant land where she saw many strange things. The third was that, while in that distant land, she met an old man who told her that he would one day leave that land to purify the world with the help of Saint John the Evangelist, Enoch, and Elijah in a reformation that would precede the Final Judgment. The fourth suspect proposition was that, having asked the old man if Saint John was dead and Enoch and Elijah were in the earthly paradise, he answered that, even though the church followed the opinion that Saint John was dead, they should know that he was alive. As far as Enoch and Elijah went, they were in the earthly paradise, which was not the same as the Hidden Isle. The fifth proposition was that, while in that land, many creatures had appeared before her and then been transformed into human beings. Because the creatures had human eyes even in their animal state, she could recognize them and often spoke and had dealings with those people. The final proposition was that she had often traveled away from that land on pilgrimages and to celebrate novenas, though she had never been able to tell how the doors to the churches she went to were opened or by whom. A final note on the list of questions stated that "the intent of this person is directed toward the things of King Sebastian."

The responses of the two *qualificadores* who were given these questions will be discussed in greater detail in chapter 7, but a few brief comments on them should be made here.[27] The first *qualificador* to send his conclusions back was Dr. João Gomes, a doctor of theology and a resident of the Jesuit Collegio de Santo Antão in Lisbon, who had been appointed a *qualificador* only the previous year, in May 1664.[28] He began by saying that he had found no "error of faith" in the propositions, although he was unsettled by the claim that a lizard had turned into a human, which might be a sign of the devil's influence. As far as the claim that Saint John was still alive, he knew that that was not the common opinion of the church, but he went on to cite many church fathers who had believed that Saint John would live until the end of the world, before coming to the conclusion that the claim that he was alive was, itself, not contrary to the faith. Even Sebastian might still be alive, he admitted, because, after all, "Sebastian himself had said he would one day reform the world," an interesting snippet that gives another contemporaneous view of Sebastian. If God wished to preserve Sebastian so that he could reform the world, Gomes argued, then it was possible. Despite all these possibilities (which are intriguing admissions in themselves), Gomes stated that the most probable case was that the claims either came from the illusions of the devil or were simply the result of fraud ("fingimento"). "The person" who made these claims might be guilty of pride or vanity, but the claims themselves were not heretical, he concluded, although he was sure to say that he would defer in his opinions to the judgment of the Holy Office.

The conclusions of the second *qualificador* were not to be quite so favorable, however. Father João de Deus was a Franciscan and a reader of theology at a convent in Lisbon and had been appointed a *qualificador* in July 1661.[29] He began his answer by stating his suspicion that the claims were fraudulent, although he conceded they might be the result of melancholic delusions to which, he noted, women were particularly prone. He was dismissive of the beliefs of the *sebastianistas*, who he said "would take as an article of faith, the biggest bunch of nonsense one can imagine," and then criticized "the person" for even more extravagant claims than the *sebastianistas* normally made. The fact that the defendant made claims about the state of Saint John and about the Judgment of Reformation that were contrary to the opinion of the church was worrying and probably merited punishment. He found no evidence of a pact with the devil, however, and said that the claims were the result of either fraud, madness, or the illusions of the devil, though he never stated to which of these possibilities he was finally inclined.

The answers of Father João de Deus were dated December 24, 1665, but the trial record does not begin again until March 6, 1666, when all three inquisitors (Fernão Correa de la Cerda simply being described as "voting again in the case" without any explanation of his absence from it) wrote a new report to the Conselho Geral.[30] They had read the answers of the *qualificadores*, one inclined toward lenience and the other mixed, but the inquisitors knew that the opinion of the *qualificadores* was irrelevant; they took the hint from the Conselho Geral's response to their previous report. The crimes of Maria de Macedo were, it turned out, much more serious now that they had reflected further upon the case. They were still sure that she was guilty of *fingimento*, but the issue of the suspect propositions she was spreading could not be ignored this time. The inquisitors were clear: if she had believed only "the beliefs held by the vulgar that King Sebastian is alive on the Hidden Isle or the other things affirmed by the *sebastianistas*, then the prisoner would not be guilty of any crime falling under the jurisdiction of the Holy Office." It was the other beliefs that she held—such as her claims about Saint John being alive or that there would be a Judgment of Reformation before the Final Judgment—that were culpable. Her claims that Sebastian would bring new laws for humanity when he returned was "more than a suspect proposition," a phrase that clearly implied that the inquisitors thought she was in grave danger of being guilty of heresy. Even though the issue of whether Saint John was alive or dead had not been decided dogmatically by the church, she should have been more fearful than to presume to make pronouncements on such a grave issue, they went on to say. She should be punished, they decided, for "the crime of faking miracles of Saints and revelations of hidden and future things, and for proposing fearful things which could result in abuses and false doctrines to the harm of our Holy Catholic Faith, such as the manner of fasting, the observance of Sundays on the aforementioned Island, and the new laws to be confirmed by God."

They then voted that Maria de Macedo should be punished by having to pay for all trial costs and by being exiled to the small town of Crasto Marim in the Algarve for five years. João de Andrade, one of the deputies who had signed off on the report of October 20, 1665, now added that, in addition to those punishments, the prisoner should be made to confess publicly to all those she had deceived that she had invented the whole thing, an addendum that was readily agreed to by the other voters, with the exception of de la Cerda, who it says did not concur with the report as a whole. No details as to the nature of his objection were recorded, but after having seen his earlier attitude toward Maria, one could probably guess with a fair degree of certainty that he was still sure she had made a pact with the devil in addition to all her other crimes.

The members of the Conselho Geral were much more pleased with this report, and they confirmed its conclusions in their response, dated March 19, 1666.[31] Needing to tie up one final legal loose end, they ordered that, before any more reports were sent to them on the matter, Maria de Macedo be put to the torment in order to get her confession at last. On March 23, she was duly warned one last time as she was shown the "instruments."[32] She refused to change her testimony and so was put to the torture. She made the whole thing up, she now confessed, and even gave her original motivation for telling the story. Up until that time, her stepmother had treated her badly, but after she claimed to have been to the island, her stepmother treated her much better, since Maria had promised that the enchanted Moors of the island would one day give her gold. She claimed that everything that had followed stemmed from that original motivation. She had told her father because she did not want her stepmother to know she had lied and start treating her badly again; she had kept on adding to the story to keep the lie going. This admission was enough for the inquisitors and for the members of the Conselho Geral. On March 26, they expressed their satisfaction with the report of her long-delayed confession and then urged that the case be wrapped up.

Before that could happen, though, Maria had to confirm the testimony she had given under torture, as specified by inquisitorial regulations. So, on the same day, she was deposed for a final time.[33] Inquisitor Fernão Correa de la Cerda began by asking if she wanted to add anything to her previous confession. She said she did and then proceeded to say that not only had she made up her stories to get her stepmother to treat her better but she also had continued to tell the stories to her father, her stepmother, her husband, and others so that they would hold her in higher regard, which might redound to her benefit. Not satisfied to leave it at that, de la Cerda then asked her how it was possible that she thought her family would hold her in higher regard for having visions while, at the same time, they were trying to find some way to rid her of them. Maria did not know how to answer that. On and on, he pestered her, questioning her about the version of events the torture chamber had "persuaded" her to tell, and one by one, she was forced to individually recant the principal claims and events of her narrative. His final question was typical of his style: Did she think that a person who pretended to perform miracles, have visions of saints, predict future things, or promulgate suspect propositions was worthy of punishment? She answered that she did not know how to judge that question. His questioning finished, he harangued her again about the great harm she had done to herself and to the faithful with her stories. Since she had finally confessed to her crimes, he ended on a positive note by saying that she had preserved her soul and would be welcomed back into the community of the faithful with great mercy. After hearing that, she was taken back to her cell to await her punishment.

Later the same day, the inquisitors of Lisbon and their deputies registered their approval of Maria de Macedo's final confession, as did the Conselho Geral, but it was the latter body that reserved to itself the authority to determine her punishment. Since she was guilty of *fingimento* of spiritual visions and revelations, her punishment would be by the book, namely, by book 3, title 20 of the Regimento of 1640: she would appear in an auto-da-fé on April 4, 1666, and publicly confess her sins. She would also be whipped through the streets of Lisbon "until the blood flowed" and then be exiled for five years, not to the Algarve, but to the lethal Portuguese colony of Angola. The verdict ratified and the sentence decided, all that was left to do was to begin her punishment.

Maria de Macedo duly appeared in the auto-da-fé held on Sunday, April 4, 1666, holding a lighted candle like the others in a long line of accused Judaizers, bigamists, and blasphemers. As recorded in inquisitorial lists of autos-da-fé celebrated by the Holy Office in this period, she had been found guilty of "falsely claiming revelations, transportations, and visions."[34] After listening to the sermon and then publicly confessing, she was returned again to the prisons of the Inquisition to await the rest of her sentence. Her husband, Feliciano Machado, who we learn from the documentation was gravely ill at the time, was working on a petition for the inquisitors to exempt his wife from one part of her sentence. She should be spared the whipping, he argued, because he was of noble blood, which was indeed a reason for which the punishment of whipping could be lifted according to the Regimento of 1640. In a traditional culture such as that of seventeenth-century Portugal, in which social shame was to be avoided at all costs, the urgency of Feliciano's plea is understandable. Along with his petition, he included a list of witnesses who could testify to his background. The inquisitors of Lisbon agreed to examine the claim and called the witnesses to establish Feliciano's parentage. The testimony of the four witnesses who were called in during the next two weeks—Francisco Vilela, Bartolomeu Sousa, Gonçalo Martins Lima, and Tocalo de Fritas—was mixed, with some saying he came from a noble family in Guimarães and others saying that he was the son—the illegitimate son—of an abbot near Guimarães, who was in fact a noble. Probably more decisive than that evidence was a letter from Gaspar de Abreu, the secretary of the Treasury, reassuring the inquisitors that Feliciano Machado was of noble stock. After a brief consideration of the evidence, the inquisitors of Lisbon and the members of the Conselho Geral accepted the petition and, on April 16, 1666, exempted Maria from the penalty of a whipping, though only at the price of an additional year of exile in Angola. Feliciano's efforts on behalf of his wife had paid off, but alas, he was not to see it, since he had died of his illness on April 11.[35]

In June 1666, the new widow put in a plea to delay the sentence of exile until she was cured of an illness she had caught in prison, a plea that was granted. For reasons that are still unknown, the inquisitors ordered her released from prison, though they stipulated that she had to remain in Lisbon. The order of exile was still in place as well. On September 4, 1667, she put in another plea that the exile order be removed, since she was a widow and had four children—aged from sixteen to seven—to take care of in circumstances of great poverty. If she was exiled, she argued, they would have no one to care for them at all. On November 1, 1667, an order came down from the Conselho Geral, written in the crabbed hand of its elderly secretary, Diogo Velho, granting her a reprieve from exile. Her only punishment would be to continue her spiritual exercises. Because the Great Lisbon Earthquake of 1755 destroyed virtually all of Lisbon's parish records up to that date, we have no idea what happened to her or when she died, making the exemption order from the Inquisition the final document in her historical legacy.

III

Understanding the Artifacts

‹ 5 ›

THE ELEMENT OF TIME IN MARIA'S VISIONS

In order to fully understand the layers of meaning in the visions of Maria de Macedo, it will be helpful to begin by examining her narrative closely in regard to a single element: the passage of time. At first glance, her story may seem to be an example of the fully developed narrative of Sebastian and the Hidden Isle that was becoming more and more widespread among the *sebastianistas* by 1650, the date of the pamphlet's original dictation. Such a conclusion would be incorrect, however, simply because the experience, in the beginning, had nothing to do with Sebastian or even with the Hidden Isle. It should be remembered that the king of the Enchanted Moors was not identified as Sebastian until May 1650, some fourteen to fifteen years after Maria's initial experience of feeling someone touching her while she was in bed, so in a real sense she could not be considered a *sebastianista* until that point. What, then, was she? An examination of the development of her story over time will help answer that question.

Maria's story begins in November 1635, when she would have been around ten years old. As has already been noted, her mother must have died when she was quite young, and it seems that her stepmother had been married to her father for no more than a few years by November 1635. In the confession that was eventually forced from her, she claimed that she made up the entire story of the lizard and the Moor so that her stepmother would treat her better.[1] Whether that admission was true or not, that detail in her confession may reveal a truth about her emotional state and the relationships within her family at the beginning of the visitations. The admission certainly has the virtue of verisimilitude, as the existence of innumerable evil stepmothers in folk tales can attest. So Maria was probably a young girl disturbed both by the death of her mother and by tension with her new stepmother.

Maria said that the night after she felt herself being touched she dreamed—which is not a word she used frequently to describe her experiences—that she was taken to a field filled with flowers and trees. This may have been only a pleasant dream, but the experience was soon to take a strange turn when she woke up to find a lizard next to her bed, a lizard that only she could see. As a result, her father consulted various clerics about the situation and even moved to a new house for a time. And although she later claimed to have heard strange voices and the sounds of walking during this period, she did not, as yet, claim that she had seen a human figure.

In fact, Maria did not say she saw a human figure until after her aunt, Apelonia de Almeida, suggested that the figure appearing to her might be an enchanted Moor. This is significant because it offers a clue regarding the origin of Maria's understanding of her initial experience, namely, the aunt's suggestion. In other words, Maria was able to fit her strange experience into a broader context only because her aunt provided her with a folkloric trope by which to understand that experience. More will be said of the Portuguese legends of the enchanted Moors in the next chapter, but for now it will be enough to say that the appearance of a mysterious lizard suggested the presence of an enchanted Moor to the aunt because, in the legends surrounding them, they often appeared in the form of animals, particularly snakes. Of course, it can be argued that Maria's vision of a lizard may have sprung from her own childhood familiarity with the legends of the enchanted Moors well before the aunt ever entered the picture, but it is still more likely the aunt's knowledge was the real impetus for Maria's conviction that her visitor was an enchanted Moor.

The primary evidence for this conclusion is that several of the other elements associated with the legends of the enchanted Moors do not appear in Maria's narrative until after she talked with her aunt. For example, when she first told her aunt about her experiences, her aunt asked her if the figure was wearing a red cap, an unusual question to ask about a lizard. Maria said that it was not wearing a red cap, but later, in May 1636, when the Moor finally appeared to her in human form, there he was, wearing a red cap. It is, therefore, probable that Maria, after hearing the stories of enchanted Moors from her aunt, not only finally imagined a human figure for her story but inserted the detail of the red cap as well. This is also suggested by the fact that the Moor did not open the magic door in her wall or show her the jars of gold—both elements well represented in the legends about enchanted Moors—until after the aunt's intervention. By that point, it seems to me that her aunt had convinced Maria that the figure was an enchanted Moor (as the narrative in the pamphlet definitely suggests), and so from that point on, the figure in her mind was going to be an enchanted Moor that conformed to the image of one supplied by her aunt's folkloric knowledge. Whatever the precise origin of Maria's initial experience of the appearances of the lizard, as a result of her aunt's influence she began to place those occurrences within a more highly defined context, that of the long-standing stories surrounding enchanted Moors. Indeed, as Maria herself stated, it was her aunt telling her to go with the Moor because it might be (financially) beneficial to her that finally convinced her to go to his house.

This contention receives further confirmation by the details involved in the next major stage of the story's development. After showing Maria the jars of gold, the Moor tried to convince her that she should go with him to his home. When she refused, he asked for various items of food, food that her father agreed to supply. The Moor would then come and talk with her while he ate the food, though no one else could see him. As it states in the pamphlet, "this continued until the Eve of St. John of 1636 [i.e., June 23, 1636]." On that date, the Moor appeared to her, first in lizard form, and then ate lunch with her in the upper room of her house. After they had finished the meal, he asked her again if she wanted to go to his house. Less afraid now because of her aunt's advice and because of her growing familiarity with the figure, she agreed to go with him.

And so it was that the next day, St. John's Day, Maria made her first voyage to the Moor's house. As in many traditional European cultures, St. John's Eve and St. John's Day were important dates in the magical calendar in Portugal. The Portuguese viewed St. John's Day, in particular, as a sort of temporal nexus for supernatural occurrences, a time when witches, fairies, and enchanted Moors were especially active in the affairs of men. Because Maria's concept of enchanted Moors was so closely based, at this point, on the traditional ideas about them, it should not come as a surprise that the next phase in the development of her story took place on a date so intimately connected with their activities.

It should also be noted that on this first trip with the Moor there is no mention of the destination being an island, beyond a rather ambiguous statement that she could see the sea from the windows of the Moor's palace. Indeed, as Maria's narrative in the pamphlet shows, the only places she saw on the first voyage were the palace proper—where she met the Moor's wife and children—and the palace's garden. These initial descriptions are very much in line with traditional lore about enchanted Moors, most of whom were connected in some way to the fabulous magical castles abandoned by the Moors during the period of the Reconquest. Even as the narrative progressed, she did not stray far from the parameters provided by the folklore about enchanted Moors, since after her initial trip, she met more and more of the Moors—all of whom were also shape-shifters—until she met thirty-six of them, all dressed as great nobles. At the end of the thirty-sixth day of this process, they gave her a great feast and then took her down into the corridors below the palace—appropriately named Alminas—where she worked with them, digging up gold, silver, and jewels and bringing water to the other workers in the mines. In the stories about them, enchanted Moors were almost always connected with hidden treasure, and so it is natural that the mining of precious metals and jewels played an important part of Maria's experiences with them.

According to the pamphlet, the experience of going to the land of the Moors to work in the mines occurred regularly for a period of two years. It was then that the Moor who had first met Maria, Bencerrage the Great, and his wife, Zygrereal, asked if she wanted to meet their king. She said she did, and so they introduced her to him. The king—who was not yet identified as Sebastian—was very solicitous of her welfare and made sure that she got a fair share of the profits for her work in the mines. While high nobles or enchanted kings would at times appear in the traditional stories of the enchanted Moors, in this part of her narrative there is the beginning of a new dynamic because for the first time she began to explicitly Christianize her experience. For example, she called herself a Christian for the first time when introduced to the king and then went on to state that in all her time with them she never had a scruple regarding the Catholic faith because she had seen images of the Virgin, the Baby Jesus, and other Christian figures, all despite the fact that the inhabitants of the palace wore Turkish clothes (in one of many times she conflated Moors and Turks). Assuming that the two years she mentioned corresponded to the passing of real time, she would have been between the ages of eleven and thirteen at the time she met the king. It may be reading too much into that timing, but it could be that the impetus to Christianize her voyages stemmed from her confirmation. While there is no evidence about when she was confirmed, after the Council of Trent, Catholic children rarely remained unconfirmed after the age of twelve. Whether this change was due to the experience of confirmation, with its attendant catechizing, remains uncertain, but what is certain was that it was about this time of her life that her visions started to take on a more explicitly Christian character. It was the beginning of a process that was to continue up to and even during her trial before the Inquisition.

This new stage of Christianized enchanted Moors lasted, apparently with little further elaboration, until May 1650, when the Moors finally revealed that their king was Sebastian. Apparently, it was not until this time that Maria was given a tour of the area outside the palace, the garden, and the mines, causing her to realize that the land was an island, indeed the Hidden Isle. In other words, the elements of the Hidden Isle and Sebastian—so crucial in the final form of her story—actually appeared very late in the process. But with the addition of Sebastian, the narrative became thoroughly Christianized and messianic in tone. For example, it is only at this point in the evolution of the story that Maria stated specifically that all the inhabitants of the island had been baptized and had taken Christian names, a claim that later got her into trouble with the inquisitors. It was also at this stage that descriptions of Sebastian's courtiers and family, as well as the eschatological goals he would fulfill, were added to her account, bringing the tale as a whole into conformity with the broad trends of *sebastianista* belief in the early 1650s. The process of the full Christianization of the vision was to continue past the period when the long version of the pamphlet was written, in May 1658, because it was only during the trial that Maria added the details that the inhabitants of the island wore Portuguese, no longer Turkish (or Moorish), clothes and that they were the descendants of the people of Iberia during the time of King Rodrigo—that is, before the Muslim conquest—which would mean they were not Moors at all but rather Christians. And because these elements were confirmed by other witnesses who had heard Maria's story before the Inquisition intervened, it is certain that she was not tailoring her narrative in a more deliberately Christian fashion to impress the inquisitors; the process of full Christianization had taken place well before she ever appeared before the Holy Office.

Timing may again have played a role in this stage of the story's development because in September 1649 Maria was married to Feliciano Machado. In the account given in her part of the pamphlet, she claimed to have revealed her experiences to him soon after the marriage, and by her own admission, her husband did not believe her. Feliciano's own version of his reaction to her visions certainly bears out her statement, though reading between the lines of Feliciano's account, it is probable that there was a good deal more tension between Feliciano and Maria than either was willing to state explicitly. So another extensive elaboration of her fantasy world came about during another time of considerable familial stress, just as the original experience had come about while she was having difficulty with her stepmother as a child.

Of course, this convergence of domestic tension and narrative evolution may just be a coincidence. The significance of the month of May 1650 may simply be that that was when Maria was exposed to the *sebastianista* legend. According to Feliciano, by May 1650 his wife's experiences were known to some people in Lisbon, and it was this notoriety that impelled João Penalvo to contact Maria's father and let him know that his sister-in-law was experiencing similar visions and that the Moors Maria had seen were the people of King Sebastian. Unfortunately, there is no corroborating evidence for or against the existence of this João Penalvo. So, whether a real man did tell her her experiences were related to Sebastian or whether João Penalvo was created as a corroborating witness by Feliciano and Maria to convince people that her visitations were real cannot be definitively settled. Despite this basic uncertainty, Feliciano's account is plausible in general terms: if Maria was known as some sort of visionary (a possibility bolstered by the testimony of her childhood neighbors), it is certainly not impossible that a João Penalvo may have contacted her and told her of the legends surrounding Sebastian. She then may have reelaborated and expanded her narrative to fit the matrix of the *sebastianista* tradition that had just been provided to her, just as she fit her original strange experiences to the legends surrounding enchanted Moors as told to her by her aunt.

Whatever the precise role of João Penalvo in the development of Maria's story, it is clear that she did not include Sebastian or the Hidden Isle until after May 1650, and it is probable that it was during that time period that she was first introduced to *sebastianismo* as a coherent legend. It was a defining moment for her story and for her within the story, as well, because after that point she no longer had to work in the mines. Instead, she is revealed as a witness of the impending return of Sebastian, and her new apostolic role privileges her to accompany Queen Aureliana to a novena in Lisbon and to accompany the Hidden One himself to the Church of Our Lady of Tribulations, where he received his commission from the prophets. By that point—which, according to the long version of the pamphlet, "took place" on April 1, 1651—her visionary world had been wholly transformed from its original parameters; it had gone from the wholly folkloric world of the enchanted Moors to a Christianized version of that legendary world to, finally, a completely Christianized and millenarian vision of

Sebastian and the people of his Hidden Isle, who are really no longer Moorish at all. The transformation of her interior world was complete.

By examining the successive strata of Maria's story, it becomes obvious that the elements of her narrative were not always consistent with each other. Each layer or stage of her account is largely coherent within itself, since each was built out of the elements provided by more or less well developed external traditions, such as the legends about enchanted Moors, the Hidden Isle, or Sebastian, but each layer was built on the foundation of the previous layer with little regard to the consistency of details between the two. Whatever the internal discrepancies of her narrative, the trend toward a greater and greater understanding of her experience in Christian terms is quite clear and, in all likelihood, is indicative of an increasingly strong identification of herself as a Christian.

‹ 6 ›

A GLIMPSE OF PARADISE

Unlocking the Meaning of Maria's Visions

The principal elements of Maria de Macedo's visions were her belief in Sebastian as the Hidden King and her belief in the existence of the Hidden Isle, so one might be tempted to say that this simply made her an orthodox *sebastianista* of the mid-seventeenth century. Such a conclusion would, however, be incorrect, and for at least two important reasons. First, as pointed out in the previous chapter, Maria de Macedo did not believe in the Hidden Isle or in Sebastian until some fourteen years after her initial experience; in 1635–36, when she first began to have her visitations, she believed only in enchanted Moors. The second reason that Maria de Macedo cannot be seen only as a *sebastianista* is that it was the elements that distinguished her from the orthodox *sebastianista* tradition that caused her trouble with the Inquisition. With these facts in mind, we will carefully examine the sources (folkloric, millenarian, and otherwise) of each layer of her vision and assess the role specific details of her account played within her overall narrative. We will then conclude with an analysis of the underlying values that framed Maria de Macedo's understanding of her visionary experience and of herself.

The first narrative matrix Maria de Macedo used to understand and articulate her experiences was that of the Portuguese tradition of the so-called enchanted Moors. By the seventeenth century, that tradition was well established in Portugal, as even a cursory reading of Maria's own narrative tends to suggest. The legends of the enchanted Moors had their origin in the Iberian Reconquest, when, it was said, the Moors had to flee the advancing Christian forces so quickly that they were forced to leave behind their great treasures, protected only by powerful enchantments and magical guardians summoned by the escaping Moors. Other variants of the legend placed the enchantments not on the

Moors' treasure but on their children, most frequently the daughters of Moorish nobleman, who had to be enchanted to protect them from the Christians. More often than not, though, the two elements were combined, with the enchanted Moors serving as the guardians of the hidden treasure.[1] Frequently, the stories about encounters with enchanted Moors centered on some task a Christian would have to perform (the sharing of food, as in Maria's case, was one of the more common tasks found in the folklore) in order to disenchant the Moor; once disenchanted, the Moor would reward the Christian's service with the vast treasure he or she was guarding.

This context explains why Maria's aunt, Apelonia de Almeida, urged her to go with the Moor and do what he said, "seeing that it could result in great good for me," as the pamphlet puts it; once she had identified the figure appearing to her niece as an enchanted Moor, it was natural for her to see an opportunity for Maria to gain great wealth. After all, that was what everything she knew about enchanted Moors told her to expect. And it was these expectations, transferred to Maria, that finally compelled her to "take the next step" in her dealings with the Moor and in the elaboration of her story.

Maria's aunt transferred more than just her expectations to her, however; Apelonia de Almeida also passed along a good deal of her specific knowledge of the legends of the enchanted Moors to her niece. In story after story involving enchanted Moors, magical palaces make an appearance, not only as the residence of the deathless Moors but also as the repository of the great wealth they guarded. The appearance of the palace and the mines full of gold, silver, and jewels in Maria's vision can be understood only in the context of this venerable element of the folklore. Even the means used by Maria and the Moor to reach the palace, the door he opened in the wall where there had been no door before, finds an echo in the magic doors found in the traditional corpus of legends about the *mouros encantados*.[2] The connection between St. John's Eve and the activities of the Moors is also well established in the literature,[3] and it has already been argued that the St. John's Eve and St. John's Day of 1636 were key temporal points in development of Maria's narrative, precisely because those dates were so closely associated with enchanted Moors in the folklore.

The physical description of the Moors in Maria's account was also heavily dependent on the broader tradition about the enchanted Moors. Enchanted Moors wearing red caps are well documented in the literature about them,[4] and after her aunt asked her if the figure appearing to her was wearing a red cap,

Maria duly included a red cap among the clothes worn by the Moor when he first revealed himself to her in human form. In the pamphlet, Maria described the man as "having a dark complexion; coarse, blond hair; colored white; of good stature, dressed in the Turkish manner, with a red cap, with a scimitar and matching boots with spurs, and many other ornaments." This depiction is almost wholly based on the appearance of enchanted Moors in the legends rather than on any exposure at all to a real Moor on Maria's part. Indeed, throughout the pamphlet, especially in the shorter version, which still includes some of the false starts of her original dictation, she consistently used the terms Turkish and Moorish interchangeably, an indication that she really had no conception of a difference between them. Even in the quote above, the Moor is "dressed in the Turkish manner"; Turkish clothing and the inclusion of a scimitar and spurs demonstrates that her conception of Moors (enchanted or otherwise) was founded not on any personal experience but rather on an exoticized depiction of the Moorish Other picked up from the culture around her. One might also wonder how many real Moors had "coarse, blond hair," but blond hair is not unknown in the stories of the enchanted Moors.[5] Similarly, the trope of the enchanted Moors being extremely beautiful is quite common in the traditional stories about them, and in answer to one of de la Cerda's questions as to whether the inhabitants of the island had any physical deformity, Maria said that, on the contrary, they had the most perfect bodies nature could form.[6]

Of course, the most striking aspect of Maria's early experiences with the Moors was that they appeared to her in the form of animals, and indeed, this was one of the elements of her story that most disturbed the inquisitors. The tradition of enchanted Moors being trapped in animal form or of being able to assume animal form when they wished is very well established in the literature.[7] The most frequent motif of animal transformation to appear in those stories was that of a *moura encantada* taking the shape of a snake, usually to guard the fantastic treasures hidden away in the legendary Moorish palaces, though bulls, foxes, sheep, lions, and toads, among other animals, also made appearances in the folklore. Maria's list of "snakes, lizards, salamanders, hippopotamuses, lions, and other kinds of animals of which I have no knowledge" is certainly comparable to the menagerie of animals that played a role in the traditional lore about the enchanted Moors. It is essential to point out that in none of the accounts of encounters with enchanted Moors was the fact that they took the form of animals understood as indicative of their malevolence or their hostility.

Instead, their ability to take animal form, even serpent form, is narrated neutrally within the folkloric tradition, and it seems that the trope of zoomorphia was interpreted as no more than a sign of the enchanted or magical nature of the Moors, not as a sign of affiliation with the forces of either good or evil. The main gist of all the stories of the enchanted Moors was not a moral choice in favor of God or the devil; rather, it was the prospect of gaining fantastic wealth, instantaneously achieved, unencumbered by the necessity to work for it, and without a lot of undue moralizing.

The nonassociation of animal forms with evil is also seen in the fact that the first Moor appeared to Maria in the shape of a lizard. In the realm of Portuguese folklore, lizards were not seen as harmful creatures. In fact, they were often associated with supernatural healing, since they were believed to have sympathetic magical properties. Thus, it was thought someone with a broken leg could heal it by intoning the proper incantations and then breaking the lizard's leg. The medical problem would thus be transferred to the lizard and the person healed.[8] The interjection "Lizard!" was often used as a verbal talisman to keep away misfortune, another example of the positive magical associations of lizards in the folklore of Portugal.[9] At times, lizards were connected to dragons—and thus to evil—in Portuguese legends,[10] but that only proves that traditional associations were not always consistent. On balance, the popular view of lizards tended toward the positive side, which was in marked contrast to the inquisitorial view of the matter. This view of lizards as bearers of good magic is at least consistent with Maria's reaction to it; to be sure, she was frightened when it first appeared to her, but it seems her fear came more from the fact that she thought there was a strange creature in her room than that she associated danger with lizards per se.

Before moving on to the other legends that provided the raw materials for Maria's construction, I should make some comments about another example of Moorish influence on her vision. One of the strangest details of her story was the claim that there was a "rooster as large as a turkey" with "very long tail feathers" in one of the three corridors that led from the first Moor's palace to its garden. In my initial readings of the pamphlet, I was at a loss to understand either the origin of this detail or what role it could have played within her vision. However, as I was doing background research, I learned that according to some Islamic legends that were known in medieval Europe, the gate to paradise was guarded by an angel who took the form of a giant rooster.[11] The similarities between a giant rooster guarding the way to the garden paradise of Islamic myth and a giant rooster walking up and down the corridor beneath the palace, in essence guarding the way to the palace's garden, in Maria's vision are simply too close to be due to coincidence. The question remains, though, of what Maria's source for this element was. It is very unlikely that she gained it directly from any of the Latin translations of the Islamic legends then available, though she may have picked up on the association as the content of those translations filtered down to the uneducated populace. However, one cannot discount the possibility that this was a folkloric relic, a relic that had survived, somehow, from the times of Moorish dominance in Portugal. Lisbon had been taken by the Christians under Dom Afonso Henriques in 1147, but legends are remarkably hardy. Even though that detail clearly had its origin in Islamic legend, by the 1660s that association was so deeply buried and vestigial that I doubt Maria even realized what its origins were. Indeed, not even the inquisitors, generally so aware of suspect details, picked up on its Moorish origins, and they did not ask her any follow-up questions about it, nor did they raise it as an issue of concern among themselves. It was a relic that had survived for so long in the folklore of Lisbon that it all traces of its origins had been obscured.

At first glance, Maria's description of Sebastian would seem to be comparable to that of a great many other messianic figures in the history of western Europe. It might, therefore, be tempting to dismiss her characterization as no more than another example of the popular reception of a traditional image of a divinely appointed redemptive leader, the analysis of which would have limited historical value. Such an understanding would be mistaken in at least two important ways, however. First, though she included in her characterization of Sebastian many elements that were part of the common messianic tradition of western Europe, she excluded others and even invented some details—an arrangement of elements that was, if not unique, at least unusual. This point leads to the next reason that her vision of Sebastian is still worth studying. To dismiss the description of Sebastian given in the pamphlet and in her testimony as no more than stereotypical would be to miss an opportunity, an opportunity to understand why she chose the elements she did. By examining her characterization of Sebastian in detail we can gain insight into the cultural values that informed it, especially in regard to how she (and others) conceived of an idealized ruler in the seventeenth century. Such an examination will help our understanding not only of her views of an externalized ideal ruler but also of the parameters of her self-conception because, after all, what is the image of a romanticized leader but the projection of an individual's or group's values, purged of the dross of human weakness?[12] By thus understanding the image of Sebastian she created (or accepted), we will better understand how she conceived of her own identity.

In terms of a physical description of Sebastian, the influence of the portrait of Sebastian Maria had seen in the Convent of St. Bridgette, as well as the fact that she aged that portrait in her mind, has already been noted. The tiny detail that Sebastian showed Maria a scar above his eyebrow to prove his identity will be discussed later, so there is little else to say regarding her visual description of Sebastian, simply because she gave very little information on the subject. Unlike many of the visionaries who were contemporaries of Maria, she provided little in the way of visual symbols. For example, she gave no description of Sebastian's clothes, crown, throne, or symbolic images around him, nor did she even mention whether he had a crown, throne, or such images around him.[13] In fact, there was no physical description of him that cannot be reduced simply to the physical signs needed to accomplish the practical task of identifying him as Sebastian. The only possible exception to this is that Maria described him as an "old man," perhaps as a sign of his dignity and authority. This possibility receives some confirmation in the fact that Sebastian's companions were said to be of "great authority and respect, both in their clothing and their persons." The noblemen of his court were also said to stand around him with drawn swords ("espadas nuas"). Since these depictions lack the level of detail needed for any type of intensive symbolic interpretation, it is probably safe to say the meaning is not abstract and opaque but transparent: such a gathering of great nobles demonstrates the sublime dignity of Sebastian as the Hidden King, as well as the trust and loyalty between him and the members of his court. The utilitarian, and even minimalist, nature of her portrayal of the physical aspects of her idealized king indicates that the source of her views on this issue was a folkloric messianic tradition rather than any type of erudite, heavily symbolic system of meanings.

This point receives confirmation when one compares Maria's visions with those of some of her contemporary visionaries in Portugal. Luzia de Jesus was a Franciscan *beata* (a celibate lay holy woman) and *terceira* (a member of the lay third order of Franciscans) tried by the Inquisition in 1645 for a variety of heterodox statements, the most important of which were that she was greater than an angel in God's favor, that she knew that the Castilians (with whom the Portuguese were fighting at the time) had fallen from grace, and that she knew Portugal was still loved by God despite the pope's refusal to recognize the Braganza regime. She claimed to have learned all this after speaking to the Guardian Angel of Portugal, and the content of her vision is mostly taken up with a description of what the angel told her. She did see King João being blessed at one point, she asked Saint Louis to bring about peace between Spain and Portugal at another time, and she once saw Saint George protecting the Portuguese and punishing the Spanish. Besides these exceptions, the vision itself is quite static (and, may I say, dull) and not visual in nature. For the most part, it is simply a series of incidents in which either a saint or an angel verbally revealed various spiritual truths to her.[14]

The vision of another *terceira* prosecuted by the Inquisition, Joana da Cruz, is quite similar. In her case, she claimed to have received a direct revelation from God that she was the most perfect creature of all and that even the Virgin Mary was not superior to her. She also said she had learned that Sebastian would be canonized and that there would an enormous spiritual battle between the saints of Portugal and the saints of all other countries; despite their inferior numbers, the Portuguese saints would, of course, emerge triumphant. If anything, Joana da Cruz's vision was even less visual than Luzia de Jesus's, and it was essentially a narrative of her being a passive receptacle of God's favors.[15] In content, these visions are very different from Maria's in that they are more narrowly focused on the issues of the war, the spiritual state of Portugal, and, most important of all, the exalted status of the women receiving these revelations; Maria's vision hinted at a much wider range of issues. Also, the tone of these visions is different from that of Maria's. They are largely didactic with the two visionaries recalling what they *heard* from various spiritual figures; Maria, however, gave a *visual* description of what she claimed she had *experienced*. These contrasts in tone and content stem from the fact that the two *terceiras* had almost certainly received a greater degree of formal religious instruction and were exposed to more standard descriptions of visions than was the laywoman Maria de Macedo.

The clearest contrasting example, though, is found in the visions attributed to Madre Leocardia da Conceição. Her vision appears in more than one of the seventeenth-century *sebastianista* collections, and the *sebastianista* apology known as "A Reposta de certa pessoa a outra" claims that she was still alive when it was written in 1658.[16] Besides this information, very few biographical details are available, since there is no evidence that she was ever investigated by the Inquisition or any other ecclesiastical court. The content of the vision largely centers on various figures, including Dom Afonso Henriques and Sebastian himself, giving Madre Leocardia reassurance that the Portuguese would triumph in their struggle against Castile and that Sebastian was the Hidden One who had been chosen by God to redeem Portugal and conquer the world for Christ.

This is fairly standard *sebastianista* rhetoric, of course, and is not all that different from what can be found in Maria de Macedo's vision; the difference between the two is seen in the different ways by which prophetic knowledge was conveyed. Compare the following passage from the text of Madre Leocardia's vision with the minimalist approach of Maria de Macedo:

> She saw that, in the interior part [of the chapel where she was praying], there was a man, completely dressed in white armor, from the bottom of his feet to his head, which was covered with a beautiful closed helmet. In his left hand, there was a shield upon which were engraved the arms of this kingdom, and in his right hand, a staff. Above this man was a tree upon the crown of which was an Image of Christ, Our Lord, Crucified, and at the foot of this tree the man was kneeling in the manner of a hermit, with his hands raised in prayer. To the right of the tree, a woman was standing, dressed in all white, with a candle near her face. Her face was quite composed and in her right hand was a pyx and, in her left, a cross. To the left of the tree, there was a noble youth holding a standard, with the sacred coins of this Kingdom [i.e., the thirty coins of the coat of arms]. Next to him was an older man, dressed in a long, red garment.

The rest of the vision is an explanation of what the various elements of this scene, and other scenes revealed later, meant. In terms of their content, there is nothing in any of them that could really be considered antithetical to the messages conveyed in Maria's visions, but the methods used to convey those meanings are quite different. Leocardia de Conceição's visions clearly demonstrate a profound exposure to symbolic imagery in an apocalyptic mode. As symbols, they are abstract visual signs that must be interpreted.

Maria's vision is notable for its lack of symbolism, for its interpretive transparency, if you will. The enchanted Moors, for example, do not symbolize anything; they are just enchanted Moors. To be sure, certain images in Maria's vision evoke further interpretation—the garden and the fountains as signs of abundance, for example, or the presence of the three churches in the island's main square as a sign of the islanders' piety—but these are not the same kind of symbols used in Madre Leocardia's vision at all. These visions from professed female religious, taken together, seem to confirm, by contrast, the folkloric, down-to-earth origins of Maria's visualizations. All four women constructed their visions from the materials available to them in their respective milieus; the results show what those materials were and, therefore, the character of their environment as well.

Maria also provided her hearers (and interrogators) with a description of Sebastian's family, and the first point that needs to be made regarding this issue is no more complex than that Sebastian was characterized as having a wife and children. The possible origin of this element will be examined later, but it is important to say that this is evidence that Maria's views on Sebastian had nothing to do with the historical record of Sebastian at all; instead, everything was derived from a mythologized construction of him that been developed over the eight decades since his death. In Maria's account, he was married to a princess, as befitted a providentially favored king, and thus the issue of the historical Sebastian's horror and aversion to women was simply moot; similarly, his six children proved beyond a shadow of a doubt that he was not impotent. But more important than understanding those details is the general picture of Sebastian presented by Maria, a picture that accords well with Catholic ideals of the king as a father figure.[17]

More important than a physical depiction or a description of his family, both to us and, apparently, to Maria, is her portrayal of Sebastian's character as a ruler. Before addressing the core value that Maria attributed to Sebastian—piety—we should examine an incident that, while only forming a tiny part of her narrative, provides an important clue as to her views of an ideal ruler. After two years of working in the mines of the island and bringing water to her fellow workers—and thus in the transitional phase of her story's development—the Moor who first brought her to the island and his wife asked if she wanted to meet their king. When she said she did, they introduced her to the king, though at that time he was not named as Sebastian. The part of the narrative that follows is the key for our purposes now: after hearing that she was named Maria and that she was a Christian, the king went on to praise her and inquire whether she had been well treated as she worked in the mines. She replied that she had been, although they had ordered her about a few times and kept her very busy. She went on to say that he continued to ask about her treatment for the next fourteen years—that is, up to the time of the pamphlet's writing. The significance of the passage is that it (again) portrays the king who was to become Sebastian as a preeminently *paternal* ruler, one who shows a fatherly concern for the well-being of all his subjects. This point is further reinforced by another part of the same narrative in which Maria said the king personally assigned her a presumably fair and probably even an equal share of what had been gained from the labors of the islanders. Above all, this small incident demonstrates that, in Maria's mind and narrative, the king was a *just* ruler.

As with almost all messianic figures, the principal's piety is the defining aspect of his character and, indeed, the character of his rule. But while piety was an axiomatic characteristic for all messianic candidates in the early modern period, this does not mean that the piety of these figures was of the same type; characterizations of piety varied according to the ideals of piety espoused by the would-be messiah or his supporters and are thus evidence of those ideals. In the case of Maria de Macedo, therefore, we will work backward from her description of Sebastian as an idealized pious ruler toward a greater understanding of what piety meant to her.

What, in Maria's mind, demonstrated that Sebastian was pious? How did she describe him to others to convince them of his piety? Two elements of piety are repeated again and again, both in her testimony and in the testimony of the witnesses: prayer and fasting. According to her description, Sebastian prayed and fasted on bread and water three times a week. The pamphlet states that Sebastian was very familiar with God and that he spoke with Christ on Mondays, Wednesdays, and Sundays, presumably the same times he was fasting. This characterization is further reinforced in that whenever Maria was given a question to ask Sebastian, he always seemed to be fasting and praying and so was unavailable to give an answer. Nor was the frequency of the fast the only indicator of Sebastian's rigor: Maria was also favorably impressed by the fact that Sebastian would, while praying, kneel on the ground "without anything interposing itself between the ground and his flesh,"[18] an observation we will see again in her description of the religious devotions of the islanders as a whole.

In answering one of de la Cerda's questions as to why she thought her visitations were from God rather than the devil, Maria revealed more information about the nature of Sebastian's piety. His devotions took place in an oratory that contained images of Christ Crucified, Our Lady of the Rosary, the Baby Jesus, Saint Joseph, and Saint Anthony, she said, which led her to conclude that, whatever the precise nature of her experience, it could not be from the devil. This scene of iconolatry emphasized the Catholic nature of the devotion; it would certainly not be indicative of Protestant piety, which could have included both prayer and fasting. More to the point, the veneration of the saints and their images would absolutely preclude it from being Islamic in any way, a point necessary to make clear. This does not mean that she deliberately made up this point to impress the inquisitors; the description is well attested in the testimony of the witnesses who heard her story before the Inquisition ever got involved. Instead, as has been said before, it was part of the natural evolution away from her initial concept of the magic palace of the enchanted Moors to her later view of the Hidden Isle, the home of Sebastian, the Hidden One favored by the Christian God.

This view of Christian piety as prayer, fasting, and veneration of the saints is further reinforced by the stories of Maria's two voyages from the island back to Portugal. The first was the pilgrimage to Our Lady of Tribulations with Sebastian, so that he, along with King Arthur and Don Jaume, could be commissioned by the prophets. The second voyage was the trip to the Convent of Our Lady the Mother of God in Lisbon with Queen Aureliana to celebrate a novena.[19] The origins of this view of piety will examined later after reviewing the religious practices attributed to the islanders by Maria, but it should be said here that this view is founded on an understanding of piety as devoted or correct practice. In other words, Maria's ideals of devotion were fundamentally ones of orthopraxy.

Of course, Sebastian's piety was not only a virtue in its own right; it would have also—in Maria's mind—qualified him to be God's instrument on earth, and we can gain a greater understanding of her ideals of a perfect ruler by examining the eschatological goals she attributed to Sebastian.[20] Sebastian would, she said, appear on a Friday on which the church celebrated a feast day, and when he returned, the sun would rise again at ten o'clock at night.[21] He would reappear in Lisbon, and when he did, there would be great revolutions in that city. He would bring new laws—only five in number—that he wrote and that were confirmed by the very hand of Christ.[22] From there, he would "reform the World, conquer the Moors and Turks, convert the heretics, put everything right and, being the Hidden One, would go to the Holy House [of Jerusalem]." In the task of the Judgment of Reformation, he would be assisted by Saint John the Evangelist and would "make all laws one law." Sebastian would rule the world from Jerusalem until the age of 120, and when he died, he would be buried in a tomb next to the Holy Sepulcher. One of his sons would then rule in his place and continue the perfection of the world until the return of Enoch and Elijah before the Final Judgment.[23]

What can we glean from this list regarding the values that informed it? Of course, it is quite similar to many other lists of goals for eschatological figures, as the Trovas of Bandarra demonstrate. But what did it mean to Maria de Macedo, to the extent that we can make that determination? The details of Sebastian's reappearance—the return on a feast day and the sun rising again at night—point to the divine timing of Sebastian's return and to God's approval of his Chosen One's mission on earth. The location of Sebastian's return is also significant: neither Jerusalem nor Rome but Lisbon. The Portuguese capital would, therefore, be significant as the starting point for the Hidden One's task of conquest and reformation. The choice of Lisbon as the venue of Sebastian's advent also emphasized, yet again, the special place of Portugal in God's plan for humankind and that his instrument on earth was Portuguese and would rule first as a Portuguese king. From this we can see that Maria de Macedo valued, as did Bandarra and others, the idea of the sacred and her identity as Portuguese. She was a type of religious nationalist, insofar as that term can be used in the seventeenth century.

Given the course of Sebastianism's evolution, such a conclusion is hardly unexpected. However, by examining the other details of Sebastian's millennial goals, we can gain still greater insight into the values of self-identification motivating Maria's acceptance of the legend. If she was a religiously motivated nationalist in the sense used above, how, specifically, was such an identity conceived? One very important way in which this identity was formulated was by way of contrast. Well in line with the long-standing Iberian tradition of the Hidden One, Sebastian would conquer both the Moors and the Turks and would retake Jerusalem for the Christians, a task that would necessarily entail the complete destruction of the political powers of the Islamic states of North Africa and the Levant. It is, therefore, not too much to say that, at a fundamental level,

Maria conceived of herself as *non-Muslim*. Indeed, this should not be surprising because if there was one thing all groups of Portuguese millenarians agreed on it was that Islam would have to be destroyed for the purposes of God to triumph on earth. From Bandarra's "dogs" and "pigs" to Castro's "sect of Mafoma" to Vieira's bloody conquest of the Turks by the resurrected João IV, virtually all millenarians (and probably most Portuguese for that matter) viewed Muslims as the most dangerous enemies of the followers of the one true faith. In essence, in early modern Portugal, Islam was the paradigmatic embodiment of the Other who had to be opposed.[24]

This is not to say, however, that Maria de Macedo was as self-consciously and virulently anti-Muslim as someone such as Dom João de Castro. Because this anti-Islamic element does not appear in her narrative outside her list of Sebastian's eschatological goals, its inclusion may be nothing more than an example of *sebastianista* rhetorical boilerplate. This does not mean, though, that she would not have identified herself as opposed to Islam; in fact, the opposite is more probable. The fact that anti-Islamic tropes were standard elements of the *sebastianista* (and millenarian) tradition is not an indicator that they were meaningless relics from a bygone age; from everything we can reconstruct about the state of Portuguese messianism in the mid-seventeenth century, it is much more likely that this is an indicator of the ubiquity of anti-Muslim sentiments throughout the millenarian communities and throughout Portuguese society as a whole.

The inclusion of the conversion of the heretics as a goal for the triumphant Sebastian probably falls into a similar category. Again, the heretic is the Other against whom the faithful define themselves; as such, he must be either converted or destroyed. Since Maria was a Roman Catholic in baroque Portugal, the heretics to be converted would certainly include the Protestants of northern Europe and probably the *conversos* and *mouriscos* that so troubled the Inquisition and its supporters in Portugal. We cannot be sure on this point, though it is interesting to note that she did not include the conversion of the Jews as a separate eschatological goal as had Bandarra or as had her contemporary António Vieira. This issue will be examined again in the next section once the issue of the source of her characterization of Sebastian has been addressed, but for now it should suffice to say that Maria thought the Hidden One would bring about the conversion of the entire world to (Roman Catholic) Christianity, or to use her own words, that he would "make all laws one law."[25]

Sebastian's goals, and therefore Maria's concerns, were not limited to those of religious purification. He would also "put everything right," and he would reform the world with the help of Saint John the Evangelist. Thus, Sebastian also had political imperatives to fulfill; beyond the goal of confessional hegemony, there was the matter of political reform, although within the Western millenarian tradition the two were inevitably linked. According to the common view, the scourge of war, with all its attendant abuses, could be truly eliminated from the world only when the power of Islam and the heretics had been broken. Then, and only then, could society as a whole be reformed. The use of the phrase "put everything right" by Maria in this regard is interesting, and it was probably related to her claim that Sebastian would bring five new laws, a new standard by which to govern the world. This new standard would place everything where it should be, which was the essence of many early modern conceptions of justice.

A concern for religious purity and the pursuit of earthly justice were the two axes by which Maria's vision of a messianic ruler were laid out. This should come as no surprise, since these were the two key elements of virtually all millenarian hopes. Because these goals were almost universally accepted, they do not, in themselves, tell us much about the origins of Maria's views or about the specific values upon which they were founded. Next we will address the issue of the sources for her views, specifically her views about the messianic figure of Sebastian.

The fact that the characterization given above was, in a great number of ways, a fairly standard view of Sebastian by the middle of the seventeenth century complicates determining the origins of Maria's views about him. Since so many people were saying roughly the same things about Sebastian (or João or Afonso), the range of possible sources for her description of him is, at first glance, rather daunting. However, by using the approach first advocated by Giovanni Morelli in which the examination of a painting's small, trifling features became the principal means by which to evaluate the artwork's authenticity, it will be possible to ascertain a good deal about the sources of Maria's view of Sebastian—in terms of traditions, if not documents.[26] I believe that this investigation will demonstrate that her *sebastianismo* was heavily influenced by Dom João de Castro or at least the school of Portuguese messianism of which he was a part.

To demonstrate the validity of this conclusion, we must examine a number of important similarities between the characterization of Sebastian found in the writings of Dom João de Castro and that found in the visions of Maria de Macedo some fifty years later. One very obvious similarity is the common emphasis on the king's deep piety, but for the reasons of ubiquity elaborated above, such a similarity is hardly solid evidence of Castro's influence on Maria. A more suggestive correlation is the fact that this piety was outwardly indicated by rigorous prayer and fasting. Speaking of the Prisoner of Venice, Castro said, "His devotion was the same in prison as when he was free: always in prayer. . . . He fasted almost the entire week: Fridays and Saturdays, on bread and water; he did not eat meat on Sundays and Thursdays, sometimes not even Mondays or Tuesdays. . . . On Wednesdays, he always fasted."[27] This is certainly comparable to Maria's descriptions of Sebastian's prayer and fasting on the island given above, though it does not prove Castro was her source.

Another notable similarity between the two descriptions is found in Maria's list of the great deeds Sebastian would accomplish after his return. She said that he would "reform the world, conquer the Moors and Turks, convert the heretics, put everything right . . . and retake the Holy House of Jerusalem,"[28] everything Bandarra had said except for the conversion of the Jews. Admittedly, this is not decisive evidence of Castro's influence on Maria, either, since by the middle decades of the seventeenth century most Portuguese millenarians had stopped making explicit reference to the goal of the conversion of the Jews. António Vieira was, of course, an exception to this rule, but even among the *joanista* apologists who supported João's policies regarding the New Christians, this element rarely received much emphasis. I have not been able to find any evidence in the *sebastianista* literature of the period that the *sebastianistas* considered the conversion of the Jews a goal for the Hidden One or that they ever had. This is not to say that because Maria failed to explicitly include the conversion of the Jews as a goal Dom João de Castro was (directly or indirectly) the source of her omission in this regard; it demonstrates only that their views on the *converso* issue may have been consistent.

Unsurprisingly, these observations about Sebastian are so generic and were so widely held that they are not sufficient to establish a firm linkage between Castro and Macedo. It is only when some of the smaller details of her account are examined that such connections can begin to be made. One such clue is found in her response when Inquisitor de la Cerda asked her whether Sebastian ever left the Hidden Isle and, if so, how. She replied that she did not how he traveled away from the island but she did know he had traveled to "Venice, to Rome, and to other parts she could not remember."[29] It is not surprising that, in her mind, a pious figure like Sebastian would travel to Rome—that most important of all pilgrimage sites in the West—but the inclusion of Venice is more significant, simply because it would not be a natural destination for a messianic figure. Did Venice appear on the list because she associated Sebastian with the figure of the Prisoner of Venice, an association shared by many people in Portugal, both *sebastianistas* and non-*sebastianistas*?

Perhaps, but the evidence for such a connection remains shaky until another small detail found in Maria's testimony is considered. When asked how Sebastian had first arrived on the island, she answered that, while "crossing the mountains of Italy" to escape the king of Spain, he, his family, and his companions had been enveloped in a cloud and had then woken up on the island.[30] According to Maria, this flight from agents of the king of Spain took place in the "mountains of Italy," presumably the Alps, since she also said it occurred on "Mount Camposallo, which is in the mountains of Germany, toward the port of Venice." This is another piece of evidence that Maria de Macedo's understanding of Sebastian was, at least in part, due to the traditions surrounding the Prisoner of Venice. Because Castro's story of the Venetians releasing Sebastian and handing Catizone over to the Spanish in his place and her story of Sebastian fleeing the Spanish across the mountains of Italy are compatible with each other, this may also be evidence of a more direct connection between her and Castro.

Of course, Maria's version of the story demonstrates a certain amount of confusion about the Prisoner's story, whether derived from Castro or not, largely because of issues of timing. According to Maria, Sebastian was fleeing the Spanish with his wife and his oldest children when he was translated to the Hidden Isle; certainly the Prisoner of Venice, even if he had been Sebastian, neither was married nor had children at the time of his release from Venice in 1600. This element is also inconsistent with the received version of the Prisoner's story from Castro and his close ally, Father José de Teixeira, in that they explain Sebastian's long absence from Portugal after Alcazarquivir as due to his penitential travels in faraway lands, followed by a lengthy period as a hermit, either of which would have precluded a family.

The question remains of the origin of Maria's contention that Sebastian had a wife and two children at the time of his escape through "the mountains of

Italy." The most likely source is the spurious papal bull attributed to Urban VIII, which of the three bulls relating to the issue of Sebastian was the only one to mention that Sebastian had a family. The bull was supposedly issued sometime in 1630, but its various versions contradict each other as to the exact date. This inconsistency did not in any way hinder it from being eagerly accepted among the *sebastianistas*, though, and it was one of the source materials that was included in the "Jardim ameno," which was written sometime around 1650, precisely the period in which Maria's visions were evolving from a land of enchanted Moors to a belief in Sebastian as the king of the Hidden Isle. This is only to say that it is possible that Maria was familiar with the contents, at least in general terms, of the forged papal bull and that this familiarity was the basis for her belief that Sebastian was married and had children.[31]

The possibility that the papal bull of 1630 was, directly or indirectly, the inspiration for this element of Maria's story may help explain other aspects of her description as well. According to the bull, Sebastian presented himself before Urban VIII "in the Castle of Saint Angelo," just as he supposedly had in 1598 before Clement VIII and in 1617 before Paul V, and begged the pontiff to issue a new ruling to Philip IV of Spain commanding him to give up the kingdom of Portugal so that Sebastian's heirs would not be further prejudiced by their absence from the kingdom.[32] Could Maria's exposure to the story that Sebastian had presented himself to the pope sometime in 1630 have provided the impetus for her belief that Sebastian had, at some point, traveled from the island to Rome? Probably, and the influence of the three false bulls may explain yet more about this part of her story. Her belief in the bulls might also account for her story of Sebastian fleeing from Spanish agents across the mountains of Italy sometime *after* his escape from Venice or San Lucar in either 1600 or 1603. If he presented himself before the pope in 1617 or in 1630, perhaps the dastardly Spanish had persecuted him yet again, or so she may have thought. This may, however, be reading too much coherence into the details of her vision. Her list of Sebastian's destinations may simply be a grab bag of disparate elements—the family and Rome from the bulls, Venice and the "other parts she could not remember" from the story of the Prisoner of Venice—that she heard at some time and then reworked into her own catalog of Sebastian's travels. While any one of these associations may be justly be questioned, the net effect of them together is the strengthening of the contention that Maria de Macedo's mental picture of Sebastian was influenced both by the traditions surrounding the

Prisoner of Venice and by the fraudulent papal bulls that formed a later part of that same tradition.

The more conclusive evidence of a linkage between Castro's Sebastian and the Hidden King of Maria de Macedo becomes clear only by using the technique of the close examination of details advocated by Morelli. As Morelli argued for the importance of fingernails and earlobes in authenticating art, so this evidence literally hangs on an eyebrow. According to the testimony of Pedro Peixoto, Maria knew that it was the true Sebastian on the island because she saw a scar above his right eyebrow.[33] One must ask the question of why such a mark would be taken as proof of Sebastian's identity, in Maria's mind and, perhaps, Peixoto's as well. The answer to this question takes us back, I believe, to the list of physical signs sought by the Portuguese conspirators in Venice to confirm that the Prisoner of Venice was Sebastian. One of the signs included on this list was a scar above his right eyebrow, generally interpreted as the result of a wound he had received at Alcazarquivir or in his subsequent battles against the Turks. Since it is quite unlikely that this correlation was accidental, we must ask how Maria de Macedo was exposed to at least this element of the list of physical marks associated with the Prisoner of Venice. There are only two printed sources that could have been the sources of that information, the *Discurso da vida* of Dom João de Castro ("over the right [eyebrow] I noticed a scar") and Teixeira's *Aventura admiravel* ("another [mark of a wound] over his right eyebrow").[34] And so her source was probably one of these two books or, more likely, the common tradition of which both works were a part.

As a result of Maria's statement about the identifying mark above Sebastian's eyebrow, Pedro Peixoto later showed her a portrait of Sebastian and asked her if she had seen the same person on the island. Predictably, she responded that it was the same person, although she noted that his cheeks were fuller and more masculine, his nose sharper, and his complexion ruddier than in the portrait he showed her.[35] The possibility that she had mentally aged the portrait she had seen in the Convent of St. Bridgette has already been noted, though the possibility that the modifications came about under a different influence cannot be dismissed. In the description of the Prisoner of Venice given by Dom João de Castro in the *Discurso da vida*, he noted that his face was neither as full nor as ruddy as it had been in his youth, *though only due to his imprisonment and his fasting*, and he also noted that Sebastian's nose was sharper than it had been when he was young.[36] This is not decisive, but the parallel descriptions are suggestive. Dom João's description did include many elements that Maria's did not, though, and this fact lends weight to the possibility that Castro's influence on Maria de Macedo was indirect rather than direct. While he might be the ultimate source of her knowledge of Sebastian, the fact that there are differences (but no true contradictories) between them suggests that that knowledge had passed through the hands (and mouths) of many intermediaries before reaching her.[37]

The evidence that conclusively demonstrates that Maria de Macedo's views of Sebastian had their ultimate source in Dom João de Castro must now be examined. It centers on the names of the companions who, according Castro's version of the Prisoner's story, accompanied him in his escape from the battlefield of Alcazarquivir. In her seventh deposition, Maria said that the companions of Sebastian she had met on the island were "the Duke of Aveiro, the Count of Redondo . . . Henrique Muniz, and Ruy de Tavora."[38] Compare this with the list found in Castro: "he [Sebastian], wounded, saved himself with the Duke of Aveiro, the Count of Redondo, the Count of Sortelha, Christovão de Tavora, and another knight whose name I forget, but I think I heard him called Tello or Meneses."[39] The Duke of Aveiro and the Count of Redondo appear in both lists; it is not too difficult to imagine that Christovão de Tavora in Castro was transformed into the Ruy de Tavora of Maria's list in the course of oral transmission; and the imperfectly remembered knight possibly named Meneses could easily have become Henrique Muniz by a similar process.

The truly decisive evidence has to do with why the Count of Sortelha appears in Castro's list and not in Maria's. Put simply, he was replaced in Maria's list by Dom João de Castro himself. If I may be forgiven for the rhetorical use of the ellipsis above, Maria's full statement was that "the Duke of Aveiro, the Count of Redondo, Dom João de Castro, Henrique Muniz, and Ruy de Tavora" had accompanied Sebastian after Alcazarquivir and ultimately had gone with him to the Hidden Isle. Of course, Dom João had not participated in the battle and so could not have accompanied Sebastian anywhere, but I believe he was included in the list because, by the period Maria was experiencing her visitations, Dom João de Castro's name was so closely associated with the tradition of the Prisoner of Venice that it was a natural mistake for Maria (or for one of her intermediary sources) to assume that he was part of Sebastian's entourage after the battle. This fact also demonstrates that his influence on the course of that tradition, and therefore *sebastianismo* as a whole, was, while profound, also probably indirect. Anyone actually reading the *Discurso da vida* could easily learn that Castro was not at Alcazarquivir and that he did not include himself among Sebastian's companions. The same cannot be said of those only hearing of the contents of Castro's works. As anyone familiar with the party game of "Telephone" knows, oral transmission often results in garbled details, even when the substance of the transmitted message remains intact. So it seems clear that Maria's Sebastianism was founded in large part on the legacy of Dom João de Castro, with some details falling out or being changed in the process of oral transmission over a period of five decades and with some elements being added during that time due to the influence of the material found in the forged papal bulls.

If this hypothesis is true, it may help explain another curious element of Maria's characterization of Sebastian. In the episode of the meeting at the Church of Our Lady of Tribulations, Maria claimed that Sebastian had met King Arthur and Don Jaume of Aragon there and that they had received divine commissions from Saint John, Elijah, and Enoch, respectively. Each of the kings was given both a sword and a piece of paper by their prophets, symbolizing the commission to conquer and to rule. The inquisitors were concerned by the claim that the prophets had been there, but our interest in the incident lies (for the moment) with the kings. The issue of why Arthur and Jaume, specifically, were chosen as Sebastian's companions will be addressed later, but first we must ask why Sebastian needed companions at all in his work of conquest and rule.

The answer goes back Dom João's view in the *Paraphrase* that Sebastian would be aided in his conquests by three other rulers, two kings and the Angelic Pope, a formulation peculiar to Castro in the history of Portuguese messianism.[40] In Maria's visions, Arthur and Jaume could fill the roles of the two kings, but what about the Angelic Pope? There are two likely answers to this question. It should be remembered that, both in the pamphlet and in the depositions, Maria stated that while on the island, Sebastian was accompanied by a Franciscan confessor, named, appropriately enough, Father Angelico, and by a Benedictine chronicler known as Father Angelo. Could Maria have imagined that Angelico would, one day, become the Angelic Pope when Sebastian began his conquests? Was the fact that he was described as a Franciscan due to some residual association in Maria's mind between the Spiritual Franciscans and the figure of the Angelic Pope they had invented in the thirteenth century? Perhaps.

There is another possibility that must be considered, however. According to Maria's own testimony, Sebastian would not be helped in the Reformation of the World by Father Angelico or by Father Angelo; instead, he would purify the world together with Saint John the Evangelist, who would leave the earthly paradise in order to accomplish his eschatological purpose. Therefore, it seems that Maria's Saint John would much more closely fulfill the role of the Angelic Pope as it had been described by Castro than would Sebastian's confessor, Angelico. Castro even speculated that the Angelic Pope might reappear after having been in the earthly paradise—another interesting correlation—though he favored the return of Elijah in such a role. He was not dogmatic on the issue of identity, however. This may, then, simply be another bit of evidence that Castro's influence on Maria was indirect rather than as the result of her reading one of his books personally.

If, indeed, Castro was the source, indirectly, of Maria's views on the three other rulers and that someone from the earthly paradise—whether Elijah or Saint John—would become the Angelic Pope, another possibility is raised because Dom João argued for the return of Elijah only in the "Aurora." While the structure of Sebastian plus the Angelic Pope plus two other kings appears in the *Paraphrase*, the identity of the Angelic Pope as someone returning from the earthly paradise never appears in either of his published works. If Maria was somehow influenced by Castro's formulations in the "Aurora," it would be the first documented evidence that his unpublished material also had an influence on the course of Sebastianism. Admittedly, such a conclusion is only speculative at this point given the lack of corroborating evidence, but if it can one day be corroborated, it could only enhance Castro's reputation as the apostle of *sebastianismo*, as well as being evidence of some kind of conduit for his thought between the Parisian exiles and the broader mass of *sebastianistas* in Portugal.

The possibility that Dom João de Castro was the ultimate, if indirect source, of Maria de Macedo's understanding of Sebastian is further strengthened by the fact that she knew the author of the "Tratado da quinta monarchia," Sebastião de Paiva, whose views on Sebastian were heavily dependent on Castro's printed works.[41] As revealed in Feliciano's section of the short version of the pamphlet, he sought out de Paiva, who he had heard was a "learned man," in order to alleviate his own doubts about the source of Maria's visions. The Trinitarian theologian told him not to worry, since it was quite possible that Maria's visions were a gift sent from God, and ultimately it was this reassurance from a respected religious figure that convinced Feliciano of the truth of his wife's claims.

Though no other details of the association between de Paiva and Maria and Feliciano are revealed in the pamphlet, it is surely not implausible to think that de Paiva had some degree of influence on Maria's newly emerging understanding of her experience. For example, although de Paiva occasionally makes negative comments about the Jews, an anti-Semitic program for Sebastian is hardly as central to his understanding of Sebastian as it had been for Castro; in Maria's eschatological version, it is virtually undetectable. Also, a number of details related to Sebastian's life after Alcazarquivir in Maria's visions are more likely to have come from a reading (or hearing) of de Paiva's version of the Prisoner of Venice's career than directly from Castro. This is all to say that it is unlikely that the relationship between de Paiva and Maria was one-way. She certainly recounted her experiences to him, but it is quite likely he also provided her with a more detailed *sebastianista* framework by which to understand what she saw, just as her aunt had done earlier with the legends of the enchanted Moors. This is especially probable given the fact that, according to the chronology revealed in the pamphlet, Maria met de Paiva some time shortly after the initial emergence of her *sebastianista* understanding of her experience in May 1650.

Whatever may be made of that possibility, the argument above demonstrates clearly that Maria de Macedo's Sebastianism fell squarely within the tradition of which Dom João de Castro was an important voice. I explore the nature and extent of Castro's influence in the development of Sebastianism in greater detail in another work,[42] and Maria de Macedo is an important example of his millenarian legacy. Castro was, however, only one of the sources Maria drew upon, even for her mature vision; in fact, the other major component of the mature vision—the Hidden Isle—became part of *sebastianista* orthodoxy independent of Castro's influence, for the simple reason that he never mentioned it in any of his works.

The transformation of the location of Maria's voyages from an enchanted palace of the Moors to the legendary Hidden Isle is one of the most important characteristics of her mature vision. Asked how the islanders sustained themselves and how they were governed, Maria replied that she did not know how they were governed, except that they all seemed to obey Sebastian.[43] In the pamphlet, she was more specific and stated that they lived "without anyone administering them" and indeed that no one even knew how to do so. Given the rest of her description of the island, why would they have needed anyone to govern them? It was a land of great abundance, where everything one could want was available without work. Cultivation was unnecessary, and people could simply carry what they needed from the fields directly to their houses, whether bread, meat, fruit, or other food. For wheat, all one would need to do was take it home from the field and grind it with a hand mill. Meat was provided by oxen, sheep, and chicken, none of which would resist the journey to the islanders' plates. The birds were so tame that they could be caught and prepared as food without any danger of their flying away.

The only profession practiced on the island was weaving, Maria stated, and one only had to shear the docile lambs for their wool, spin it, weave it, and then make clothes from the cloth. No additional steps were needed or wanted in this simple process, and Maria made sure to note that the islanders wore clothes according to the original color of the wool—black or white—without any vain and useless colors being added to God's original design. In fact, no one even knew how to dye cloth or make colors.

The plenty of the Hidden Isle was not limited to concerns of food and shelter. In contrast to Maria's original characterizations of the hard work and sickness in the mines digging up gold with the enchanted Moors, by the time the stable vision had evolved and was written down in the pamphlet, gold was so abundant on the Hidden Isle that one could simply pull it out of the fountains of the city by hand. Each person could take what he or she wanted, but even then the prosperity of the land was such that gold was not really necessary.

Maria de Macedo's experiences began with a dream of a great field full of flowers and trees, and this trope of lushness continued through all the versions of her experience. The Moorish palace contained a beautiful garden; the developed vision of the Hidden Isle was, according to the pamphlet, "very full of flowers and flying birds." This motif of vitality can be seen again, not only in the fountain of the Moorish garden—with all the deep associations attached to it—but especially in the fact that the main square of the island was the location of three great fountains. The evolution of one fountain into three is not only another possible trace of the Christianization of her understanding of her experience—in a reference to the Trinity—but also a further elaboration of the trope of abundance: one fountain is good, but three is a sign of superabundance, of divine provision even beyond the needs of the inhabitants of the island.

Of course, the main square of the city on the island was not only the location of the three fountains; it was also the location of three churches. In this, and in many other ways, the islanders were characterized as exemplary Catholics. In addition to obeying the precepts of the church just as they were obeyed in Portugal (which, according to the Ourique traditions, was taken as a model of faithful devotion),[44] the islanders practiced a piety that was, in some ways, superior even to that found in Portugal. To prepare themselves for Sunday Mass, for example, they would abstain from all work and pray continually from the Saturday evening before until late the Monday morning after,[45] a practice that impressed Maria and several of her hearers, though not Inquisitor de la Cerda. In Pedro Peixoto's testimony, extended fasting and praying were also done before and after a saint's day, though this might be another example of his conflation of separate details in Maria's account.[46] In another series of questions, she explained that Sebastian was not the only one who knelt on his bare knees while praying; the islanders did as well.[47] In any event, Maria and those hearers took these practices as indications of the loyalty and devotion of the islanders to the Roman Catholic faith.

There were several other signs of Catholic piety that reassured her as well. As Maria stated in her pamphlet, she felt no scruple about traveling to the island because she saw images of Mary, Christ Crucified, Saint Joseph, and the Baby Jesus on the island and in Sebastian's oratory and because the people of the island were always speaking about the things of God. Also, when asked if anyone on the island had ever asked her to perform any kind of devotion or other religious act, she responded that no one had, except to tell her to commend herself to God and to Our Lady of the Rosary.[48] And, after being pressed to explain how the island could truly be Catholic if it had no communication with the pope, she replied that she did not know what to say to that, although she did point out that the island had a bishop of its own and so presumably remained in the fold of the Catholic faithful.[49]

Of course, Maria was in the position to make these claims of Christian piety for the people of the island only because of the earlier transformation of her own understanding of it. By 1665, and even by the 1658 version of the pamphlet, the people of her world no longer wore Turkish clothes as the figures had at first; instead, they wore Portuguese clothes. They were no longer the enchanted descendants of the Moors driven out in the Reconquest; instead they were the descendants of the Christians who had fled the Muslim onslaught in the time of King Rodrigo.[50] This is a clear reference to the very old Iberian legend of the seven Portuguese bishops and their followers fleeing to the land of Cíbola to escape the Moors after King Rodrigo's fall. In fact, this association was so well established in the culture that Dona Isabel Soares de Britto said that, at least as well as she could remember, the island had seven bishops, misquoting Maria, who only claimed one.[51] The main point, though, is that Maria's reimagining of the enchanted Moors into the descendants of the legendary inhabitants of Cíbola also allowed her to further reinscribe her voyages into a more acceptable, Christianized matrix, a process that had begun, it should always be remembered, well before she ever came into contact with the Inquisition.

Returning to the Hidden Isle itself, what was life like in this fruitful and faithful land? "They live in common, without having dissensions among them over anything," was Maria's answer.[52] Even in the earlier, "enchanted Moor" phase of her vision, the work in the mines was shared equally among her and all the exotically dressed, shape-shifting Moors.[53] The Hidden Isle was thus an idyllic, even utopian, land of prosperity and peace, the reasons and inclination for social conflict being wholly absent. And this land of abundance and tranquility allowed its inhabitants to dedicate themselves to the spiritual disciplines of prayer, fasting, and communion with God. It was Maria's vision of an ideal life, as we will see in greater detail shortly.

One question that needs to be addressed before such an examination is the issue of the source of Maria's characterizations of her perfect land. It is very unlikely that the erudite and sophisticated utopias that were a literary fashion during the sixteenth and seventeenth centuries, such as More's original *Utopia*, Bacon's *New Atlantis*, or Campanella's *City of the Sun*, played any role in Maria's conceptions.[54] Beyond the critical question of how she could have been exposed to those works, even indirectly, the truth of the matter is that her descriptions of the Hidden Isle differ so substantially in tone and character from those works that is almost certain that her beliefs were not derived from any of those writings.

A more likely source would be the legends of the land of Cockaigne and the cognate realms of Luilekkerland, Schlaraffenland, and the sensuous Islamic paradises whose descriptions were guilty pleasures for many medieval Europeans. These were among the longest lived and most widespread folklore traditions in western Europe during the medieval and early modern periods.[55] Remarkably stable in its core elements but incredibly diverse in its details, the tradition surrounding Cockaigne told of a land where no one ever had to work and where food and drink were free for all. Fasts came only once every hundred years, and the major holidays of the religious calendar were all quadrupled in frequency. Not only was work unnecessary, but it was positively forbidden, and the unending supply of food did not even require effort: candies and pastries would rain from the sky, sausages would grow on trees, birds would fly into people's mouths to be eaten, cows and dogs would defecate pies and pancakes, pigs would wander around with knives in their back, ready and eager for their flesh to be sliced away and consumed. Nature, in the form of the weather and the fauna, was kind to visitors in Cockaigne, and even the architecture of the land's buildings was edible: fences were made of pastries or sausages, houses were built of waffles, roofs were tiled with tarts.

Gluttony and sloth were not the only vices that could be practiced with impunity in Cockaigne; so, too, could their close ally, luxury, in some versions of the Cockaigne legend. Sexual license of all sorts, including homosexuality and incest in some of the more libertine traditions, was encouraged, and the presence of a rejuvenating fountain ensured a state of perpetual youth that guaranteed permanent erections for men and renewable virginity for women. As the trope of an unending variety of food had a psychological basis as compensatory fantasies for food shortages, real or feared,[56] so the element of unrestrained sexual activity was an imagined abrogation of the strict sexual morality enjoined by the church. Cockaigne was a largely anticlerical place, or perhaps antiecclesiastical would be a better term, since clerics often appeared in the accounts of Cockaigne, though as fellow participants in, rather than critics of, the delights of that land.

In his book *Cocanha: A história de um pais imaginário*, Hilario Franco Jr. lists four defining characteristics of Cockaigne: it was a land of abundance, a land of sloth, a land of youth, and a land of freedom.[57] Returning to the question of Maria de Macedo's sources, how does the Hidden Isle of her imagination compare with the land of Cockaigne as described above? Without a doubt, the Hidden Isle was a land of abundance, and some of the same elements appear in both constructions. However, it is also clear that the Hidden Isle is less generous than Cockaigne in this regard. In Cockaigne, effort is wholly unnecessary, since birds would fly into peoples' mouths already cooked; on the Hidden Isle, while cultivation and planting are unnecessary, the food must still be prepared. If one was hungry in Cockaigne, one simply needed to pull a sausage from a tree or eat one of the waffle roof tiles; on the Hidden Isle, the architecture was not so accommodating.

Sebastian's land was also less generous in terms of the variety of food available. In the pamphlet, Maria had the islanders eating only "bread, meat, a little wine, pork and fruit," a diet quite consistent what she would have been exposed to as a skilled artisan's daughter and the wife of a royal bureaucrat. Absent was the great variety of delicacies, sweets, and spiced foods that make such a prominent appearance in the descriptions of Cockaigne. The sedateness of Maria's imagined world is further emphasized by the appearance of bread among the foods eaten on the Hidden Isle; bread, the monotonous staple of western European diets, was rarely included in the Cockaigne texts.[58] After all, who would choose bread when you could simply slice off a piece of roast pork instead?

More than either the variety or the availability of food, though, it was a difference in attitude toward food that distinguished the Hidden Isle from Cockaigne. In Cockaigne, the abundance of food was simply the necessary condition for gluttony, and the two ideals—limitless food and unrestrained consumption—were inextricably linked in the stories about that wondrous realm.[59] Gluttony makes no such appearance in the Hidden Isle; instead, it is clear that Maria admired the people of the island for their pious fasting, in fact, for their very vigorous fasting. Fasting as an ideal was antithetical to the very conception of Cockaigne. At most, fasting occurred there once every hundred years, and in only some versions of the legend. This fundamental difference in *ideals* will only be noted here, but an extended discussion of the reasons for this difference will be undertaken at the end of this chapter.

How does the Hidden Isle measure up as a land of sloth? As in Cockaigne, work was unnecessary, except for some minor food preparation and some weaving, but a difference remains between their ideas of what all the resulting free time should have been used for. In Cockaigne, the fact that work was unnecessary needed no justification: the opportunity to do nothing was its own reward. The only activities that seem to have filled up time in Cockaigne were eating, drinking, and having sex with any and all of one's companions. The situation on the Hidden Isle was different; though Maria mentioned that the inhabitants sang, played music, and danced—all good, clean fun, or at least potentially so—in their free time, she actually portrayed them as spending a good deal of time fasting and praying. Though they were not described in the exemplary terms by which Sebastian was depicted—fasting and praying three times a week—the islanders at least fasted on the saints' days, and their rigorous preparations for Sunday Mass should not be forgotten. So, while the characterizations of both Cockaigne and the Hidden Isle as lands where work was unnecessary shared many of the same elements, the values that informed these descriptions—laziness for its own sake or free time for devotion—were radically different.

The Hidden Isle as a land of youth fares even less well, if for no other reason than the fact that the issue of youthfulness was never mentioned at all in Maria's narrative. Traces of the importance of youthfulness may be found in the inclusion of the fountain motif or in the fact that all the inhabitants of the island were "the most beautiful nature could produce," but even these elements received very little emphasis. This seems especially clear given the fact that Maria consistently calls Sebastian a "velho," an old man, although this may be more of an attempt to invest him with the dignity and authority of age than a rejection of youth. Youthfulness may sneak in through the back door if the description of Sebastian given by Pedro Peixoto—"he seemed to be much younger than he was, because his beard and hair were more blond than white"[60]—is actually a reflection of something Maria had told him, though with Peixoto one can never be sure regarding the accuracy of details. But even if these elements truly are traces of a vestigial motif of youthfulness, they are no more than traces, whereas in Cockaigne, youth was central to the ideals being fantasized about.

If there are no more than vestiges of the ideal of youthfulness in the Hidden Isle, Cockaigne's emphasis on freedom is entirely absent. The prospect of casual fornication was joyously proclaimed in many, though not all, of the versions of the Cockaigne legend that were circulating in medieval and early modern Europe; the issue of sex is not even hinted at in Maria's narrative. The only possible exceptions to this rule—the mention of the Moor's family and of Sebastian's family—only serve to emphasize the main point: sex, if present at all, is limited to the venue of a monogamous marriage. Nothing could be further from the ideals embodied in the land of Cockaigne.

Returning, then, to the issue of the sources of Maria's characterization of her idealized land, were the Cockaigne legends the ultimate source of her portrait of the Hidden Isle? Several tropes, such as the supply of food without work, the docile animals, and the presence of archetypal fountains, are found in both depictions and so might be evidence of a genetic linkage, though seemingly only of the traces. If the Cockaigne myth was the original model of the Hidden Isle, its fundamental character was highly modified in the process of reception and further articulation by Maria, as even the brief comparison of the two lands given above demonstrates.

What would have driven this process of modification? The best way to find the answer to that question is to look at the results of that process. Taking a generic land of wonders in the Cockaigne mode as the starting point and then looking at the end result of the Hidden Isle as described by Maria, it is clear that the original utopian and fantastic characterization underwent a process of transformation to make it meet Catholic moral and devotional norms. Illicit sex was eliminated; sloth and debauchery were replaced by rigorous prayer and fasting; edible architecture, by three great churches surrounding the city's central square. Activity in Cockaigne had no purpose beyond self-indulgence; the Hidden Isle was not only the repository of Sebastian until his revelation, but also the key mustering grounds for his coming war of conquest, as Maria's description of his vast armada and his army of 200,000 troops indicates. Thus, the hedonistic paradise of Cockaigne was transformed not only into a Catholic utopia but into an eschatological one as well.[61]

Assuming that the legends of a wondrous land such as Cockaigne were the ultimate source of Maria's characterization of the Hidden Isle, the question remains as to when the transformation from a land of sensate wonders to a land of rest and prayer took place. One possibility is that it occurred during Maria's lifetime because the process of Catholicization was an individual one. Maria originally fit her vision into the preexisting matrix of the enchanted Moor traditions, only to recast her experiences in a Christian/*sebastianista* mode as she matured. It is therefore possible that a parallel process of Christianization in regard to her understanding of an ideal land took place at roughly the same time and as a result of the same cultural imperatives. The fact that Restoration Portugal was precisely a time in which there was a great deal of cultural pressure from above to recast popular religious beliefs to conform to the ideals of the Council of Trent lends credence to this possibility.

It is also possible that Maria received the elements of the Hidden Isle in an already Catholicized form and simply used them as the building blocks of her mature understanding of her experience, as we have already seen her do before with the legends of the enchanted Moors. As best as can be reconstructed, myths of the Hidden Isle were spreading in Portugal precisely around the period she developed that mature understanding—that is, around 1650. More will be said later about why the element of the Hidden Isle began to be attached to the older *sebastianista* tradition in that period, but the fact that the major transformation of her vision came about at that time cannot be without significance. Of course, the fact that the matrix by which she understood her vision changed at that time does not tell us when the tradition that she received was transformed and Christianized in the broader culture.

Clearly, the messianic elements of the myth came about as a result of cross-fertilization with the *sebastianista* tradition of the early seventeenth century, but the recasting of Cockaigne into a Catholic paradise may have taken place much, much earlier. One possibility is that the Hidden Isle was not based directly on Cockaigne but on the Joachimite vision of the Third Age, the more detailed versions of which were based on the same classical stories of wondrous lands such as the Isles of the Blessed and the legends of the Golden Age that were models for Cockaigne itself. Whereas Cockaigne diverged from the aesthetic utopias of the classical writers (and their later Renaissance imitators) by becoming a gustatory, fornicating paradise of the poor, the ideal world of the Third Age was a time when Adam's curse would be lifted, making work unnecessary and freeing people to engage in continual praise and contemplation of God. In many ways, the core elements of Maria's vision of the Hidden Isle fit better in a Joachimite context than as an example of a popular, folkloric tradition being transformed (and tamed) as result of Counter-Reformation ideals. If it is true that the Hidden Isle was more Joachimite than Tridentine, it would mean that the process of Christianizing the land of wonders legends (at least far as Maria's sources are concerned) would have taken place sometime in the thirteenth or fourteenth century rather than the sixteenth or seventeenth. Given the key role of Joachimism in the development of Portuguese millenarianism, this possibility cannot be discounted. Or it could be the case that both sources played a role, with details from the Cockaigne tradition being added to and fleshing out the spiritualized vision of the Third Age during the course of that tradition's long evolution. But whenever the process occurred and under whatever auspices, it seems clear that, at some point, the more fantastic elements of the land of wonders tradition, which dates from ancient times, had been modified or eliminated outright to bring Maria's narrative into closer agreement with Catholic norms.

Before addressing the broader question of the values that provided the foundation for Maria's vision, we must deal with one final issue related to the sources of her views about the Hidden Isle. One tradition that may have served as such a source would be the biblical stories of the Garden of Eden, since all Western views of paradisiacal lands were influenced by it to some extent. And while it may indeed have served as the impetus for the idea of a utopian land for Maria, as it clearly did for countless others, the scriptural description lacked many of the details that characterized her account. The interesting aspect of this issue is that the question of the Hidden Isle's connection to the earthly paradise raised concerns among Maria's contemporaries, both among the inquisitors and among some of her hearers. The issue was first raised by Father Luis de Madre de Deos after Maria had told him her story. The last of the three questions he asked her in response dealt specifically with the question of whether Saint John, Enoch, and Elijah were located in the earthly paradise and whether the earthly paradise was synonymous with the Hidden Isle.[62]

What is the significance of the question, though? First, it is prima facie evidence of the long millenarian tradition that Enoch and Elijah were waiting in the earthly paradise until the end of time, and it is also evidence that Maria's description of the Hidden Isle naturally caused people to associate her claims with the idea of the earthly paradise.[63] Second, and more important, though, is her answer to the question because she stated that it was doubtful that the Hidden Isle was the earthly paradise. This does not mean that the stories (biblical and otherwise) she had heard about the earthly paradise had no influence on her description of the Hidden Isle; rather, it is evidence of the eclectic nature of her sources. The reason she gave for her doubts on this subject stemmed from the fact that she had asked "many sailors and others about the earthly Paradise, [and] they say it is certain that it is confined to the land and not in the sea."

Let us consider for a moment the implications of Maria's statement. The reason she did not think the Hidden Isle was the earthly paradise was that she had heard that the earthly paradise was located on the land and was therefore not an island. She was therefore *aware* of the traditions surrounding the earthly paradise, whether from biblical sources or as part of the extrabiblical elaborated tradition. However, since her own ideal land did not conform to that expectation regarding location, she concluded that the Hidden Isle was probably not the same as the earthly paradise. Although she does not mention it explicitly, it is also quite possible that her understanding that the Hidden Isle was located somewhere near the island of Madeira in the Azores, west from Portugal—following in the long line of Western wonder islands from Hy Bresil to Avalon to Saint Brendan's islands—also caused her to conclude that it was not the earthly paradise, located by the Bible and by venerable tradition as somewhere "in the east."[64] What this tiny detail shows is that Maria had a variety of legendary matrices by which to understand her experience and that, for whatever reasons, she made choices (consciously or unconsciously) among them.

Maria's story of her journey with Sebastian to the Church of Nossa Senhora da Pena represents the most developed form of her vision, and it was also one of the episodes of her account that caused the greatest concern for the inquisitors. Recounting her story, she said that on April 1, 1651, she traveled with Sebastian to the church, where they met the prophets Elijah, Enoch, and Saint John the Evangelist, as well as King Arthur of England and King Jaume (I) of Aragon. While there, the prophets delivered a divine commission to the monarchs, giving each a sword and a piece of paper before bestowing a final blessing on them. According to the description given by Maria, this meeting had been arranged beforehand,[65] and it is clear from the series of letters supposedly exchanged by the monarchs' messengers that the point of the meeting was to ratify an alliance between the three kings, almost certainly as a prelude to their campaign of world conquest, although this point was never made explicitly.

First, it is necessary to examine the reasons that this particular group of legendary figures was chosen to attend this momentous meeting and then to analyze the meaning of the meeting as a whole. Enoch and Elijah, as the two people in the Bible who were said to have been "taken up" without dying (Gen. 5:24 and 2 Kings 2:11, respectively), had key roles in almost all the eschatological schemes conceived in the Christian West. They were almost universally held to be the two witnesses who would reappear to preach against the Antichrist at the end of time (Apoc. 11:3–12), and it was also very widely accepted that they had been deposited by God in the earthly paradise to await their roles at the consummation of the ages.[66] The belief was particularly strong among those influenced by Joachim of Fiore and his disciples,[67] and so, given the influence of Joachimism in Portugal, it should come as no surprise that these two figures appear in the role of prophetic legitimizers in Maria's vision.

The inclusion of Saint John the Evangelist among the participants in the meeting was due to similar considerations. From the earliest days of Christianity, there have been those who have believed that Saint John never died, largely on the basis of a passage found in the Gospel of John in which Jesus told Peter that if he (Jesus) wished John to remain alive until his return, that would be his business and not Peter's (John 21:22). Similarly, Saint John's role as the visionary of the Apocalypse clearly associated him with the coming millennium in the minds of many. While the belief that Saint John the Evangelist lived beyond the first century has never been part of the official doctrine of the Roman Church, even one of the inquisitorial *qualificadores* in Maria's case conceded that many eminent church fathers had held that belief.[68] Most millenarians, in Portugal and elsewhere, were considerably less skeptical on the point, and Saint John was widely seen, if not quite so widely as Enoch and Elijah, as a figure of eschatological destiny. In Joachimite tradition, his role in the end times was even more secure, and many saw him as the Apostle of the Spirit, as opposed to Peter as the Apostle of the Father and Paul as the Apostle of the Son.[69] This view of Saint John as an initiator of the millenarian Age of the Spirit accords well with Maria's understanding that he would aid Sebastian in the Judgment of Reformation, and it may be the decisive clue in determining the origin of her views about Saint John. With such an illustrious prophetic pedigree, in many ways, it would have been more surprising had Saint John not appeared in Maria's vision.

The legends of the Arthurian cycle were well known in early modern Portugal,[70] though, unfortunately, there are no systematic studies of the diffusion of the stories about Arthur at the popular level in Portugal during that period, so it would be virtually impossible to try to track down a specific source for Maria's knowledge about him. In all likelihood, she picked it up as a part of an oral tradition about the English hero-king. In fact, her reception of the Arthurian detail may have been no more than a hearing of his name and an understanding of his legendary role at the most basic of levels, since little beyond Arthur's name and an understanding that he was a great Christian warrior is evident in his appearance in Maria's vision. This is not to say, however, that the rather circumscribed picture of Arthur we find in Maria's narrative was the only way in which the Arthurian legend influenced her account. Arthur was taken as a model for Sebastian, even during Sebastian's lifetime, and so certainly King Arthur played an important role in Maria's vision both as the archetypal Christian warrior-king and as a legitimizing symbol of Sebastian's greatness and destiny. It is an open question, though, as to whether Maria herself would have grasped all these connections at a conscious level.

King Arthur's companion in Maria's vision, the great conqueror of the Moors, Jaume I of Aragon, clearly played a similar role. Unfortunately, though, there is no well-defined Iberian tradition connecting Jaume to broader messianic expectations. Still, it is surely significant that he was described by Maria as "Jaume of Aragon"—that is, that he was not a Castilian. It is also intriguing to speculate that the inclusion of this Aragonese/Catalan king may have been inspired by the example of the Catalans, who in 1651—the year during which this episode supposedly took place—were, like the Portuguese, fighting against the forces of Castile. It is doubtful (to me) that Maria consciously included Jaume in her vision for geopolitical reasons; nevertheless, his inclusion does give another peek into the possible influences on her thinking.

The role played by all these legendary prophets and kings can be summed up in one word: legitimization. If a leader was endorsed and commissioned by the three most eminent prophets in history, who could dispute his identity as the Hidden One or deny that he and his upcoming mission of conquest were most favored by the Almighty? Similarly, what could be greater proof of the greatness of Sebastian's role in the divine plan than that he was to be the leader of an alliance that included two of the greatest Christian heroes in history, King Arthur and Don Jaume? The presence of these five legendary figures thus served to legitimize Sebastian both in terms of his character as a pious ruler and in terms of his mission as a conqueror under the sign of the Cross. If legitimization was the rhetorical role the incident at Our Lady of Tribulations played within Maria's larger narrative, that episode also provides more evidence that she chose elements from a wide variety of folkloric, legendary, and millenarian traditions in order to construct her own messianic world.

We have looked at the details and the possible sources of major elements of Maria de Macedo's envisioned world, but what can we now conclude about the cultural values that underlay those elements? Piety—as revealed by both Sebastian and the islanders—was central to Maria de Macedo's value system. At a fundamental level, her understanding of piety was one of Catholic orthopraxy, and on multiple occasions she said that she felt reassured that nothing about Sebastian or the islanders was contrary to the Catholic faith because she saw them praying and fasting, speaking about the things of God, or venerating the saints. The more fantastic elements of the Cockaigne-type legends upon which her vision of the Hidden Isle may have been based were reduced to a more sober and restrained level; the licentious elements were eliminated entirely.

The folkloric elements of Maria's vision, whether based on the enchanted Moor traditions or legends of Cockaigne, were systematically Christianized in the mature version of her narrative, and the prominence of the islanders' orthopraxy is evidence in favor of that conclusion. However, it is evidence, I believe, of another conclusion as well; it is also proof of the interiorization of those religious values by Maria de Macedo herself. This personal connection can be seen in the bit of religious autobiography she gave to Inquisitor de la Cerda in response to his question as to whether she performed any special spiritual exercises or devotions to commend herself to God. Her answer was that she followed no special exercises; instead, she "commended herself to God with the prayers of the Catholic Church."[71] She expanded on this in her genealogical deposition when she claimed she "went to Church, heard Mass and the sermons, confessed, took communion, and did the other *works* of a Christian."[72] In the *contradittas* submitted on her behalf, her counsel described her as "very inclined toward praying the Rosary,"[73] a depiction echoed in the testimony of her childhood neighbor, Pedro Nunes, as "praying with her beads in her hand and going to church on Sundays and saints' days." His son, António Perreira, had similar sentiments: he said Maria "prayed and went to Mass."[74] So the portrait provided by Maria of herself as a pious Catholic woman who "did all the works of a Christian" is borne out by the testimony of others.

But if this is evidence of the interiorization of the values inculcated in the Catholic laity of Tridentine Portugal, the evidence also points out that the kind of religiosity that most appealed to Maria was interior in nature, as her repeated identification of piety with prayer and fasting demonstrates. The intensely inward nature of Maria's devotion is to be contrasted with religious practice of the French *dévotes* described by Louis Châtellier in *The Europe of the Devout.* To be sure, much of the *dévotes*' spirituality was interior as well, and their Jesuit mentors heavily emphasized both prayer and communion, but there was also a widespread interest in performing works of charity.[75] Maria de Macedo reveals nothing of that kind of outward orientation in her religious practice.

This is entirely consistent with the most common term used by the witnesses in Maria's case to describe her, which is also the word she used to describe herself—*recolhida*—which can be translated as retired, withdrawn, contemplative, even resigned. And when de la Cerda asked if she had gone with the people of the island in order to obtain a spiritual or temporal benefit, she said that she had received no benefit except that the islanders had told her to have patience and to commend herself to God during times of trouble, an attitude that she described as the highest good of all.[76] The picture of her as a woman of devout resignation and prayerful faith in God becomes clearer still.

This interior devotion did take on a particular form, however, and that form was prayer, specifically prayer to the Virgin Mary. The fact that Maria was often seen with her rosary beads in her hand and that she was inclined toward praying the rosary has already been noted above, but there is additional evidence to prove this point. When asked if the natives had encouraged her to practice any new devotion, she answered that they had told her simply to commend herself to God and the Virgin by means of prayer. Surely these are the clues we need to understand why she chose a "Dona Maria Maior" (Mary the Greater) as her patroness ("ama") on the island. Although it caused Inquisitor de la Cerda concern that Maria had made a pact with the devil, it seems clear enough that the figure of Dona Maria Maior was an avatar, in Maria's mind, of the Virgin, for what Mary could be greater than she? And, was not the principal church of the island named "Maria Maior" in honor of the Virgin? It thus becomes clear that the veneration of Mary was a very important component of her spirituality.

Although Maria never listed fasting among her own spiritual exercises, given its importance within her narrative, it is almost inconceivable (to me) that she did not practice fasting to some extent. The fact that she may have engaged in rigorous fasting may also explain, in part, the intensity of her visions, the connection between self-mortification and visionary/hallucinatory states being well established by the examples of countless mystics.[77] What portrait can we form from these elements—resignation, prayer, devotion to Mary, and fasting? As Susan E. Dinan argues in her essay "Spheres of Female Religious Expression in Early Modern France," the Council of Trent's insistence on cloistering communities of female religious limited the scope of women's religious expression (especially for poor women) to one of two basic categories: a *dévoté* life within marriage, or the life of a nun in a cloistered convent. Independent, uncloistered *beatas* were to be suppressed.[78] While Dinan's essay comments only on the situation in France, her conclusions are probably even more characteristic of Portugal, given that the Portuguese ecclesiastical establishment and various royal dynasties were more enthusiastic about implementing the decrees of Trent than were the French, who accepted them only in part. To be sure, the situation was less stark in practice, as individual bishops and other ecclesiastical authorities decided how to enforce those decrees.[79] But the fact that there were exceptions does not change the fact that there was also a general rule.

What does this have to do with Maria de Macedo? It is my contention that the character of her religious devotion demonstrates a strong affinity for a cloistered, contemplative life, a life she could not lead because she was married and had children. In many ways, she seems to have had a particular affinity for the rigorous devotions of the stricter female religious orders. And the combination of prayer, fasting, and vision immediately recalls the example of Saint Teresa of Avila, the paradigmatic Counter-Reformation female saint. In reality, this similarity may be more than casual. When asked whether any of the islanders asked her to fulfill a vow or perform any religious act on their behalf, she answered that the only time she had been asked to do anything like that was when one of the women on the island asked to hear Mass in the House of the Discalced Carmelites, the religious order formed (or rather, reformed) by Saint Teresa in the sixteenth century.[80] Since the Discalced Carmelites were widely known for their disciplines of prayer, fasting, and general rigor, is it too much to conclude that Maria's experience of visions pointed her (consciously or unconsciously) in the same direction of intense interior spirituality that had been followed by Saint Teresa?[81]

We might ask, did the visions encourage the vocation, or did the vocation prompt the visions? This is a very difficult question to answer, although it was probably a dialectic process with each reinforcing the other, her sense of vocation becoming stronger and stronger as her vision became more and more Christianized, and the more Christian the vision, the stronger her vocation. Her stepmother vouched that Maria had experienced the visitations from the age of nine or ten, and her childhood neighbors described her as "recolhida" even while in her parents' house. In regard to the issue of timing, it is notable that the major transformation of her vision into a fully Christian and fully millenarian vision came about within the first year of her marriage—that is, at a time when the chances of her following a solitary vocation would have been much diminished—though this may be nothing more than coincidence. Given Feliciano's initial reaction to her claims, however, she hardly could have been encouraged to think she could follow the path of a visionary within marriage. And, on a more macro scale, it is understandable why a young girl growing up in the period in which she did would turn to a more interior form of religion. It was a time of revolution and war, a time in which the Vatican did not recognize the new Braganza regime and the kingdom of Portugal was under papal interdict. As a result, ecclesiastical offices could not be filled as they fell vacant, and the church in Portugal found it more and more difficult to maintain its institutional integrity and its mission of pastoral care. With the institutional avenues to God becoming more problematic, it is not surprising that some turned to a more personalized and interior expression of their religious devotion. Whatever the issues of timing, though, it is clear that Maria de Macedo both understood and experienced religion in a profoundly interior way, outwardly manifested by prayer and fasting, but interior nonetheless. This view of piety as both correct practice and internal devotion was the most important cultural and individual value that informed Maria de Macedo's conception of religion, an understanding that she projected onto her imagined ideal world and leader.

Another value evidenced by Maria's narrative is that of nationalism, though because the nature and extent of early modern nationalism are still hotly debated by historians, perhaps the term "patriotism," in the sense of having a love for one's homeland, would be better. Whatever the theoretical considerations involved, it is clear that Maria de Macedo identified herself as fundamentally Portuguese, as opposed to any other ethnic identification, just as Bandarra, Castro, and many other millenarians had. This identification carried over to Sebastian, of course, but also to the chosen and blessed people of the Hidden Isle, whom both she and her husband described as speaking Portuguese, albeit somewhat crudely. In the mature version of her story, they no longer are dressed as Turks but, rather, like the Portuguese.

Sebastian's identity as Portuguese was not merely one of passive ascription, however. He apparently continued to take an active interest in the goings-on of the kingdom he had once ruled, even going so far as to question Maria about what was happening in Portugal, at least according to the testimony of Pedro Peixoto.[82] Also, Manoel da Costa reported that Maria told him that Sebastian secretly (and perhaps even invisibly) visited Lisbon and that he had watched the Jesuit father as he had gone about his business in São Roque.[83] But Sebastian's active interest is most clearly seen in Maria's claim that, somehow, Sebastian helped the Portuguese troops against the Spanish invaders during the Battle of Linhas de Elvas, which took place on January 14, 1659.[84] The battle was the first important military victory for the Portuguese in the War of the Restoration, and it is significant that Maria attributed that victory, in part at least, to Sebastian's intervention, casting him almost in the role of the patron saint of Portuguese independence. Whatever the details, the patriotic foundations of the claim should be clear for all to see.

The value of primitivism was also a key component of Maria de Macedo's worldview. Though subtle, its influence is strong throughout her narrative. One might miss it upon the first reading, but the value espoused in Maria's claim that the clothes of the islanders were made of uncolored cloth, according to the natural color of the wool, is that of primitivism.[85] The message is that one should not seek to improve on what God has provided, especially by means as vain and artificial as dye. None of the islanders even knew how to color cloth; what could be a greater statement of their commitment to primitive purity? Similarly, the statement that there was no government on the Hidden Isle (besides Sebastian's benevolent word) and that there was no need for one was a look back to a mythic age of freedom, when fathers ruled their own families and no other hierarchies were needed. Maria's claim that gold nuggets could simply be plucked from the fountains, and that no one really needed them in any event, also sprang from a desire for a more primitive age, an age in which money was not necessary. In this, she had the same attitude that drove many of Bandarra's prophetic criticisms a century earlier, a view of prosperity defined by the simple possession of food and clothing, coupled with a deep suspicion of money and the grasping ways it inspired. Even the seemingly insignificant detail that all families could grind their grain at home with a hand mill has a primitivist resonance, since it would eliminate the opportunity for robbery by millers, who were stock villains of much early modern thought.

The fact that primitivism was an important value underlying Maria's millenarian vision should come as no surprise. Certainly the Protestant reformers of the sixteenth century saw themselves as trying to bring the church back to an earlier, less corrupt age, but this could equally be said of many Catholic reformers as well. Indeed, the reforming impulse that drove the Council of Trent was fired, in large part, by a desire to return the church to a more primitive, apostolic stance, if not in terms of doctrine—which was viewed as fixed by both papal authority and tradition—then certainly in terms of practice. And while some apocalyptic radicals in Europe sought to create something new on the earth, many millenarians saw in the coming age a return to a more pristine age of the church and of the world. The value of primitivism was thus widely held among European and Portuguese millenarians of all kinds.[86]

Primitivism is closely related, both in the narrative of Maria de Macedo and in the broader messianic movement, to another key value—utopianism—for implicit in a desire for a more primitive time is a critique of the complexities and corruptions of the present age. Now to say that utopianism was a key value of Maria's *millenarian* vision may seem banal, but the issue needs to be addressed simply because the type of utopianism displayed in her visions needs to be examined. From her faith that Sebastian would one day conquer the forces of Islam and convert the world, we can see that her utopia was a Christian utopia, and the future age of peace would simply be the ultimate extension of the Christian triumphalism that had begun with Constantine.

There was also an undercurrent of something less conventional in Maria's utopian vision, however. Not only would Sebastian conquer the world, but he would also "put the world right," he would bring "new" laws by which to govern the world, there would be "revolutions in the city" when he reappeared in Lisbon. A popular egalitarianism also flowed deep beneath the surface of her vision; in the model land of the Hidden Isle, did not all people work equally, when they had to work at all? And who could forget the king's *just* division of the spoils of the mines? And did the islanders not "live in common," just as the early Christians had, without private property to divide and cause dissensions among them? Ideals that had deep popular resonance, they were also the claims that made the inquisitors nervous.

But for all these elements, the more radical tendencies of Maria's vision remained muted, and one does not get the impression that there was a call to action lurking beneath the fertile fields of the Hidden Isle. Instead, it seems that it was more of a call to patience, to wait until the supernaturally chosen Redeemer was revealed. The vision never challenged anyone to take measures to accelerate the appearance of Sebastian's millennial kingdom; as far as the timing of his return and conquest was concerned, that was "all in the hand of God" and thus beyond human control. These facts underline the essentially conservative nature of the world created or imagined by Maria de Macedo.

Indeed, it seems that the appearance of the Hidden Isle as part of the legends about Sebastian in the late 1640s is indicative of the growing political conservatism and quietism of the *sebastianistas* as a whole. Both Castro, who truly believed that Sebastian was alive and would one day return to save Portugal, and the Braganza apologists of the late Hapsburg period demonstrated a degree of political realism in that they sought a savior in a person who was alive, or at least conceivably could be. This is not true of the *sebastianistas* of the Restoration Period, however. By that time, the real Sebastian would have been between eighty and one hundred years old, and his followers' continued faith in him can be interpreted only as a retreat into political fantasy. The Hidden Isle solved the issue of aging; as the century wore on, the descriptions of it became increasingly elaborate, more and more in a land-of-Cockaigne mode. In Maria's case, it is clear that the Hidden Isle was a land of fantasy where all the aspects of life that worried her—food, money, social peace—would be supernaturally resolved and where she could have time to fast and pray without distraction. Once being led back to paradise by a providential leader became the goal, there was little incentive to work for change on earth.

In one sense, the *sebastianistas* were right; only supernatural intervention could have brought about the radical reform of society or the rise of Portugal to preeminence among the nations that they hoped for, but the continued clinging to these fantasies bred in the true believers a habit of political passivity. By the end of the seventeenth century, the elites of Portugal had largely abandoned messianism of all varieties, though the popular classes continued to believe in Sebastian. Among them, *sebastianismo* was both everywhere triumphant and everywhere irrelevant in political terms. Waiting patiently for Sebastian to return, they could no longer bestir themselves to real action, as they had in Évora in 1637 or in Lisbon in 1640. There is no evidence as to when Maria de Macedo finally died, but it is very likely that when she did, she was still waiting quietly for her visions to be fulfilled.

‹ 7 ›

UTOPIA'S JUDGES

Understanding Inquisitorial Subculture

In the previous chapter, I appraised the varied and sometimes disparate elements of Maria de Macedo's vision as artifacts, discovering the origins and assessing the value of those elements. The result was a glimpse into the world of seventeenth-century popular culture in Portugal, as Maria selected, worked, and reworked elements of different traditions into a millenarian construction of her own making. This mental world is a window on the cultural values that informed it. Admittedly, it gives us insight only into a very specific case, though the virtue of such an approach is found in its concreteness, a concreteness that helps us, in turn, understand some of the ways by which Maria de Macedo understood herself.

Maria's self-identification is only half of the story, however; we can discuss her today only because she appeared as a defendant before the Holy Office and so was a subject of identification by the inquisitors as well. It is now to this half of the story, the half in which Maria de Macedo is evaluated and classified by the officials of the Inquisition, according to their own standards, that we now turn. And by understanding how the inquisitors understood Maria de Macedo and her claims, we will also gain a deeper insight into how they understood themselves and into the values that guided them.

Before Maria de Macedo ever appeared before the Inquisition or uttered one word of testimony, the *promotor* of the Tribunal of Lisbon had already evaluated the testimony of the initial witnesses in her case and had come to a conclusion that would set the parameters of how the case would be decided. After reviewing the more unusual parts of Maria's narrative (as recounted by those witnesses), he concluded that "because the aforementioned things cannot occur, it is easier to believe that it must be a fraud and invention of the accused, although it should be kept in mind that it could have come about by the deception of the Devil. Therefore, an investigation must be conducted in order to resolve this matter."[1] The *promotor*'s decision echoed the tripartite schema found in the testimony of many of the witnesses in the case: they could not decide whether Maria's story was true, fraudulent, or a result of an illusion by the devil.[2] In the *promotor*'s case, though, the possibility that her story was true had already been excluded, since he deemed what she said impossible.

In his report, the *promotor* also excluded the possibility of madness by neglecting to mention it at all, though his reasons for doing so remain unclear. All the judges in Maria de Macedo's case were aware of the possibility that she suffered from mental incapacity or insanity and did ask the various witnesses a rather boilerplate question as to whether Maria retained her reason. One of the unusual aspects of the case is that they never seriously pursued the possibility of insanity as the source of Maria's visions and they never discussed it among themselves. Perhaps, the witnesses' universal assessment that Maria was not mad convinced the inquisitors early on that, whatever Maria's problem, it was not due to a flaw in judgment ("uma falha no juizo").[3] Time and time again, both the witnesses and the inquisitors would return to the three possibilities of true, fraudulent, and demonic in their testimony about and discussions of the case. Keep these options in mind throughout the rest of this chapter because it would be this limited set of options that would ultimately determine Maria de Macedo's fate.

"As a baptized Christian and, as such, obligated to hold everything held and taught by the Holy Mother Church of Rome," the *libello* against Maria de Macedo began, "she did the opposite, forgetting for a time her obligation, [and] she departed from the common usage due from faithful Christians."[4] This phrasing was part of the well-established formula of inquisitorial justice and appeared in virtually all formal charges against those who were tried by the Holy Office. In many ways, it was legal boilerplate from the theologians and canon lawyers who ran the Inquisition, but its formulaic nature does not imply that it was meaningless. If nothing else were to be said about the culture of the inquisitors, this example of stock phrasing is evidence of a profound truth: the inquisitors saw themselves as the preeminent guardians of orthodoxy within Portugal, the principal correctors of those who "departed from the common usage" of the Roman Church. In early modern Portugal, crimes often fell into various legal jurisdictions—inquisitorial, episcopal, and several secular authorities—a fact that frequently resulted in disputes between the different prosecuting powers as to who had primary jurisdiction over a given crime. This was not true in the case of heresy, though; no one doubted or disputed that the Holy Office had sole jurisdiction over the realm of heretical or suspect teachings and practices. It is banal to say that the Inquisition was the guardian of orthodoxy in the world of the Counter-Reformation; it is somewhat less banal to be reminded that the inquisitors defined themselves in such a way. It was their guiding ethos, the ethos of one of the elite ecclesiastical subcultures of early modern Portugal.[5]

In the case of Maria de Macedo, the standard phrasing of the introduction to the charges reveals what the officials of the Tribunal of Lisbon thought was the central problem in her case: in their view, she had departed from the norms of Catholic usage and so needed to be corrected. The issue of whether Maria was guilty of disseminating suspect propositions was raised repeatedly in the trial record,[6] and it needs to be pointed out again that it was the issue of the suspect propositions embedded in her claims that caused the Conselho Geral to reject the first, more lenient decision of Inquisitors Baretto and Castilho.[7] So, unsurprisingly, this is evidence that the Inquisition was concerned with issues of heterodoxy in and of itself. In the end, though, Maria de Macedo was not found guilty of heresy; instead she was condemned for *fingimento*, or fraud. The connection between the inquisitors' concern about suspect propositions and their final decision that she had made up her visions will be established later, but the point is worth bearing in mind as the material is examined below.

Of course, while the inquisitors were worried by the issue of false doctrine in general, there were some specific aspects of Maria's narrative that caused them to suspect her of heterodoxy. The issues that, by their own admission, concerned the inquisitors most are found in the list of propositions presented to the *qualificadores* by the Conselho Geral after the first, lenient decision had been rejected.[8] The first, second, and fifth questions all dealt with the issue of animals turning into humans and Maria's willingness to have dealings with them. The third and fourth concentrated on the issues of the participation of Saint John, Enoch, and Elijah in the Judgment of Reformation, whether the Hidden Isle was the earthly paradise, and whether Saint John was alive or dead.[9] Why, of all the possible issues that could be raised from Maria's narrative, were these the questions the members of the Conselho Geral were most concerned about? Why did they view them as suspect propositions worthy of close examination? The answers to these questions will form the remainder of this chapter.

Moving to specifics, the first, second, and fifth propositions will be examined in detail later in this chapter, so for the moment, we will concentrate on the issues of Saint John and the prophets, the Reformation of Judgment, and the status of the Hidden Isle. Interestingly, the inquisitors' disquiet on these matters was echoed in the list of three questions asked of Maria by Father Luis de Madre de Deos, as related in the pamphlet. As an examiner of books, Father Luis de Madre de Deos was associated with the Inquisition, but the fact that he asked such similar questions about Maria's story some fifteen years before she was called to the Holy Office suggests that these questions were not merely the narrow concerns of the inquisitors but rather a more generalized response from members of the Portuguese ecclesiastical elite. So, why did these claims concern members of that elite in the first place?

Although the various inquisitorial officials who commented on the case were concerned that Maria said she had seen Enoch and Elijah, the claim that most disturbed them was that Saint John the Evangelist was still alive and that he would one day return with Sebastian to help in the Judgment of Reformation. Why did Saint John's fate and future cause them such unease? In the first instance, it was the assertion that Saint John was still alive, "contrary to the common sentiment of the Church,"[10] that caused suspicion among the inquisitors. The situation was probably not helped by Maria's rather bald answer to de la Cerda's questions on the subject: "the same King [Sebastian] told her that, while the Church followed the opinion that St. John the Evangelist was dead, he knew that he was alive."[11]

The fact that there was no universal agreement on the matter even within the church—a point noted by the *qualificador*, João Gomes—did nothing to lessen the conviction of the inquisitors that Maria had stepped over an important line with such a statement. Gomes's uncertainties on the issue were contained in a private letter, written by a theologian for theologians; Maria's statements were well publicized. Gomes clarified that the belief that Saint John was dead was both the more common and the most probable, despite the testimony of some eminent church fathers; the tone of Maria's answer was less accommodating. And, finally, the *qualificador* made sure to say that he "submitted everything to this Holy Tribunal";[12] it is unlikely that the inquisitors interpreted the bluntness of Maria's answer as indicative of a submissive attitude to the ministers and teachings of the church, a point that will be examined in greater detail later. The seriousness with which an apparently defiant attitude was taken can be seen in the comments of Gomes's acerbic fellow *qualificador*, João de Deus. Even after conceding that the church had not ruled definitively whether Saint John was alive or dead, he stated that the sense of the church was that he was dead. Since the church "cannot err," he felt that sense should be respected, and he concluded that section of his response by quoting Saint Paul's Letter to the Galatians, saying, "if even an angel teaches another gospel, let him be anathema" (Gal. 1:8).[13] The underlying issue and the underlying value could hardly have been put more starkly.

Beyond the issue of showing a willingness to defy or ignore the "common opinion of the Church," there was another aspect of the issue of Saint John's fate that was viewed with suspicion by the Inquisition. As was noted in the previous chapter, the prophets Enoch, Elijah, and Saint John played legitimizing roles within Maria's narrative. Even though there was a large cultural divide between the inquisitors and Maria, this clash of subcultures did not lead to any misunderstanding of her meaning by the inquisitors but rather to a difference in valuation, at least on this issue. The inquisitors understood quite clearly the legitimizing role that Saint John, above all, played in Maria's story, and that was precisely what made them suspicious because the endorsement of a saint, especially one as illustrious as Saint John, of the eschatological program laid out by Maria was tantamount to an endorsement by God himself.

This was of particular concern because of Saint John's connection to the Judgment of Reformation within Maria's schema. In response to her assertion that the beloved apostle would return with Sebastian to perfect the world in the Judgment of Reformation, Inquisitor de la Cerda said that such an opinion was "without foundation" and that it was "an article of faith that there would only be one, final judgment."[14] In terms of the institutional church, de la Cerda knew of what he spoke, since, from at least the time of Augustine, the leaders of the Catholic world had been skeptical, if not downright suspicious, of millennial or terrestrial interpretations of the end times. Also, Thomas Aquinas had firmly advocated the position that there would be a single judgment without intermediate ages of bliss before the Resurrection Day.[15] Since scholasticism was the epistemological standard by which most of the leaders of the Counter-Reformation church, and especially members of the Inquisition, understood truth, the importance of his endorsement of the single judgment position cannot be underestimated. Because of the weight of the Angelic Doctor and indeed the entire scholastic tradition, the dogma of the singularity of the final judgment, unlike the issue of the status of Saint John, was largely fixed among educated clergy. It is this fact that helps explain why Maria's statement caused de la Cerda such disquiet and why his tone was so confident when he rejected it as outside the common usage of Catholics. Of course, in reality, this would apply only to the common usage of theologically trained Catholics, since the multiplicity of millennial schemes of all sorts shows that popular Catholicism had very different views of the matter. The divergence in expectation between an imminent, physical, and earthly paradise and a temporally distant, spiritual, and otherworldly heaven points to a difference in values, which is, in turn, an indicator of a significant cultural distinction between elite and popular Catholicism, in Portugal and elsewhere.[16]

Another issue of concern for the Holy Office was Maria's prediction that Sebastian would bring "new laws" by which to rule the world. In fact, this was the proposition that prompted the gravest suspicions among the inquisitors. So serious was the issue that, during the sixth deposition, de la Cerda asked her about the subject twice, pressing her for a clear answer when she denied that she thought that the law of Christ would be changed before the end of the world. Since that answer was so clearly at variance with her previous testimony, the testimony of the other witnesses (including Feliciano), and the evidence in the pamphlet, the inquisitor rephrased the question and asked her again: Would God give new laws to "mankind" before the end of the world? Again, she said she did not believe that new laws would be given.[17] It remains unclear why she changed her story then, though perhaps by that point in her experience with the Holy Office, she recognized that it was a claim she would be best to distance herself from. Whatever the reason for the change, it did not change the inquisitors' view of the issue; as they describe it in their final, more rigorous report on the case to the Conselho Geral, the idea that Sebastian would bring new laws was "a more than suspect proposition."[18]

Given the atmosphere of intense confessional loyalty in baroque Portugal, it is easy enough to see why the prediction of a new law would be unsettling to many within the Catholic ecclesiastical hierarchy, even outside the realm of specialized heresy-hunters such as the inquisitors. This is true because the faith was viewed as fundamentally fixed and unchangeable and contained in scripture, tradition, and the teachings of the Magisterium, all of which were subsumed under the aegis of papal authority. To be sure, new practices and procedures could be promulgated on the basis of that same papal authority, but these changes were viewed as specific elaborations of the unchanging truth of the gospel, not as anything fundamentally new. The new was, by definition, suspect, and it certainly did not help Maria's case that the promise of new laws was closely connected to the prediction that there would be great revolutions in Lisbon when Sebastian returned; the prospect of scandals among the faithful was one of the reasons the inquisitors felt they needed to suppress Maria's story.[19] Without a doubt, this reasoning was hyperbolic, but just because it was exaggerated does not mean it is not evidence of a real fear among the inquisitors.

Perhaps, though, the inquisitors were not as irrational in their fears about the effect of Maria's claims as it might first appear. The origin of their fears regarding these matters could have been what they may have perceived—correctly—as its foundation: the radicalism of the Spiritual Franciscan followers of Joachim of Fiore. Indeed, radical Joachimism, along the lines of Gerard de Borgo San Donnino's belief in the Eternal Evangel, is the thread that binds together all these issues—the identification of Saint John as an apostle of the future; the belief in a Reformation of Judgment to usher in a time of blessedness along lines comparable to the Joachimite Age of the Spirit; and the proclamation that a new law that would replace the law of Christ. Given that the overall tone of Maria's vision is one of resignation, it seems that the influence of radical Joachimism on her story was largely vestigial in nature, however. These tropes were probably included in her narrative, not as a result of a conscious desire for more revolutionary outcomes, but rather because they were part of the specific millenarian traditions from which she gleaned the elements she needed to cobble together her own vision of the future. Whether the inquisitors consciously associated these claims of Maria's with the Spiritual Franciscan apocalyptic tradition (and therefore rejected them) is an open question, but it is clear enough they felt they did not conform to Catholic dogma. The possibility that the inquisitors understood the historical roots of Maria's beliefs better than she did herself cannot be excluded, and this possibility may help explain both Maria's sincere insistence that nothing she saw or heard on the island contradicted her view of Catholic orthodoxy and why the inquisitors so readily rejected that claim.

The undercurrent of heterodox Joachimism found in Maria's vision was not the only matter that made the inquisitors of the Lisbon Tribunal suspicious about her commitment to and understanding of the Catholic faith. The religious practices of the islanders, as described by Maria, were also suspect. In several places, Maria favorably described the great devotion of the islanders to the Catholic faith, and her understanding of piety as orthopraxy has been previously established. In a positive tone, she stated that the islanders' devotion, especially as evidenced by their rigorous form of prayer and fasting, even went beyond what was normal for the Portuguese and was an example of true piety. Her judges in the Inquisition looked at the islanders' exceptional exercises in a very different light.

The attitude of the Holy Office on this point is most clearly seen in one of de la Cerda's follow-up questions. After hearing Maria's glowing description of the islanders fasting and praying with nothing to protect their knees as they knelt, the inquisitor asked how could she say that those people were in complete conformity with the Church of Rome when they practiced an observance so different from the common usage of the Catholic faithful and when such practices *because they were different* ("por ser differente") necessarily led to a suspicion of heresy.[20] This demonstrates that, for the inquisitors, any devotion, however exemplary it might have seemed, would fall under suspicion for the simple fact that it was different and therefore unauthorized. This is the institutional view of religious practice in its starkest terms, and Maria's response to the question that embodied this attitude is significant: it was incomprehensible. The only thing she could say in reply was that she did not know what to say beyond what she had already said. This breakdown of comprehension will be explored in greater detail later, but it should be noted that this series of questions reveals a real gulf in expectations and values between the inquisitors on one side and Maria de Macedo and her supporters (including some educated Jesuits) on the other. For the officials of the Holy Office, orthopraxy was not enough.

The issue of the orthodoxy of religious devotion on the Hidden Isle was also closely related to the question of papal authority in the mind of Inquisitor de la Cerda. After hearing that the island was located somewhere near the Azores, he asked Maria how it was possible that the islanders lived in conformity to the Roman Church if they had no communication with the Apostolic See.[21] Given that Portugal itself had no relations with the Holy See at the time, it was an interesting question for de la Cerda to ask, but whatever the geopolitical context, the underlying expectation of the question remains clear: only those Christians who were in submission to the bishop of Rome could be considered true

Catholics. The fact that the inhabitants of the Hidden Isle apparently had no such communication only served to increase his suspicions about the nature of Maria's claims. Again, Maria said she did not know how to respond to the question, but she did say that she had heard that Sebastian had traveled to Rome and that there was a bishop on the island. Apparently, this answered the question in her mind, though de la Cerda was not impressed.

Another aspect of Maria's description of the Hidden Isle caused suspicion in the mind of the inquisitor: the idyllic nature of the Hidden Isle itself. Maria's depiction of the Hidden Isle was a utopian one, a land in which nature was so bountiful that work was unnecessary, in which the people lived in common, and in which there was no cause for dissension of any kind. While this was clearly, for her, a fantastic vision of a life in which the worries of everyday life would be banished, Inquisitor de la Cerda viewed her narration in a dim light. He wondered how it was possible that such a land could exist given that, because of Adam's sin, discord had entered the world and as a punishment for his transgression Adam and all his descendants were cursed to live by the sweat of their brows.[22] De la Cerda's response to Maria's hopeful portrayal of the Hidden Isle is a very clear example of a fundamental cultural difference between them. She believed in the Hidden Isle because it offered the hope of an imminent release from earthly troubles; it was, in many ways, a form of innocent escapism. Looking at it through an exclusively doctrinal prism, de la Cerda rejected it, since it did not conform to the norms of the doctrine of original sin.[23]

His suspicion that Maria's vision was full of unacceptable doctrinal innovations colored her trial throughout its duration. The issue arose early in the process, as can be seen even in the first report to the Conselho Geral, which was written immediately after her first deposition. In that report, Inquisitors de la Cerda and Barreto stated their concern that Maria was spreading "suspect propositions which were without reason, according to the rules of *true theology*."[24] It was the suspect propositions of her account that caused the Conselho Geral to reject the lenient decision of Barreto and Castilho and order that those propositions be sent for qualification. It is interesting that almost the same point was made, at almost exactly the same period in time, during António Vieira's trial before the Inquisition, since one of the specific charges against him was that he "took as a criteria for belief in prophecies simply whether they have been fulfilled and *not according to their doctrine*."[25] Thus, doctrinal purity (or at least submission to same) was, in the view of the Holy Office, the sine qua non of one's identity as a Catholic; anything that failed that test of orthodoxy was suspect, if not downright heretical.

Inquisitor de la Cerda's growing conviction that both Maria and her vision were untrustworthy was further reinforced by other aspects of her account that he viewed as contradictory to Catholic dogma. For example, he asked her how she could have claimed both that Saint John the Evangelist was alive on the Hidden Isle and that there was a church there named for him when it was not the practice of the Catholic Church to canonize or name churches for people who were still alive, and she admitted she could give no satisfactory answer to that question.[26] Similarly, she could not answer how the islanders had both Moorish and Christian names, since such a policy of hidden names was forbidden to Catholics. And when he asked a follow-up question as to how she could reconcile her claim that the islanders had never lied to her and her statement that they had concealed their names from her for a period of years, all she could say was that she had forgotten that detail when he had first asked about it. His final follow-up question hits at the core of the matter as far as he was concerned: If the islanders lied to her about their names, how could the appearances she experienced be from God, since God did not lie?

The cumulative effect of all the doctrinal missteps, heterodox claims, and inconsistencies within Maria's account led the inquisitors (not just the punctilious de la Cerda) to the conclusion that, whatever the precise nature of her vision, it could not have come from God. Once this conclusion had been reached, it was simply a matter of determining the nature of her vision's error; since the possibility that it was true had been definitively excluded in the inquisitors' minds, the only options left were that it was the product of an illusion by the devil or that it was a deliberate invention by Maria de Macedo. And so we now must turn to an examination of the reasoning and values that led the inquisitors to choose between those options and to reach their final decision.

If there was one issue, besides the heterodox components of her account, that convinced the inquisitors that Maria's vision was not from God, it was the claim that she had witnessed the transformation of animals into humans. Since the claim was seen by some as a possible indicator of diabolical influence over Maria, we will use the issue of zoomorphia as a point of departure for an examination of inquisitors' views of the possible role of the devil in Maria's vision.

However, before we proceed to the specific case, we should first set the context by a discussion of the broader issue of how the Portuguese Inquisition understood witchcraft and the role of the devil in human affairs.

Though the vast majority of Europeans who lived in the sixteenth and seventeenth centuries—both educated and uneducated—believed in witchcraft, there were wide variations in how that term was defined and in how people felt they should respond to the phenomenon. Thanks to the work of Julio Caro Baroja, Gustav Henningsen, and others, we now know that the Spanish Inquisition played a large role in sparing Spain from the witch craze that unsettled many parts of Europe in the early modern period, and the Inquisition played a similar role in Portugal as well.[27] Historians have offered a variety of reasons to explain this somewhat curious fact,[28] but we will concentrate on only one of these factors as we look at the trial of Maria de Macedo: the degree to which the Portuguese inquisitors accepted or rejected the "cumulative concept" of witchcraft, to use Brian P. Levack's term—a concept that asserted the reality of the Sabbat, night flights, the pact, *malefice* (harmful magic), and animal transformations.

José Pedro Paiva, in his excellent study *Bruxaria e superstição num país sem "caça às bruxas,"* 1600–1774 (Witchcraft and Superstition in a Country without a "Witch-Hunt," 1600–1774), points out that all the major elements of the cumulative concept of witchcraft were known in Portugal and did make appearances in the judicial proceedings against accused witches, though he notes that those elements were generally given credence in secular courts rather than in inquisitorial tribunals. But while all these beliefs were known to Portuguese judicial authorities, stories about the Sabbat, flight, and transformations into animals were generally viewed with skepticism. In Portugal, it was the pact with the devil that was the central issue of concern to all authorities investigating the possibility of witchcraft, and even the issue of *malefice* was seen as derivative of (and therefore secondary to) the demonic pact.[29] The pact was even more central in the case of inquisitorial prosecutions because it was viewed as a violation of the First Commandment to worship God alone and thus heretical.

Of course, one could be concerned about the pact without believing in the other elements of the cumulative concept, and it seems that this was the situation that prevailed in early modern Portugal. Paiva notes that there was virtually no production of demonological tracts in Portugal during the period—only two were published in the seventeenth century—and that when the subject of witchcraft was discussed, Portuguese authors generally consulted theological texts rather than demonological treatises; the major works on demonology written in Europe during the period were rarely cited. The exceptions to this rule were the *Malleus maleficarum* of Sprenger and Kramer; the *Praxis et theoriae criminalis* of the Paduan jurist Prospero Farinacci; and the *Disquisitiones magicae* of Martin del Rio, with del Rio's work being by far the most popular.[30] These exceptions tend to prove the general conclusion, however, because each of them (including the infamous *Malleus*) spent a good deal of time on questions of procedure and evidence for trials against accused witches. Again, the popularity of del Rio's work proves the main point because, while he accepted the theoretical possibility of most of the elements of the cumulative concept, he was more skeptical of them than were French (secular) demonologists such as Bodin and Rémy, and he attributed many of the fanciful aspects of witch narratives to the devil's power of illusion. He also spent a considerable amount of time discussing criminal procedure, including the issue of false accusations, and giving advice to confessors as to how best deal with the problem of those caught practicing magic, not all of whom he considered witches.

I will say more about del Rio's influence on the officials involved in Maria's case later, but it can certainly be said that the Inquisition as a whole exhibited an attitude toward the problem of witchcraft that was, in many ways, consistent with his approach, though the inquisitors tended to be even more skeptical of the fantastic elements of the witch myth than del Rio had been. It is doubtful that the attitude of the Inquisition (speaking of the institution rather than of individual officials) was derived directly or exclusively from the *Disquisitiones magicae*, but it is very likely that the similarity of approach did spring from a source common to both: a deep reverence and respect for canon law and the well-ordered procedures of the Roman law tradition that underpinned it. The inquisitors were nothing if not sticklers about following their own procedures—the vaunted "o estilo da Inquisição"—and it was probably this underlying respect for "good order" and proper criminal procedure that endeared del Rio to many judicial officials in Portugal, both inside and outside the Inquisition.[31] So we may conclude that, generally speaking, the inquisitors in Portugal were skeptical of the fantastic elements of the cumulative concept, that they focused their attention on the issue of the pact, and that they were determined to conduct an orderly criminal prosecution that met the standards of canon and Roman law. It will be important to keep all these conclusions in mind as we now turn back to Maria de Macedo's trial and to the issue that helped convince the Inquisition that her visions were not from God: the issue of animal transformation.[32]

Within the folkloric context in which Maria de Macedo developed her vision of the Hidden Isle, the fact that her Moorish interlocutors could take animal form was viewed as indicative of their magical nature rather than of any affiliation with the forces of evil. Even from the earliest stages of her questioning, though, the reaction of the inquisitors was that Maria's claim was "horrendous and ridiculous," a phrase repeated throughout the course of the trial to describe the possibility that humans could take animal form.[33] In the first report of Inquisitors de la Cerda and Barreto to the Conselho Geral, they both agreed that "because of the horror they cause and because of the ridiculous transformations during which creatures turn into men [these appearances] cannot be from God."[34] The *qualificador*, João Gomes, concurred that the figure of the lizard who turned into a man could not be a "good angel sent by God" because "good angels had never appeared in the form of lizards, vipers, or snakes." Instead, given the devil's scripturally demonstrated propensity to appear in the form of a serpent, the appearance of the lizard-man could be a sign of the Evil One's influence, Gomes concluded, citing del Rio's *Disquisitiones magicae* as his immediate source.[35] One should not make too much of Gomes's comments, though; they prove that some officials of the Inquisition were familiar with the connection between transformation and demonic influence, but the tone of the inquisitors themselves was that zoomorphia was a problem because it was absurd and vaguely unseemly. Although obviously disturbed by the claim, the inquisitors themselves never directly connected it with the presence of the devil, concluding only that it was so grotesque that it could not have come from God. And even Gomes seems to have been more distressed by the fact that the Moor took the form of a lizard than that he could take the form of an animal per se. In any event, the very different responses of the officials of the Holy Office and Maria to the issue of animal transformation constitute more evidence of real differences in cultural understandings.

Of course, even before Gomes was asked to evaluate the matter of transformations, Inquisitor de la Cerda had already begun his own line of investigation into the possibility that Maria's vision had its origin in the demonic realm. His questions regarding whether she felt pain, fear, "interior consolation or disconsolation," or greater or lesser fervor for spiritual matters when she was with the people of the island were all part of his quest to see if her testimony revealed the emotional traces of a demonic encounter.[36] The series of questions about whether the islanders exhibited a bad smell, a physical deformity, a disproportioned body, or the parts of an animal had a similar intent, since the list of signs he asked about was consistent with the telltale signs of demonic figures as described in many of the treatises on witchcraft of the day.[37]

The fear of the demonic was also the motivation behind another series of questions having to do with the measures Maria had taken to rid herself of the appearances.[38] Did she not know, he asked, that people who experienced such appearances should do everything possible to free themselves of them, simply because they might be from the devil? She replied that she knew very well that that was her obligation. Did she know then, he continued, that the devil, although he is an evil angel, could appear as a good one, to thereby deceive the faithful and so cause them to sin? She replied that, as a Christian, she understood that well. The next few questions and answers in the series dealt with whether she knew she had an obligation to consult with educated and pious men to rid herself of the visions, and after stating that she also knew that very well, she proceeded to give the details of her consultations with various clerics on the matter, both while a child and as an adult. De la Cerda then asked her if any exorcisms had been performed on her behalf and whether she had been instructed to perform any spiritual exercises by those clerics in order to free herself of the visitations. She answered that exorcisms had been performed and that she had been told to hear several Masses, though neither of those steps had caused the visitations to cease.

De la Cerda's response to Maria's answer here was typical of his suspicion; he was openly skeptical that she had truly "taken advantage of the exorcisms and the other spiritual things" she had been given to do. If she had, how then was it that she continued to have the visitations? Maria admitted she did not know how to answer that question, so he pressed on. Why, if she was truly intent on freeing herself from her visions, had she not continued on with these spiritual "diligences" and ceased to have any familiarity with the people who appeared to her? Here Maria was more self-assured. She replied that she did continue with the Masses, although still to no effect, and as far as the communication she had with the islanders went, she did not view it as a bad thing because they said nothing against "Our Holy Faith" and the only thing they had told her to do was to commend herself to God and to Our Lady of the Rosary.

This series of questions well illustrates the fundamental difference in how the two parties to the questioning thought. For Maria de Macedo, the fact that the exorcisms and the spiritual exercises had not caused the appearances to cease, combined with the fact that those within her vision only made spiritually positive comments, was proof that the appearances were from God, or at least a result of benevolent forces. Her aunt, as described in the pamphlet, apparently shared a similar style of reasoning: "she did not think this could be anything else but enchanted Moors, because neither the holy things nor relics that I carried, nor the exorcisms that were performed, caused them to leave." So it seems that the bottom line for Maria and her aunt (to speak only of specific individuals) was that, since exorcism was understood to drive evil spirits away and since it did not drive Maria's visitors away, the islanders were, therefore, not evil. De la Cerda took a very different approach and so came to very different conclusion. As with Maria and her aunt, there was no doubt in his mind that exorcisms were effective against evil spirits, but unlike them, there was also no doubt that the visions were not from God, with the elements deemed "horrendous and ridiculous" being enough to prove that point in his mind. So if exorcisms were valid (and how could they not be, since they were approved by the church?) and the visions were clearly not divine, the only explanation for the exorcisms' lack of effectiveness was some fault on Maria's part. The sense of his questions leads one to believe that he thought the exorcisms had failed because Maria did not truly want to be rid of her visitors, and it was this conclusion that was to inform Inquisitor de la Cerda's understanding of Maria's case until its end.

Having rejected the possibility that Maria's visions were true in some way, the inquisitors of Lisbon had to determine whether her story was the result of demonic influence or the product of conscious invention on her part. Demonic influence could have contributed to her claims in one of two ways: Maria could have been the victim of infernal deception, having fallen prey to the devil's power of illusion, or she could have been shown the elements of her vision as a result of a pact that she had already made with the demon. The issue of the pact was central to most investigations of witchcraft in Portugal, and it was this line of investigation that de la Cerda was to pursue vigorously throughout the course of the trial.

The suspicion that Maria's visions may have been a result of a demonic pact seems to have been present in Inquisitor de la Cerda's mind even from the beginning of the questioning, and he was continually trying to find evidence that she had made some kind of agreement with or was obeying the instructions of the forces of evil. In the first deposition, for example, he made sure to note that she had said "Yes" to the Moor's request that she share her lunch, and later he lectured her in the form of a question: Did she not know that it would have been better not to have had any communication with clearly supernatural beings, since they could have been agents of the devil in disguise? Maria admitted that she could have been deceived but insisted that she thought they were good because they had never said anything against the faith.[39] This answer was insufficient for de la Cerda, and immediately after the first deposition, he noted to the Conselho Geral that she had obeyed the command of the one called King Sebastian and taken a letter to the king of Denmark at his behest. Of course, according to Maria, this incident had not actually taken place, and it seems clear that de la Cerda included it on the basis of the mistaken testimony of Manoel da Costa and others. However, for the purposes of this investigation, it does not really matter whether it was part of Maria's narrative or not; what is important is that de la Cerda made special note of it. He clearly saw the episode as potential evidence that Maria had made a pact (whether explicit or implicit) with the devil disguised in the form of Sebastian.

In the second deposition, de la Cerda tried to establish Maria's possible motivation for making a pact by asking if she had gone to the island "in order to gain any spiritual or temporal benefit," using fairly standard phraseology for what supposed diabolists hoped to gain from their association with the devil.[40] Given that her original motivation to go with the enchanted Moor as a child was almost certainly a desire for enchanted treasure, the pious answer she gave to the inquisitor's question—that the islanders had told her to have patience and commend herself to God, which was the greatest of all benefits—in all likelihood rang hollow in de la Cerda's ears. His long series of questions dealing with Maria's claims about "future contingencies" could have been related in his mind to the issue of the pact,[41] for speaking of those future contingencies smacked not only of heresy (since the future was known absolutely only by God) but also of diabolism, since the ability to predict the future was often characterized in the demonological literature as one of the illicit gifts given by the devil to his adherents. In the third deposition, the first question was whether her trips to the island were voluntary and whether she was allowed to stay in her house if she refused to go. If she had answered that she had gone willingly, it would have been evidence (in de la Cerda's mind) that she had made an explicit pact with the devil. As it was, she answered that her voyages to the island had always been involuntary, which became yet more evidence for the inquisitor that she was lying.

Matters came to a head during the fourth deposition with de la Cerda asking Maria several times and in several ways if she knew that those who made agreements or promises with unknown, supernatural persons might, in fact, be making an agreement with the devil. Maria's response to this question, in all its variations, was always the same: she had not known that, but she knew it now.[42] The inquisitor was also very concerned that Maria had called Dona Maria Maior her "mistress." He missed entirely that that character was clearly an avatar of the Virgin in Maria's narrative; instead, he asked her whether she had realized that Dona Maria Maior could have been the devil in disguise and that by calling her "mistress" she could have rendered homage to the Evil One. Probably under a great deal of strain, given her situation and de la Cerda's relentlessness, Maria merely replied that she had called Dona Maria Maior her mistress of out of ignorance and because Dona Maria had always been kind to her on the island.[43]

This line of inquiry by Inquisitor de la Cerda culminated in the lecture he gave Maria before ending her fourth session.[44] He began by informing her that, by that point in the investigation, there was "sufficient foundation that [her claims] were her own creations or illusions from the Devil." He then went on to demonstrate why she was not a viable candidate for God's special favors (a subject that will be revisited in the next section): her life was not sufficiently virtuous, and her account was filled with horrible, false, and suspect elements, as well as opinions that went beyond the common usage of the church and so were without authority. He then raised an issue that provides a key insight into his thinking: he stated that the confessors she had consulted to rid herself of the appearances had been mistaken to think that they were merely the product of her imagination because the appearances included "facts in reality." After all, had not someone truly eaten the lunch she had brought at the Moor's request, and had she not brought back answers from the island several times to satisfy the curiosity of her listeners? This indicates that de la Cerda truly believed that a supernatural being or beings had appeared to Maria, eaten her lunch, and given her the information she sought. Given that he believed that, his next statement is hardly surprising: "Whether all the repugnant elements [of this account] persuade that she invented these things to be held as favored by God and to disseminate false doctrines, *or that the Devil collaborated in it*, it has the same effect and [results in] the same damage to her soul."[45] He went on to say that the presumption of a pact was even greater given that she had been able to obtain information "in an extraordinary manner" and that she had witnessed the unseemly sight of animals turning into humans. He concluded by noting that all her voyages to seemed to be quite voluntary to his way of thinking, and her account included several episodes in which she obeyed the actions of the islanders in exchange for some benefit.

All of this was sufficient proof for Inquisitor de la Cerda that Maria's visions and visitations stemmed from a previous pact she had made (perhaps unwittingly) with the devil. He made his conclusions clear in the report he wrote to the Conselho Geral immediately after the end of the fourth deposition.[46] After repeating the major points of his reasoning, he again reached the same conclusion, "there are illusions and appearances of the Devil, which lead one to presume a Pact," and he then went on to emphasize the voluntary nature ("accões livres") of Maria's associations with the figures who came to visit her. This is a snapshot of inquisitorial reasoning in action that also provides insight into elite ecclesiastical understanding of the diabolical in Portugal. Comparing de la Cerda's pattern of reasoning with the general description of the elite ecclesiastical view as given above, we can see that his approach was comparable to the general view in that he concentrated his efforts to determine whether a pact had been made. De la Cerda's beliefs in regard to the reality of the other elements of the "cumulative concept" were more credulous than what would be indicated by the general view, though even then he seemed to be more inclined to a belief in the reality of the infernal figures who were party to the presumed pact than obsessed with details of the Sabbat or *malefice*, neither of which he ever mentioned.

It should be pointed out here that in the same report to the Conselho Geral his fellow inquisitor Francisco Barreto expressed his doubts regarding the possibility that Maria had made a pact with the devil. His reasoning is also of interest. After stating that he was inclined to the possibility that she had invented her story, he said that "presumption of a Pact can be eliminated, because the Doctors who have spoken of this matter and who have listed the signs [of a pact] require as the most important sign that there must be actual evidence of a crime, a point which has not been proven here. Even if one concedes that the visions of creatures and other transformations were true, this is not sufficient because these things should have been sought out by this woman by some deed or action if there is to be a presumption of a Pact."[47] He went on to say that since neither of these points had been proven, there could be no presumption of a pact. He concluded by stating that the crimes of which Maria de Macedo was guilty (and he did not dispute that she was guilty of something) were mitigated by the fact that she was a woman and so more easily "carried off by curiosities."[48]

This more skeptical view was repeated in the lenient report of October 25, 1665, to the Conselho Geral.[49] Barreto and the newly appointed inquisitor João Castilho argued that since there was no evidence of witchcraft ("feitiçaria"), superstition, or sacrilege, there could be no presumption of a pact because the evidence in the case did not meet the standards for such crimes as set out in the Regimento of 1640.[50] They also decided that the nature of Maria de Macedo's consent—the most vital issue involving a possible pact—was no more than that she had consented to the reality of "visions and representations" she had been shown, and that since she had never understood the visions to be of demonic origin, none of her actions could be construed as rendering obedience to the devil. In her favor in this regard was the fact that she had consulted many clerics in order to rid herself of the visitations, and this was not consistent, in their view, with someone who had pledged herself to the devil. They rejected the possibility that Maria had made a pact with the devil; therefore, there were only two possibilities left—that she had been deceived by demonic illusion or that she had made up the entire story—and the inquisitors considered both possibilities in the body of their report without coming to a conclusion as to which was true. Since they could not decide between the two options, they advised that she be put to the torment to determine the truth. The entire report was endorsed by both Barreto and Castilho, along with all of their *deputados;* Inquisitor de la Cerda either did not wish to sign or was unable to do so. Although the report was ultimately rejected by the Conselho Geral as too lenient on the question of the suspect propositions in Maria's account, the fact that the members of the Conselho Geral did not criticize the inquisitors' reasoning regarding the possibility of a pact stands as a tacit endorsement of their position by the members of the council. It was thus the institutional view of the Inquisition that Maria de Macedo was not guilty of having made a pact with the devil.

What should be made of this decision? First, it confirms that the representatives of the Inquisition were, indeed, generally more skeptical of witchcraft claims than were their judicial counterparts in many other areas of Europe. It also confirms the centrality of the pact in Portugal. Both de la Cerda and the inquisitorial officials who ultimately disagreed with his conclusions focused their efforts on trying to determine whether Maria had pledged herself to the devil. What, though, can be made of this disagreement within the Inquisition itself on this issue in this case? Does this undermine the contention that there was a common subculture among those who ran the Inquisition?

Not really, though it may add a certain amount of nuance as to how that subculture is understood. The nature of the disagreement between de la Cerda and the other inquisitors was primarily evidential rather than theoretical in nature. De la Cerda thought that the weight of the evidence tilted in favor of Maria's diabolism; as the quotes above demonstrate, the other inquisitors did not think that the evidence met the standards of good criminal procedure in general or the standards of the Regimento of 1640 in particular. Thus the skepticism of the inquisitors in regard to the more fantastic elements of the witch myth was due, in the case of Maria de Macedo at least, not to some theoretical objection to the possibility of witchcraft in a rationalist mode but rather to a feeling that the evidence in the case did not meet the Inquisition's self-imposed standards of proof. We have already seen that the elite ecclesiastical subculture of Portugal, as embodied in the Inquisition, valued orthodoxy in and of itself; the discussion of the devil in Maria de Macedo's case highlights an equally important value of the inquisitors: their legalism. Because the idea of the law was valued so highly by the inquisitors, however they may have individually rated the infernal potential of the elements of Maria's story—night voyages, animal transformations, discussions with a "Prince," heterodox statements and practices—their commitment to good (or at least authorized) legal procedures and standards of evidence prevented them from reaching the conclusion that Maria had made a pact with devil. This gives us an important insight into the inquisitorial subculture of Portugal and also helps explain why the witch craze did not take root in Portugal during the seventeenth century.

The issue of the devil was not fully resolved when the Inquisition decided that Maria de Macedo was not guilty of a pact, however. In their report to the Conselho Geral, Inquisitors Barreto and Castilho left open the possibility that Maria was the victim of demonic illusion. The end of the story, though, was that Maria de Macedo was convicted of fraud. How, then, did they choose between their two remaining options and reach their final judgment of the case at last? Fortunately, the inquisitors, in their penultimate report to the Conselho Geral, dated March 6, 1666, dealt extensively with this issue.[51] After not being able to decide between fraud and illusion earlier, they concluded that her visions were not the result of illusions of the devil. They had reached that conclusion, they said, "considering the quality of her person, the mode of her life, the information from her proceedings, the form of her visions, and the things which they contain." They went on to mention the many spiritual exercises Maria had been given to free herself of her visions, before moving on to a seemingly unrelated topic, because they then discussed their doubts that the appearances in Maria's visions fit the category of a demonic illusion. They agreed that the devil could appear as angel of light, but neither the lizard nor the Moor of Maria's story was (or claimed to be) an angel. How, though, are these two issues—spiritual exercises and the form the devil could take as a disguise—connected, since both were used as evidence by the inquisitors that the devil had not produced the visions Maria had seen?

Remember that Maria and her aunt had concluded that the ineffectiveness of the exorcisms and the spiritual exercises in driving away the figure of the Moor was proof that he was not evil. The inquisitors, however, thought that their ineffectiveness was proof that the devil had not made an appearance. Underlying both conclusions was a profound faith in the rituals of the church as remedies against the powers of the Evil One.[52] If the exorcisms did not produce the desired effect, it was for no lack of efficacy on their part but rather because the ritual was misapplied to drive away a being that was not evil. This at least was the conclusion of Maria and her aunt; the conclusion of the inquisitors was that the exorcisms had not worked because they were misapplied to drive away a being that simply did not exist in the first place, since it was deemed to be the invention of Maria herself. This conclusion is confirmed by the fact that the inquisitors went on to argue that, despite her claims that she wanted to be free of her visions, at several points during the course of her visions she took voluntary actions to interact with the people she met. This was proof in the inquisitors' minds that she had, in reality, not wanted to be freed of her visions and so was also evidence that she had made up her entire story in an attempt to be viewed as favored by God. Similarly, both the inquisitors and Maria (as proven by her testimony) believed that the angel could disguise himself as an angel of light, but that was the limit of their agreement. Maria concluded that the figure was not an avatar of the devil; the inquisitors concluded that since the figure of the Moor did not match a category they understood, he was no more than the invention of Maria herself.

So, in a very real sense, Maria de Macedo was ultimately found guilty of fraud by a process of elimination, simply because that was the only category the inquisitors felt was left open to them. They never strayed from the tripartite schema originally outlined by the *promotor*—truth, fraud, or illusion, the last possibility subcategorized to include the question of whether a pact was involved, and when both truth and illusion had been eliminated, it was a matter of simple deduction that she was guilty of fraud. Even with two of the three categories eliminated, was a verdict of *fingimento* inevitable? Could they not have simply let her go because the evidence in the case was insufficient to convict her of fraud?

The possibility that Maria would be freed without punishment of any kind was eliminated early in the process because the officials of the Inquisition had decided that, since her claims were clearly not from God, she had committed a crime;[53] it was only a matter of determining what crime she was guilty of and then sentencing her to the appropriate punishment. There is another, more important reason that a judgment of fraud was probably inevitable in this case, though. There was more to the decision that found Maria guilty of *fingimento* than merely the process of elimination; if she did not fit the categories of either a true visionary or a victim/participant of demonic influence very well, there were several ways in which she met the inquisitors' expectations of someone guilty of making fraudulent claims about special revelations. Because she fit inquisitorial expectations of this category so well, it was virtually foreordained that she would eventually be convicted on this charge, even though the officials of the Holy Office never adduced any evidence that she was lying (with the dubious exception of her confession under torture). A discussion of these expectations will follow in the next section.

In its simplest form, the answer to the question of why Maria de Macedo fit the expectations of the inquisitors in regard to people who falsely claimed special revelations from God was that she was a woman. It should be clear by now that, from its inception, the prosecution of Maria de Macedo was gendered in important ways, ways that would ultimately decide her fate. The inquisitors of Lisbon, like most other members of the ecclesiastical elite of Portugal, held very definite views about the propriety of various forms of religious expression by women, but all those views were tinged by a basic suspicion of women, by an attitude of misogyny. Women were, of course, excluded from the priesthood, and even their participation in lay sodalities was circumscribed. During the Counter-Reformation, there were two approved venues for female religious activity: as a cloistered nun dedicated to prayer and contemplation or as a married woman dedicated to performing good works through authorized charitable institutions, such as the Misericordias in Portugal. As has also been mentioned, in practice the situation was more fluid than the schema described above might lead one to believe, but the branching path of either cloistered contemplative or married worker of charity remained the stated norm of baroque Catholicism.[54]

This fact is significant in the case of Maria de Macedo because the inquisitors were concerned primarily with the stated norms of Tridentine Catholicism, and women who demonstrated a desire for forms of religious expression outside that pattern were viewed with heightened suspicion by institutions such as the Inquisition. The figure of the *beata* merited their particularly hostile attention in this regard, and while most *beatas* never appeared before the Inquisition, the numbers of them brought before the Holy Office, both in Spain and in Portugal, were still noteworthy.[55] Often overlapping with the figure of the *beata*, both in terms of sociological role and therefore also as victims of inquisitorial prosecution, was the tertiary, or *terceira*. The Holy Office watched the *terceiras* with a wary eye, as it did with all groupings of women speaking about religious matters outside the parameters of authorized teaching by parish priests or other acceptable (male) preaching orders. The questions that Inquisitor de la Cerda asked Maria regarding whether she followed a special mode or life or practiced any special spiritual exercises are indicative of his concern that he might have had a rogue *terceira* on his hands,[56] and in fact, both of the other women cited by Jacqueline Hermann as examples of inquisitorial prosecution of *sebastianistas* were Franciscan *terceiras*.[57] Even women in regular, cloistered orders who professed to have had special revelations from God could run afoul of the Holy Office, as the example of Saint Teresa of Avila demonstrates. Of course, she was eventually judged innocent of heresy and later canonized, but few women were as eloquent or as rigorously orthodox in their claims as she was.

It was not simply the fact that women such as the *beatas* and the *terceiras* were grouping themselves to discuss and practice religious devotions that made the members of the Inquisition uneasy. They also had very definite ideas about the kinds of spiritual trouble those women would get into (and cause) without the proper guidance of a sound male cleric. Women were widely viewed, in the literature produced and read by the ecclesiastical elite throughout Europe, as particularly inclined toward flights of fancy and toward accepting unusual events as signs of divine communication. This characterization of women's spiritual gullibility was so widespread among ecclesiastical authorities of the time that it is almost impossible to trace any individual's beliefs in this regard to a single source. Rather, the source was a tradition of suspicion of female religious expression dating from the earliest days of Christianity. However, to illustrate the point, I will quote the one contemporaneous author cited by an official of the Inquisition dealing with Maria de Macedo's case: Martin del Rio. In his *qualificação*, the acerbic João de Deus quoted del Rio as saying that women, because of their "humid" and "vehement" nature, were particularly prone to "receiving and believing figures that appear to them." The *qualificador* went on to add that because women "have less judgment and reason, they are more easily deceived by the Devil with false semblances and appearances, as this same Author himself adverts."[58] Even Maria's own defense counsel bought into this understanding and argued for the charges against her to be mitigated because she was "a woman, and so of weak judgment."[59]

There was an observable phenomenon that tended to confirm these conclusions about women in the eyes of the inquisitors: the fact that more women than men were found guilty of making false claims about special revelations. While the statistics of inquisitorial prosecution bear this contention out, one may justly wonder about the causes behind the statistics. Were the high prosecution rates a function of some culturally determined predisposition among women to make these claims, or were they a function of inquisitorial prejudice and stereotyping? Whatever the answer to that question is, the fact stands that many more women than men were prosecuted for falsely claiming visions, apparitions, and revelations, and these facts of institutional experience and practice probably inclined the inquisitors toward the view that Maria was guilty of *fingimento*.[60]

Many of the women charged under the heading of claiming false revelations and favors from God were more specifically prosecuted as mediums that had access to the world of the dead. In almost all the cases I have reviewed, the medium would be consulted by a neighbor in order to find out the state of a departed loved one's soul and for advice on the best way to alleviate that loved one's torments in purgatory. The prescribed remedies were generally a combination of charity and special Masses for the dead. It is easy to see what kind of sociological role women who could provide such information would play in the world of early modern Portugal, but the Inquisition took a dim view of all such activities. It is also clear that de la Cerda had this possibility in mind as he questioned Maria. His many questions about whether she had an unusual interest in dreams, or in hidden things or future events, or whether the people of the island had ever told her to perform special devotions or Masses were potentially related to a fear on his part that Maria, in reality, thought she was a medium.[61] It almost seems as if de la Cerda was testing each of his stereotypes of visionary women to see which one fit best.

Not all women who said they had received visions from God were condemned by the Holy Office, but given the high level of suspicion of such claims by the Inquisition and other ecclesiastical institutions, the women who were eventually acknowledged as true visionaries had to meet very restrictive criteria in order to be approved by the church. First, the visions themselves had to be judged completely orthodox in content, and, as we have seen in Maria de Macedo's case, this was one reason the inquisitors ultimately rejected her version of what she had experienced. The character of the visionary's life also had to meet a highly defined standard, and in this regard, too, Maria was found lacking by the judges in her trial. In the second report to the Conselho Geral, both de le Cerda and Barreto agreed that the visions could not be from God "because she is not of such a virtuous life that the Lord would show her particular favors."[62] They did not elaborate on why they had reached their conclusion, but by the end of the trial they had more concrete evidence against Maria in this regard. "The witnesses the prisoner nominated in her defense testified that, while in an unmarried state, she admitted into her house a person with whom she had an illicit friendship," the inquisitors declared, referencing the testimony of Maria's childhood neighbors about her purported relationship with Alexandre de Sousa.[63] Not only did this youthful indiscretion preclude divine favors for her, but it also provided the inquisitors with a possible motivation for making false claims: "one must believe that the prisoner ordered everything to a particular end, [hoping] by means of similar false claims she would cover up her defect." Since Maria began to experience visitations around the age of nine or ten, the chronology does not really add up in favor of the inquisitors' argument here, but whether the argument was valid is beside the point; the important aspect of this is that it is another example of the rigorous standard by which the Inquisition judged women claiming to be visionaries.

There was a final criterion that had to be met for a woman to be accepted as a true visionary by the Inquisition, and on this point as well Maria de Macedo was judged lacking, and this criterion was one of due submission to established religious authorities, especially to the inquisitors themselves. This standard was left unstated in her trial, but this does not mean that it was any less real in its effects. The fact that Maria refused to confess to the charges on which the inquisitors repeatedly pressed her was simply more evidence in their minds that, whatever her precise motivations in telling her story, they were not godly in nature. How could her motives be pure when she showed such a stubborn and impenitent attitude to the wise council of inquisitors given in an attitude of "great charity"?[64]

The evidence that her refusal to confess may have caused resentment in Inquisitor de la Cerda is found in a somewhat unusual place. During her sixth deposition, de la Cerda asked a quick series of rapid-fire questions dealing with the licitness of spreading superstitions and of making agreements with the devil.[65] Her answers were a rather terse "no" to each of his questions as to whether she thought any of those prohibited activities were permitted. One can learn something about what the Inquisition thought about each of those items by studying those questions separately and in detail, but that would be to miss the main point of the exercise as far as de la Cerda was concerned. The hectoring questions he asked during the sixth deposition were not designed to elicit information but rather to demonstrate to her who had the religious authority in that setting. De la Cerda probably felt that, after his unsuccessful harangue to get her to confess at the end of the fourth deposition (the fifth being simply the standard genealogical session), Maria, whom he was increasingly viewing a stubborn woman, needed to be reminded of her proper place in the world of Tridentine Portugal.

So, in the final analysis, Maria de Macedo was convicted of making fraudulent claims by the Portuguese Inquisition, not because the inquisitors had gathered positive evidence that she was lying but because the elements of indirect evidence in her case—the heterodoxy of her vision's content, the imperfections of her moral life, and her continued refusal to confess—were all consistent with the inquisitors' stereotypical expectations of a woman falsely claiming a special revelation from God.[66] In other words, Maria de Macedo was convicted because her general profile matched a certain mental category, a category that, helpfully, was the only one left to the inquisitors after they had systematically eliminated the other possibilities within their restrictive tripartite schema. To understand how these mental categories were constructed requires that we examine the nexus between knowledge, education, and religious power in early modern Portugal, and this examination will serve as a final look at the values that informed the Portuguese Inquisition in Maria de Macedo's case and, therefore, in their activities defending Catholic orthodoxy more broadly.

During Maria de Macedo's sixth deposition before Inquisitor Fernão Correa de la Cerda, there was more going on than just a reassertion of traditional gender roles; the inquisitor's intent was not only to remind her of her place as a woman but also to demonstrate her ignorance and to remind her of her place as an uneducated layperson appearing before the preeminent tribunal of orthodoxy in the land. The sixth deposition was, in many ways, de la Cerda's response to Maria's answers during the prior sessions. Or perhaps it would be better to say that the sixth deposition was his response to her nonanswers because it was during the third and fourth depositions that Maria was forced to concede that she simply did not know the answers to several of the questions the inquisitor had asked her. The unrelenting nature of his approach is clearly demonstrated by her exasperated exclamation, after a series of those questions, that she simply did not understand "these points and subtleties."[67]

Carlo Ginzburg has argued that judicial records such as inquisitorial depositions can, at times, be dialogic in nature and that the presence of two competing or clashing voices in the record can provide historians with the opportunity to catch a glimpse of the native or subordinate voice, a glimpse that is (relatively) unmediated by inquisitorial prejudice or ideology. As he demonstrates, inquisitorial incomprehension allows the defendant's voice to "leak" through the record.[68] Here, I will argue from the flip side of the same coin, namely, that incomprehension on the part of the defendant is an indicator of a real cultural divide between him or her and the interrogating party. In Maria de Macedo's case, I take at face value her statements that she simply did not understand either the content or the point of some of de la Cerda's more complicated questions, and I take this as evidence that she was not working with the same mental categories as those used by the inquisitor and indeed that she often did not understand those categories. We have often seen that the inquisitors, because of their different value system, misinterpreted the intent and function of many elements in Maria de Macedo's account; the examples of her incomprehension are proof that, similarly, she often did not understand the intellectual, ideological, and cultural frames of reference by which she was being judged.

At first glance, it seems that the cultural and intellectual gap between Maria and the inquisitors could be reduced, in its simplest terms, to the difference between an oral culture and a literate one, low culture and high culture, if you will. That conclusion would be wrong, however, because Maria de Macedo's case does not fit into that easy, dichotomous schema. As shown in previous chapters, neither Maria de Macedo as a person nor the content of her vision stands well as a pristine example of low, popular, or oral culture. Certainly, many of the elements of her narrative, such as the figures of the enchanted Moors or the Cockaigne tropes, came from popular folkloric sources, but we have also seen that these elements were progressively modified as she grew older to conform to the norms of Tridentine Catholicism she received from above—that is, from another, higher culture. As has been said before, Maria de Macedo was caught in the middle of many conflicting and even antithetical cultural trends, from both above and below.[69]

The influence of Dom João de Castro on Maria's understanding of Sebastian is perhaps the best illustration of this process. As an educated and sometimes well-connected figure, Castro would generally be considered an elite (or perhaps counter-elite) figure, and so the influence from above on Maria's Sebastianism would be clear; however, it is almost certain that Maria was exposed to Castro's views only indirectly, via oral transmission of the broader tradition to which he was an important contributor, and even then she incorporated elements from Castro in an attenuated and sometimes garbled way. So, in this case, we have evidence of an interesting cycle of popular-elite cultural dialectic: the preexisting oral tradition about Sebastian (keeping in mind the trial of Balthasar Gonçalves in 1584) was reworked and formalized by the erudite Dom João de Castro, whose views were, along with the tradition of the falsified papal bulls and the Hidden Isle legends, (partially) reincorporated into a new popular/

oral synthesis of *sebastianismo* by the mid-seventeenth century. It is a case of cultural recycling at its best.[70]

A sharp division into elite/written and popular/oral also falls apart in this case given the fact that, before the Inquisition was ever involved, Maria's story was written down—in the pamphlet—and at least partially disseminated by educated Jesuits. Does the mixed nature of Maria's sources and production mean, however, that no distinction can be made in this regard between her subculture and the subculture of the inquisitors who judged her? No, because if Maria's sources were mixed, the inquisitors' were not. And what were those sources? Books—to be more precise, ecclesiastically approved books of law and theology.[71] Although it was not the practice of Portuguese inquisitors to cite specific authors, Inquisitor Barreto still revealed his orientation toward written authorities when he referred to "the Doctors who have spoken of this matter and who have listed the signs" when speaking of the standards of evidence to be used in establishing a pact with the devil.[72] And, of course, the inquisitors often referred to their own handbook of procedure, the Regimento of 1640, when speaking about evidential standards, procedures, and sentencing guidelines in Maria de Macedo's case.

The influence of erudite books on the thinking of the officials of the Inquisition is more clearly seen in qualifications submitted by João Gomes and João de Deus.[73] Perhaps the best place to start this discussion is by looking at the two sources quoted by both men: the Bible and Martin del Rio's *Disquisitiones magicae.* The authority of the quotes from the Bible—from the Apocalypse in the case of Gomes and from Galatians in the case of João de Deus—should be clear enough in a case like this, but del Rio's influence requires further comment. It is interesting indeed to see how legal categories and principles enunciated by del Rio in his work reappear time and time again in the course of Maria de Macedo's trial. Both del Rio and the Portuguese inquisitors evince a theoretical belief in witchcraft and yet remain rather skeptical of the claims about it. It is clear in del Rio that this skepticism stems from a desire to follow good legal procedure, and, in fact, one of the six books that make up the *Disquisitiones magicae* was dedicated to the issues of proper trial procedure in the case of a witchcraft investigation. For example, he reminded his readers how to evaluate the credibility of witnesses and tells them how to determine whether a witch's confession is the result of delusion.[74] And it is clear that the Inquisition ultimately rejected the possibility that Maria had made a pact with the devil because the evidence in her case did not meet the standards set out in the Regimento.

Del Rio and the inquisitors also shared a suspicion of female visionaries as a group, though this could be said of most early modern ecclesiastics. It is at the level of details that the correlation becomes more interesting. Del Rio was dismissive of revelations to women because he thought women made too much of dreams and were too easily led astray by the lies of evil spirits. Those women who claimed divine revelations had to meet a high standard to prove it: not only did they have to be devout Catholics, but their lives had to be morally spotless, and the content of their visions had to be pious and good. Visions that contained both pious elements and "repugnant" elements were to be held suspect.[75] Of course, this is the same standard that was applied in Maria's case. For del Rio and the inquisitors, the pact was central to any investigation of witchcraft, and even many of the specific questions asked by de la Cerda to establish whether Maria had been in the presence of the devil (e.g. feelings of horror, deformities, scandalous statements) find an echo in del Rio.[76]

The inquisitors of Lisbon did not always follow del Rio's lead, though. While he commented extensively on *malefice* and the Sabbat, they never mentioned either issue, though this may be simply due to the fact Maria's case had nothing to do with those issues. Generally speaking, del Rio displayed more credulity toward claims of witchcraft than the inquisitors of Portugal did, though this statement would have to be somewhat qualified because del Rio dismissed animal transformations as nothing more than a demonic illusion, whereas the inquisitors may have accepted its theoretical reality.[77] Unfortunately for Maria, the Inquisitors of Lisbon never seem to have read del Rio on the phenomenon of women who sleep so deeply that they imagine they truly see and hear wondrous things.[78] So it would go too far to say, on the basis of this available evidence, that del Rio had direct influence on the inquisitors in this case, simply because a large number of theologians were saying similar things about these issues at the time. The degree of consistency in approach between del Rio and the Portuguese Inquisition is intriguing, though, and deserves further research. His influence on the *qualificadores* (and, perhaps, on the inquisitors themselves) is indisputable, however; so if the figure of Dom João de Castro was lingering in the background of Maria de Macedo's vision, it is not hard to imagine the shade of Martin del Rio peeking over the inquisitors' shoulders as they decided her case.

Besides scripture and del Rio, João Gomes cited several sources for his views on the propositions he had been asked to qualify, including works by Saint Vicente Ferrer, Saint Hippolytus, and Saint Ambrose; a sermon by the papal saint Leo I; even a Portuguese "Life of St. Teresa de Jesus," among others. João de Deus quotes from Leo I, his fellow pontiff Saint Gregory the Great, and extensively from Saint Augustine. The specific works cited and the specific ideas gleaned from them are less important, for the purposes of this study, than what they tell us about the attitude of the inquisitors toward books and authority. The whole of their understanding of the doctrinal and experiential issues they discussed was circumscribed by the authority of their written sources. Even when their views did not originate in a written source, they always, eventually, had to be validated by an authorized book.

This attitude can be contrasted with the view evidenced by the pamphlet and by the testimony of Maria herself. After receiving a simple reassurance that the first Moor was not the devil, she evinced no doubts as to the reality or the origin of what she saw and heard; the foundations of her claims to truth were personal and experiential, not based on either the literary or institutional authority the inquisitors depended on. Her vision was often internally inconsistent, though unselfconsciously so, and it followed no elaborate rhetorical structure; instead, it was organized in a rough chronological fashion. The erudite literature to which the inquisitors appealed for both their knowledge and their authority (since the two were inextricably linked) sought, though did not always achieve, internal logical consistency and was often ordered according to the formalities of scholastic rhetorical theory. The evidence presented in Maria's vision was immediate, sensory, and largely presented raw; in the inquisitors' books, arguments were made on the basis of formal reasoning from evidence that had been evaluated and categorized. The language of Maria's vision was open to a wide audience because it was informal, nontechnical, and Portuguese; the message and meaning of erudite books were restricted to a few well-educated specialists because this literature was formal, full of legal and doctrinal jargon, and, very often, written in Latin.

Of course, all these contrasting descriptions were equally true of the media used to convey each kind of message. As has been noted before, the readers of the *sebastianista* manuscript pamphlets of the seventeenth century were a generally poor, minimally literate lot, and Maria's vision as recorded in the pamphlet was certainly narrated and structured in a way that was accessible to such an audience, even though it was apparently copied and read by several educated Jesuits. The tomes consulted by the officials of the Inquisition did not have such multiclass appeal, and, besides, they required money to purchase, fluency to read, and education to understand. All these differences show why one kind of literature and one group of readers sat in judgment on the other; perhaps the difference between Maria de Macedo and the Inquisition is best exemplified by the difference between pamphlets and books and those who read them.

CONCLUSION
The Intersection of Two Worlds

What have we learned from this examination of Maria de Macedo's vision and her trial? Certainly, in the case of Maria herself, we have seen that her vision was a composite creation, a mosaic made of pieces from a wide variety of popular legends and beliefs. It began as a strange dream experience, the exact psychological dynamic of which is unclear, that occurred when Maria was a child. She understood it, though, only when she was given an interpretive matrix—the long-standing Iberian tradition of the enchanted Moors—by which to comprehend it. Although Maria's understanding of her visitations became progressively more Christianized as she matured, it did not reach a fully Christianized form until sometime around May 1650, when she began to reinterpret her experience according to the messianic tradition surrounding King Sebastian. While *sebastianismo* was the core of her newly formulated understanding, elements from other popular traditions such as the legends of the land of Cockaigne (disguised as the Hidden Isle) or the stories of the Arthurian cycle were also incorporated into what became the most developed form of her eschatological vision.

Maria de Macedo's account was not merely an amalgam of elements taken from a variety of popular traditions, however. It also shows the marked influence of cultural trends from above. The sexual license and gluttony of the Cockaigne myth were eliminated in her vision, and, in general, her mature narrative conformed to Tridentine moral and devotional norms. This transformation of the original tropes of the Cockaigne/land of wonders tradition into an identifiably Catholic utopia could have been the result of Maria receiving those elements in an already Catholicized state or because they were changed from a more original form by the same process of interiorization that we have already noted. In either case, the result was a fully Christianized and eschatological vision.

Of course, Maria de Macedo's acceptance of Catholic teaching about sexual morality and proper devotion was not enough to spare her from the judgment of the Inquisition, and so it might seem that, in terms of orthodoxy, there was an area in which she was not fully receptive to the imposition of elite values. In reality, one's understanding of this issue depends on whether one sees the glass as half empty or half full. Certainly, the inquisitors saw it is as half empty, but that does not mean we must as well. Despite the fact that Maria was not always able to answer Inquisitor de la Cerda's "points and subtleties," many of her responses reveal that she had internalized many of the views propounded by the ecclesiastical elite of Portugal. For example, she agreed with de la Cerda that those who had visions should try to free themselves of them; where they disagreed was in regard to how that principle applied in her case. She was convinced that since she had tried to free herself from the visions without success they were from God; de la Cerda, however, concluded that she was insincere. Similarly, she repeatedly told him that she knew that the devil could take the form of a good angel in order to deceive the faithful. This is a clear example of her acceptance of a elite understanding of the devil's wiles, the basis of which was Saint Paul's statement that the devil could appear as an angel of light (2 Cor. 11:14) and the subsequent tradition that had been elaborated upon that foundation by a long line of Catholic demonologists and theologians, Martin del Rio among them.

The clearest evidence that Maria de Macedo had already accepted much of the Inquisition's view on spiritual visitations is found in her sixth deposition. As stated earlier, Inquisitor de la Cerda used the session to remind her of her ignorance of theological details and thereby put her in her place. It should also be noted, however, that in response to his long series of questions regarding the propriety of claiming or spreading revelation, she agreed that no one should claim or proclaim those visions without being sure they were of divine origin. She gave a similar answer to his next series of questions regarding the permissibility of communicating with the devil: she did not think it was right to have any dealings with the devil. This pattern repeats itself in the common understanding between Maria and de la Cerda regarding, for example, the power of exorcism or the necessity that the people of the Hidden Isle be in contact with the Roman See in order to be true Catholics. In all these cases, Maria and the inquisitor disagreed as to the application of these principles in her case, but they agreed on the principles themselves. So, while the trial of Maria de Macedo was certainly the venue for a clash between two different subcultures, the record of that trial is also evidence for many shared cultural understandings, largely because that record also demonstrates that Maria de Macedo had internalized many of the doctrinal precepts of the ecclesiastical elite in Counter-Reformation Portugal.[1]

This is important to point out because the conflict that took place between the middle culture of Maria de Macedo and the high culture of her inquisitorial judges was almost completely one-sided, in terms of both power and intent. Maria de Macedo clearly wished to avoid a conflict with the Inquisition not only because she wished to escape punishment but also because she saw no reason for her to be prosecuted; she conceived of herself as a faithful Catholic. It was the Inquisition that took the initiative in the cultural struggle between Maria de Macedo and the Holy Office, in order to correct her errors and to so prevent a scandal among the faithful.

What were the errors that the inquisitors felt they needed to correct? Oddly, they were not connected to her claims about Sebastian. This point receives confirmation from the final decision of the case, in which the inquisitors of Lisbon stated, "If she had only held to the beliefs of those vulgarly called *sebastianistas*, such as the claim that King Sebastian is alive, that he is on the Hidden Isle, that he will return to this kingdom, or the other things affirmed by the *sebastianistas*, she would not have committed any crime that falls under the jurisdiction of this Holy Office."[2] This statement proves that her beliefs about Sebastian were not an issue for the inquisitors; it was only elements she had added to the *sebastianista* core—especially the traces of Joachimite radicalism, which were not present in all the versions of the *sebastianista* legend extant in Restoration Portugal, and the motif of animal transformation—that caused the inquisitors concern. Assuming that the inquisitors were informed of the beliefs typically held by the *sebastianistas*, Maria's characterization of both Sebastian and the Hidden Isle can be seen as representative of the broader *sebastianista* movement if the elements questioned by the inquisitors are excluded. Of course, this may be giving the inquisitors too much credit (and too much interpretive power), but even if her narrative as a whole is not representative of Sebastianism in all respects, it still reveals much about the beliefs that were represented by the *sebastianista* legend. We will return to a more detailed examination of how this case can help illuminate Sebastianism in the final section of this chapter, after turning to an issue that has been deliberately passed over until this time: the reception of Maria de Macedo's claims by the witnesses who testified in her case.

Another important reason that Maria de Macedo's case has historical interest is that her vision was accepted as a valid narrative by others. While Diogo Fernandes's claim that Maria's visions were being talked about throughout the city of Lisbon is an exaggeration, it highlights the important fact that her story found some sort of resonance among her contemporaries. At the point of its acceptance (or even its rejection) by others, her story ceased to be a construction of individual scope and became one that had social value among her contemporaries, which can, in turn, help us understand their values and beliefs.

The first witness in the case, Dr. António de Sousa de Macedo, can hardly be considered as someone distant from the elite ecclesiastical culture of Portugal, and so it should not be surprising that he anticipated the inquisitors' final decision that Maria was guilty of *fingimento* by some eight years. What, though, of the Jesuits of São Roque who were among her earliest listeners and supporters? The appeal of popular Sebastianism is quite clear in the case of Manoel da Costa, who, by his own admission, first came into contact with the rumors about Maria's voyages while "speaking casually about the things of King Sebastian" with Manoel Soares de Britto. The closeness of his account and the version of Maria's story found in the pamphlet, coupled with his admission that he had spoken with her many times about her voyages, is proof of his receptivity to what Maria was saying, and the fact that he, like Maria, emphasized the great piety of the inhabitants of the islanders may be a clue to the values that underlay his acceptance of her message. After making the rather incredible claim that he had not decided what his opinion of Maria's story was, he later admitted that he was inclined to believe her, interestingly saying that he was open to claims of "wondrous things" because of what he had read in Martin del Rio, the opposite reaction of the *qualificadores* who cited del Rio during the trial.[3]

Pedro Peixoto, despite his claims that his judgment of Maria's story was "suspenso," was clearly intrigued by the messianic figure of Sebastian and his purported role in the end times, and his fellow Jesuit Diogo Fernandes unabashedly stated that he believed that Maria's visions were truly from God. It is clear from his brief deposition that the utopian aspects of Maria's description of the Hidden Isle found a particular resonance with him. Manoel Soares de Britto, Feliciano's friend and the link to Manoel da Costa, was also impressed by the deep piety of the islanders and even said that the people of the island "followed the Law of Jesus Christ with greater observance than in Portugal." He, too, was inclined to believe Maria and said that he could see no motive for her to make the story up, since she had not benefited materially from it. The testimony of Maria's stepmother, Maria de Almeida, shows that she completely accepted her stepdaughter's claims about her experiences with the enchanted Moors and said she had never even considered the possibility that Maria had been making up her story. Unfortunately, the depositions of most of these witnesses reveal too little information to try to reconstruct their beliefs and values, and none of them provide the material to attempt the kind of comprehensive analysis we have attempted for Maria de Macedo. Still, traces of those beliefs and values can still be found in even the short texts of their depositions.[4]

Not all of these witnesses were completely credulous when they heard Maria's story. Pedro Peixoto tested Maria by asking her a question he thought Sebastian would know, and let us not forget the portrait of Sebastian he showed to her to find out if she had seen the same person on the island. Isabel de Britto believed Maria's story until Maria's prediction regarding when de Britto's husband would return home did not come true. Father João Ribeiro seems to have been truly undecided and said that "only God knew" whether what Maria was saying was true. While hardly up to inquisitorial standards of proof, these details demonstrate that millenarian claims about Sebastian (or anyone else) were not always accepted at face value in seventeenth-century Portugal.[5]

This point is even more clearly made when one looks at the witnesses who were dismissive of Maria's narrative. Bento Perreira (a *qualificador* for the Holy Office) refused to accompany Peixoto to hear Maria's story in person because he "did not believe in such things." Skepticism of Maria's claims was not confined to theologically educated figures associated with the Inquisition like Sousa de Macedo and Perreira; António da Costa, Feliciano's co-worker in the Treasury, testified that he had never tried to find out more about Maria's story, simply because that sort of thing did not interest him.[6] While his reaction is more properly described as indifference rather than skepticism, it still shows that there was a wide variety of responses to what Maria de Macedo had to say. And, taken as a whole, the testimony of the witnesses in this case shows that those responses cannot be easily broken down along class or gender lines in a consistent way.

While the fact that there was a range of responses—from complete credulity to outright rejection and several opinions in between—to Maria's claims is of some interest, even more significant are the reasons behind the varied reception of her story. Pedro Peixoto needed more evidence to believe Maria's account and ultimately said that he could not decide whether it was true, fabricated, or the result of an illusion by the devil. Bento Perreira not only did not believe in such tales but also said that it was unseemly that Maria's story included a lizard being transformed into a man. In an echo of what his fellow *qualificador* João Gomes would later argue, he said that he had never heard of a good angel appearing in such a form and the lizard's appearance in Maria's vision might be a sign of the devil's influence. Before admitting that he believed Maria's claims, Manoel da Costa said that he could not decide if it was a case of a true vision, an illusion of the devil, or *fingimento*. Similarly, João Ribeiro stated that he was unsure whether Maria was making her story up or whether it was all an illusion from the devil, though he added that she did not seem to be an impostor to him. The fact that Peixoto, da Costa, and Ribeiro cast their options in terms of the same tripartite schema used by the inquisitors is noteworthy.

But why should it be surprising that these Jesuit fathers were working with the same mental categories as the inquisitors? Were they not the product of a theological education along scholastic lines similar to that of the inquisitors themselves? Might the difference in responses to Maria's claims between the Jesuit believers and the inquisitorial skeptics be due to issues of an evidential rather than a theoretical nature? In other words, were the Jesuits and the inquisitors using the same set of mental categories to evaluate Maria and her story, with the difference in their responses stemming from the rather more generous interpretation of the evidence by the Jesuits compared with the suspicious inquisitors?

Quite possibly, though the difference in attitude toward the evidence needs to be explained. The most likely explanation is that the Jesuits of São Roque did not share the inquisitors' value of legalism. Since the Inquisition was primarily a judicial organization, a deep reverence for the concept of law and legal procedures was fundamental to its outlook and to its very identity. The same commitment to good legal procedure and high standards of evidence that made the inquisitors relatively skeptical of claims of witchcraft also made them suspicious of Maria's story. The Jesuits, however, especially those of São Roque, were a preaching order; they were in the business of communication and education rather than judgment. It should not be surprising, therefore, that the idea of law was considerably less central to their self-concept than in the case of the inquisitors. The fact that the Jesuits were members of a preaching order also meant they almost certainly had more normal social interactions with nonclerics than the inquisitors did and thus were probably more sympathetic to some popular beliefs. Manoel da Costa was "speaking casually about the things of King Sebastian" with Manoel Soares de Britto; it is hard to imagine any inquisitor doing so. And we have also seen that, by the 1660s, the Portuguese Jesuits had already had a long tradition of interest in messianic beliefs generally and in Sebastianism particularly, a point that may explain why some of the Jesuits of São Roque were so receptive to Maria's story.

Whatever the precise reason certain Jesuits were open to Maria's *sebastianista* claims, the evidence given above proves that the Jesuits involved in the case, whether they believed Maria or not, were working with mental categories that were very similar to those of the inquisitors. The most important common link between the Jesuits and the officials of the Inquisition was a background of education in scholastic theology, and the tripartite schema used by both the inquisitors and the Jesuits to evaluate Maria and her visions was scholastic both in structure (a discrete set of formal, authorized categories, and a final decision made by a deductive process of elimination) and in content (categories established by scholastic demonologists, theologians, and canon lawyers). Does, therefore, the use of the three options (and, therefore, of scholastic mental categories) indicate a cultural dividing point based on education? After all, this formal set of three categories never appears in the testimony of Manoel Soares de Britto, Isabel de Britto, or Maria de Almeida, none of whom, presumably, had received a theological education anything like that received by either the Jesuits or the inquisitors.

Although this may be a tidy division to make, it is not borne out by the testimony of the most important nonclerical witness in the case, Maria's husband, Feliciano Machado. Throughout his section of the pamphlet, he said that he attributed his wife's visions to "the Enemy of the Soul" and said it was "the most diabolical thing in the world." After hearing from João Penalvo that what his wife was saying was true, Feliciano remained unconvinced and even said that he took the whole thing to be "the illusion of the Demon." He did not finally believe that his wife's experiences were from God until he spoke to Sebastião de Paiva, who reassured him and said that Maria's visions could have been a gift from God. The important point to note here is that Feliciano was using the same three categories to judge his wife's claims that the inquisitors were.[7] It seems that, at first, he was very inclined toward the possibility that it was all a demonic illusion, accepting it as true only after receiving counsel from a respected religious authority. The last of the three options—fraud—does not appear explicitly in Feliciano's account, but it is still there. He almost certainly did not mention that possibility simply because he knew she was not faking it; after all, he was the principal witness of the trancelike state into which she would fall when she "traveled." Feliciano's failure to mention this possibility finds a parallel in the inquisitors' quick dismissal of the possibility that what Maria was saying was true. Both eliminated one of the three options available to them very quickly because they felt they had the evidence they needed to do so, but the elimination of that option did not change the basic parameters of how they evaluated Maria's case, either for the inquisitors or for Feliciano.

This shows that, at some time during his life, Feliciano heard and accepted some form of the scholastic/demonological view of special revelations. Unfortunately, since we are given no details of Feliciano's educational background, it is impossible to reconstruct how he came to accept this view. Although we cannot know the exact mechanism of transmission, this is clearly a case of a successful imposition of an elite ecclesiastical view on someone who was neither elite nor an ecclesiastic, at least on the relatively narrow point of the interference of the devil in human affairs. We know that Feliciano received this from above, simply because current scholarship suggests that, at the truly popular level in Portugal, visitations by supernatural beings (and magical occurrences more generally) were viewed with considerably more theological flexibility than was demonstrated by the inquisitors.[8] In other words, a variety of attitudes toward spiritual visitations were displayed at the popular level, whereas the inquisitors, for all intents and purposes, displayed one. Does this mean, then, that Feliciano had accepted the elite view of supernatural visitations without reservation? Probably not, since it seems that he did not have any difficulty accepting (eventually) the existence of enchanted Moors and he never made any connection between the zoomorphia of the enchanted Moors and the presence of the devil, as the inquisitors did.

The important point here is that Feliciano and all the witnesses who testified in the case were, like Maria herself, influenced by a wide variety of cultural trends, both from above and from below, a fact that complicates attempts to place any of the witnesses in a neat elite-popular pigeonhole. As Mikhail Bakhtin pointed out, the relationship between elite and popular culture was reciprocal and dynamic, with each influencing the other in ways that are sometimes hard to reconstruct.[9] This is particularly true because, as Maria de Macedo and the other people who appear in this case prove, the interaction between elite and popular cultural trends was taking place *within* single individuals, with each individual accepting, rejecting, modifying, or even combining elements of those trends according to his or her background, values, and social environment. We have seen that education did have an influence on the ways people approached Maria's claims, but even a background that included a scholastic theological education did not mechanically determine final judgments of Maria's story. This is all to say that the very categories of elite and popular culture are abstractions—often historically useful abstractions—but abstractions nonetheless.[10] With this in mind, it should always be remembered that the objects of history (or this history at least) are the people who experienced the past concretely, not abstractly, and that, if we wish to gain a truer insight of the past as real individuals lived it, they should be permitted to be inconsistent and hold beliefs of mixed cultural origin. This is not to say that searching for an underlying consistency in the views of individuals or groups is invalid, but it is rather a cautionary note that that consistency will more often be found in the realms of values held rather than propositions believed.

This holds true even in the case of the particular elite subculture we have examined, that of the inquisitorial officials themselves. João Gomes, for example, was open to the claims of the *sebastianistas*, unlike his fellow *qualificador* João de Deus, who dismissed their beliefs as nonsense; Inquisitor de la Cerda was more open to the possibility that Maria had made a pact with the devil than his fellow inquisitors were. These points prove that even the inquisitors themselves did not always hold exactly the same beliefs or follow the same thought patterns. The inquisitorial subculture did enjoy an important advantage in terms of the coherence of its worldview when compared with the most of the other subcultures of early modern Portugal, though, and this advantage is best exemplified by the closing statement of Gomes's *qualificação*, namely, that he would defer in all his opinions to the judgment of the Holy Office. It is this value of deference, not only to the authority of approved books but also to the authority of approved (and approving) institutions, that is a key to understanding the institutional subculture of the Inquisition. Gomes thought that Sebastian could have been alive, de la Cerda might have believed Maria was a diabolist, and Inquisitors Barreto and Castilho might have thought that Maria's crimes were so minor that the time she had spent in prison was sufficient punishment, but they all, in the end, deferred to the judgment of their superiors in the Conselho Geral. The opinions of individual officials may have been varied, but the Portuguese Inquisition spoke with one voice.[11]

The principal reason that Maria de Macedo's visions were received by others at all is that they were framed within an extant system of belief that was accepted by many of her contemporaries: Sebastianism. And although the Inquisition was ultimately indifferent to her beliefs about Sebastian, it is reasonable to say that had she not been a *sebastianista* she would not have come to the attention of the Holy Office, since considerably fewer people would have been interested in her story, and even fewer would have been concerned enough to bring her to the attention of the Inquisition. So what can Maria de Macedo's case reveal about the nature of Sebastianism in seventeenth-century Portugal? I believe that there are two significant ways in which this case, uniquely, can help us understand *sebastianismo*: by revealing the way in which the Holy Office viewed Sebastianism, and by providing a detailed case study of the values that underlay the reception of the faith in Sebastian's return.

The first way in which Maria de Macedo's trial record can help us understand *sebastianismo* is that it provides us with what are the clearest statements yet found regarding the Inquisition's attitude toward Sebastianiam. The basic attitude of the Holy Office can be found in the dismissive appraisal of the *qualificador* João de Deus: "In these matters about King Sebastian, we see even people of great judgment writing about and taking as an article of faith, the biggest bunch of nonsense one can imagine." Later, he described the *sebastianistas* as holding to "extravagant futilities" and rejected Maria's claims about Sebastian and the Hidden Isle as utter nonsense. Though they were less caustic in their language, the inquisitors seem to have held a similarly disdainful view of Sebastianism, referring to its adherents as those "vulgarly called *sebastianistas*." Using the same phrase, Maria's first defense counsel, Domingos Vieira de Santo, said that "the beliefs common among those vulgarly called *sebastianistas* are notorious in this kingdom as fantastic and without foundation, and which, for legitimate or illegitimate reasons, appeal to people of uncertain judgment." De Santo also argued that Maria should not be held responsible for speaking about Sebastian, since she had heard many learned ("doutos"), religious and grave people speaking about it. He contended that Maria, "as a woman, and so of weak judgment," could not have known that such talk may have involved suspect propositions. As has been noted, in their final decision in the case, the inquisitors downplayed the significance of Maria's *sebastianista* beliefs even more than her defense counsel had. "If she had only held to the beliefs of those vulgarly called *sebastianistas* . . . she would not have committed any crime that falls into the jurisdiction of this Holy Office." For a precedent-bound institution such as the Portuguese Inquisition, this was tantamount to saying that *sebastianismo* itself was not heretical.[12]

This is a somewhat odd conclusion given the heterodox flavor of even the elements the inquisitors listed, especially the belief that Sebastian would one day return to Portugal and the Joachimite and *bandarrista* provenance of the legend as a whole. The Inquisition gave Maria de Macedo a pass on her beliefs about Sebastian, as it seems to have done with the vast majority of *sebastianistas* during the seventeenth century. It is simply a (somewhat surprising) fact that there is no evidence that the Inquisition ever contemplated a general crackdown on the *sebastianista* movement in that period, and this requires an attempt at explanation.[13]

It is my belief that the inquisitors of Portugal did not think Sebastianism needed to be suppressed because they did not view it, however ill informed its tenets and speculations, as a danger to orthodoxy, to the activities of the Inquisition, or to the political status quo. As argued in chapter 6, much of the *sebastianista* movement had reached the peak of its political activism in the period beginning with the Alterações de Évora and ending with the Restoration of 1640. After the expulsion of the Castilians and the return of a native dynasty, it seems clear that most *sebastianistas* retreated into a stance of political passivity and fantasy, as exemplified by the introduction of the Hidden Isle into the legends about Sebastian within a few years of the Restoration. As a group waiting for the supernatural return of Sebastian in God's own time, they posed no real threat to the extant political or religious structure and so did not come under the suspicion of the Holy Office on that count.

Also, given the increasingly decisive influence of Dom João de Castro on the course of Sebastianism by the Restoration period, it is only to be expected that the *sebastianistas* of the time would have exhibited attitudes decidedly against the *conversos* and therefore in favor of the activities of the Inquisition. This conclusion is borne out by a number of *sebastianista* texts from the Restoration period.[14] It should, therefore, not be surprising that the inquisitors may have sensed that the *sebastianistas* were allies (uneducated allies, to be sure) in the great struggle that was their raison d'être: the campaign to suppress crypto-Judaism among the *conversos*. Perhaps the best way to prove this point is by way of contrast. The Inquisition certainly knew how to pick apart millenarianism (and millenarians) when those beliefs were used for goals that were contrary to the Inquisition's own, as its vigorous prosecution of Antonio Vieira demonstrates. So, in the end, perhaps the Inquisition never targeted the *sebastianistas* because they felt that, on the fundamental question of the *conversos*, they were all on the same side.

Whatever may, ultimately, be made of this possibility, Maria de Macedo's *processo* clearly demonstrates that the Holy Office in Portugal was not actively hostile, and may have even been guardedly sympathetic, to the *sebastianistas* as long as they did not stray into more heterodox territory. An exhaustive study of the social composition of the *sebastianista* movement remains to be done, but this evidence will have to play a part in any such study, since it reveals the attitude of the Holy Office toward that movement at an important moment in its evolution. This may, in turn, help explain at least one reason that Sebastianism was so long lived and enjoyed a greater degree of political success (if only in mobilizing Portuguese opinion against the Hapsburgs in 1637 and 1640) than most popular messianic movements did.

The second way in which the case of Maria de Macedo can help us better understand the *sebastianista* legend as a whole is by providing us with a concrete case study of not only the details of *sebastianista* belief but also of the values that informed those beliefs. No systematic study of the social composition of the *sebastianista* movement has yet been done, and as one who has looked into this issue, I can say the principal reason is a lack of source material on individual *sebastianistas* upon which to build any sort of detailed hypothesis. This is largely true because the judicial authorities of seventeenth-century Portugal, including the Inquisition, did not think the *sebastianistas* (in general) were worthy of investigation or prosecution and so kept relatively few records related to them. While undoubtedly a very good development for the *sebastianistas*, it does pose a considerable problem for historians trying to understand their historical legacy.

This is where a case like that of Maria de Macedo comes in. To quote Ginzburg and Poni again, "But the 'normal exception' can also have another meaning. If the sources are *silent about* or systematically distort the social reality of the lower classes, then a truly exceptional (and thus statistically infrequent) document can be much more revealing than a thousand stereotypical documents."[15]

I believe Maria de Macedo's case fits this definition of a "normal exception" as well. She is exceptional for the reason that she appears in the documentary record at all, and this was, of course, because there were aspects of her narrative that were both atypical of Sebastianism and disturbing to the inquisitors. But the fact that the inquisitors were ultimately rather uninterested that she believed in Sebastian's return or the existence of the Hidden Isle does not in any way diminish the fact that her *processo* is also a record of those beliefs. Given the relatively widespread silence on individual *sebastianistas* in the documentary record (as it is now understood), this fact alone makes her case worthy of historical interest.

There is another, perhaps more important way in which the case of Maria de Macedo is exceptional, and that is in terms of its level of detail and elaboration. There is so much material about Sebastianism (and other beliefs) in her trial record that it allows us to examine her worldview in a very thorough manner to see how elements of those beliefs were used and what they can tell us about the values that motivated her to believe in those traditions. This examination can, in turn, suggest the values that motivated the *sebastianista* movement as whole. For example, we can see that Sebastianism had an appeal well beyond urban artisans—as we might be tempted to conclude on the basis of only a synthetic, statistical approach to studying messianism—not only in case of Maria de Macedo herself (who had strong artisan roots) but among educated functionaries like her husband and his friend Manoel Soares de Britto, among the theologically trained Jesuits, and even for one official of the Inquisition itself, João Gomes.

Maria's case also sounds a cautionary note against viewing the phenomenon of *sebastianismo* with an attitude of socioeconomic reductionism. While Sebastianism had its roots in social and economic distress, in Maria's case it was not social or economic distress but probably psychological turmoil of an individual nature that gave first the legends of the enchanted Moors and, only later, *sebastianismo* appeal in her eyes. Although socioeconomic problems and inequities almost certainly provided the primary impetus for the development of a belief in an intermediate messiah like Sebastian, they probably played only a limited role in Maria's life; after all, as the daughter of a skilled craftsman and the wife of a royal bureaucrat, she probably was not doing too badly in a material sense. Thus, while socioeconomic factors may explain the origin of messianic beliefs, they do not always explain its reception by individuals.

To be sure, we will never understand what drove thousands of people over a period of several decades to believe that Sebastian was the Hidden One to the same degree that we can now understand why Maria de Macedo was a *sebastianista*. Nor is it particularly likely that, to take another example, most of the *sebastianistas* viewed Catholicism primarily in terms of orthopraxy because they had a deep need to experience their religious faith by interior devotion, contemplation, prayer, and fasting as Maria de Macedo did. Maria's example cannot tell us that about other *sebastianistas;* it can, however, suggest the values that may have motivated some of them, for, if it is certain that not all *sebastianistas* shared the same values, it is equally certain that they shared many.

There is one final reason that Maria de Macedo's case is of historical interest. Even if there were no other reasons, Maria's case file would be an exceptional document because it contains copies of the pamphlet she dictated to her husband. In that pamphlet we have an almost unique opportunity to hear a popular voice without any mediation by an elite institution. Admittedly, Maria de Macedo did not fit the stereotype often evoked by the term "popular voice." It is certain, however, that her pamphlet did contain distinct and authentic echoes of popular beliefs, and through that remarkable document we can hear, in an unusually clear way, that voice. Perhaps, in the end, this study has contributed something to historical understanding by simply allowing Maria de Macedo to speak for herself.

APPENDIX
Transcription of Maria's Pamphlet

Author's note: As indicated for the translation in chapter 3, the text of the original, shorter version is followed here and is given preference when there are minor differences of word order or vocabulary. Passages found only in the long version are denoted by the use of braces { }; the few sentences found only in the short version are denoted with angle brackets < >. Parentheses ( ) are used when they were used in the original text or when they would be in English usage. Italics indicate letters inserted to expand the numerous contractions in the original. Brackets [ ] are used for all editorial additions and comments, with those of a more speculative nature noted by a reference to the translator (myself). Ellipses and illegible words and passages are denoted by a dash—and a question mark in parentheses (?).

COUSAS
ADMIRAVEYS Q' SUCCEDERAM
A

MARIA D'MACEDO
de cujo principio dâ prim.^{ro}

húa breve noticia; &
depoys a dâ (inda que
nam de tudo) mays
ao extensum seu
Marido

FELICIANO MA
Chado

Lx^{a} 12 de mayo do anno de 1658.

(page I)

Em o mez de Novembro de mil seiscentos trinta e cinco senti me apalpavão de noyte na cama, sendo neste t'po de dez para onze annos de idade, e com o grande temor q' tinha gritava inquietando a meu pay e toda a caza sem ver algue,' nem quem me apalpava. Considerando meu Pay, q' isto seria imaginacão minha, me mandou deixar de noyte candea aceza, e me levou *para* sua cama, aonde nem sentia entender comigo, porem ouviram na caza grandes inquietações. E tornado en huã noyte *para* a minha cama q' estava aos peés da de meu Pay, com candea aceza, acabando de sonhar q' me levarão a hu' campo, a onde me mostravam muita variedade de arvores e flores, vy ao lado de minha cama hum bicho q' pelo conhecim*iento* q' depois tive, e ao diante refirirei, era hu' lagarto grande q' entam por não saber o q' era, de me Representou ser a figura d' hu' cão, inda q' lhe nam descubri os pez, e aos grandes gritos q' dei acodio meu pay, perguntandome o q' tinha e mostrandolhe eu aquelle bicho e a mais gente de caza elles o não vião. E tornandome meu pay a levar para sua cama, agastandose de q' eu o inquietava e era insofrivel a vida q' de noute lhe dava me disse q' me havia de deitar por sua ianella fora, se me não aquietame e tratasse de desterrar de min a immaginação q' me cauzava todos estes medos, e recolhido na mesma noute depois de estar dormido com os braços de fora de roupa, lhe derão huã panquada tam grande em hu' q' dahy a *muitos* dias o não sentio.

Logo na noute segu*in*te me apareceo a mesma figura, E como tornei a gritar

(page IV)

com o temor q' tinha, se queixava cada vez mais meu pay de min dizendome havia de castigar neste interin ouvimos logo grande reboluço na caza quebrandosese quanta louça nelle havia para cujo effeito nos apaguarão por duas vezes a candea; E p*e*la manhã se achou somente huã quarta quebrada, E toda a mais louça espalhada por hu' almario donde estava descomposta e fora de seu lugar.

Vendo meu pay q' os temores se me continarão E desconolação em q' vivia tratou de dar conta de tudo a homens doctos e Religiosos como foi a frei nicolau dos anjos, Frei Manoel Falcão, Frei Thomas de villanova, todos da ordem de S*anto* Agostinho; E a outros de Nossa S*enhora* do Carmo q' todos me confessarão E examinarão minha vida a quem se relatou todo occazo, E depois de confessada me derão m*ui*tas reliquias esconjurando a caza, sem couza alguã ser bastante para deixar de me não apparecerem as mesmas figures. E como a penna e tormento em q' vivia fosse tal qual se deixa considerar p*e*la variedade e incerteza com q' muitas pessoas falarão nesta material, o q' a cada hu' lhe parecia sem remedio de me evitar o damno dos temores tratou meu pay mudarse destas cazas para outras, junto as as Lazazo q' para este effeito alugou; por parecer de alguãs pessoas por vez se cessavão os aparecimentos, inda q' não a cauza q' era minha, mudandonos *para* novas cazas, em q' estivemos dous mezes me não appareçeo nellas couza alguã, supposto se sentia e ouvia sempre andar na caza de noute alguã couza

(page 2)

E em huã occazião aq*uel* dia fiquei sô, sobindo a huã caza de sima ouvy huã vox q' me disse, aqui te colho eu agora a minha vontade, e pondo me as mãos nos peitos, sem eu ver quem, me deitou pela escada abaixo, de q' fiquei tam maltratada q' nem a porta podia abrir a meu pay quando veyo: nem responderlhe por não poder falar, E tornando por largo espaço de tempo sobre min, lhe dei conto do q' me havia succedido.

Neste *tempo* q' era no mez de mayo de seiscentos trinta e seis, succedeo vir de Castella huã tia minha por nome de Pelonia deAlmeida irmãa de minha may para caza de meu pay, como viviamos todos, se lhe deu conta do principio de meu succeso; E Fazendo esta minha tia grandez dilig*encias* por ver se podia alcançar o q' isto era, lhe não pode dar alcançe. E depois de me fazer grandes inquirições, e meu pay me levar a alguãs novenas a santos E a huã q' minha may havia prometido quando morreo, q' não havia dado cumprim*ento* e eu o fez por ella, me disse esta tia, q' não achava que isto pudesse ser, senão mouros encantados, por se não abzentarem com as cousas sagradas, E reliquias q' eu trazia, nem outros exorcismos q' se fizerão; perguntandome mais se me aparecera alguã destas figures com barrette vermelho, ao q' lhe respondi q' [a]the aquelle *tempo* o não tinha visto; sem embargo de q' me animou esta tia m*ui*to dizendome não tivesse temor de nada E q' quando outra vez me appareçece q' lhe dissesse o q' queria de min, suposto eu o fazia ia no principio abracada com hu' Christo em nunca me differirem, porem não deixei de ficar mais aliviada como o q' esta tia me

(page 2v)

disse por me asegurar q' não era couza inimiga dalma o q' me apparecia, E q' sendo mouros encantados, como ella entendia serem, me poderia rezultar delles grandes bens.

E logo na noute seg*ui*nte forão ter commigo a cama de noute, e me pegarão em huã mão apertandomem*ente*; e como ja estava mais soçegada do animo, p*el*o q' esta tia me havia ditto, não gritei como costumava, supposto me acompanhava grande temor. E a outro dia estando meu pay em sua caza (q' supposto alugou ao em q' me tinha não largou as em q' de antes estava porq' nellas trabalhava de dia) immaginando na desconsolação em q' vivia por ter duas cazas dividias, lhe disserão em huã vox q' ouvio sem ver alguem: vente para tua caza; o q' logo no mesmo dia a noute fez trazendome bem contra minha vontade p*el*o temor q' eu nellas tinha mayorm*ente* por se me continarem nellas mais os appariçementos.

Em tudo o discurso deste tempo q' (como atras hei referido) forão dous mezes, me não deixarão os Religiosos de asistir sempre como de antes E da noticia q' tiverão de q' dizião serem mouros encantados o fizerão a saber algu's delles ao seu provincial de nossa Senhora da graça q' então era parente da caza de Aveiro por nome o qual mandou chamar a capitulo, sobre o cazo, para so se saberse poderia haver mouros encantados ou não, e como as suprestições sejão todas contra nossa sancta fee, E não contasse haver tal, foi

(page 3)

a questão vintilada de feição q' quazi todos concordarão entre milhares de duvidas q' tal não podia haver E so hu' religiozo trouxe hu' livro de q' constava poder haver encantos entre os mouros.

E sendo chegada a minha antiga caza em q' este successo se me principiou me buscarão logo em huã noute apalpandome como de antes E perguntando eu o q' me queria a quem me apalpava, me respondeo se me queria levantar da cama aoq' eu disse q' sy: e o fez pegando lhe no vestido q' a meu parecer era de chamalote de seda, E levandome para huã ianella da caza vi hu' homen moreno de rosto, cabello louro e crespo, pintado de branco, de boa estatura, vestido a turquesca, com barrette vermelho, alfarje e botas atamaradas e esporas E todos os mais adereços o qual me disse porq' tinha temor, se me não fazia mal algu,' E eu lhe respondi q' se soubera, quem era q' não teria medo E q' a culpa era sua pois se me não havia discuberto mais sedo; E tornandome a dizer q' isso ia não aproveitava pois era passado, me perguntou se queria eu ira donde elle me levasse, e por eu ver seu disignio e intento lhe Respondi q' sim e Levandome então a hu' canto da caza, se abrio huã porta na parede q' eu claramente vy, sem ali estar porta alguã, E elle se passou da outra parte Ficando eu de dentro em minha caza, E de la me mostrou huã carrinha de ouro, errindosse me deu com a mão me voltasse; o q' eu logo fiz, E pelo discurso de alguãs noutes seguintes, continuo isto mesmo, mostrandome cada noute hu' brinco daquelles, de differente feitio sem eu nunca passar da caza de meu pay, porq' somente passava pela porta q' se abria E

(page 3v)

se punhada de parte de fora mostrandome os ditos broncos e nesta forma E continuação se passarão sete noutes. E na ultima dellas me perguntou o q' eu havia ceado, E dizendolhe eu q' huãs sardas, me fez queixa porq' lhe não guardara da minha çea? E dando eu de tudo conta a meu pay; ordenou deixar lhe todos as noutes q' comer como era biscouto quiejo, azeitonas, vinhos, e do mais q' em caza se comia, E se lhe buscarão couzas separadas como doces e regallos ou outras das q' senão comião em caza, lhe não tocava nem comia nada; E a meza se lhe punha iunto da cama de meu pay; o q' le a mais gente da caza ouvia estar commendo e falando commigo, depois de meu pay estar na cama e a caza recolhida, mas eu somente ovia e outrem não.

Isto se me continuo [a]the vespora de são João Bauptista de seiscentos trinta e seis em q' este mesmo homen me disse se querria eu hir hu' dia com elle para huã caza de sima q' então meu pay tinha de vazio, e por ser de dia lhe disse q' sim, Respondeome q' levasse commigo a minha merenda, o q' fiz como o q' meu pay me deu q' foi hu' pastel, pão, fruta, e outras couzas q' deixo por não parecer superflua: Estando pois na dita caza sentada iunto de huã ianella esperando q' este mouro viesse vi na caza hu' lagarto q' vinha para min dando saltinhos, E chegado donde eu estava rodeadome toda, me pos a cabeça no regaço olhando para min, a que eu não sem falta de temor (inda q' muito menos do costumado pela experiencia q' ia tinha como pelo q' me offereçi) pus a mão pela cabeça

(page 4)

E em lha pondo se transformou mediatamente no mesmo mouro q' de antes havia visto, E depois de commezemos a merenda q' eu havia levado, me disse se queria eu hir a sua caza; E como hia ja aliviando o temor peloq' te aquele tempo havia passado com elle aceitei o offerecimento q' me fez, supposto não sem grande reçeo porq' inda q' havia passado com elle todo o referido, era em caza de meu pay, E la na sua não sabia o q' me succederia, porem como o meu pensamento e discurso nesta material atribria todo a nosso senhor; vendo q' não havia solicitado modos ou meyo algu' per nehuã via, para este cazo, nem tratado com pessoas q' a elle, nem a outros me persuadissem por ser naquelle tempo grande a minha innocençia me rezolui ir com elle em dia de são João Bauptisita da dita era de 1636.

Na caza q' hei referido donde estão, em hu' canto della, q' ficava na direita da de baixo, se me abrio a mesma porta q' tinha visto na de baixo. E comandome o dito mouro pela mão, passei atras delle livremente E depois de ter passado a porta, fomos andando por huã escada pelo baixo e acabada ella, por hu' corredor q' pouco mais ou menos teria de cumprimento quinze varas: E acabado elle entrei em huã caza grande e Fermoza q' constava de sete ianellas, rasguadas em areos, tres para o Mar q' estava iunto della E quarto para a terra as paredes de liza pedra e lavrado, E o terreno lageado da mesma pedra, E por huã das ianellas se deçia por huã escada de pedra larga q' hia ter a hu' iardin q' tinha muitas ervas, como era alecrin, man-

(page 4v)

manjerona, salva, rozas, e hua fonte onde costumei sempre buscar agoa pelo discurso de quinze annos como adiante Referirei, E logo se seguião mais sinco cazas, não tam grandes como a primeira, mas lavradas da mesma pedra e festro E da ultima dellas seguia outra escada em caracol q' tinha cento ointenta e sete degrãos q' hia dara huã sala muito grande da mesma pedra aquel tinha sinco mesas de jaspenegro; huã grande no meyo da dita sala, E as outras quarto cada huã a seu canto. Debaixo de todas estas cazas estevão tres corredores cumpridos muito fundos escuros donde andava hu' galo tam grande como hu' perû q' não tinha crista mas barbas muy cumpridas aos quaes corredores la chamão Alminas; não tinhão estes lus alguã mais q' a que se vinha de huã porta q' ficava iunto do mar, donde lhe vinha alguãs varidade mas como erão cumpridos, a pennas se via couza alguã nelles, senão fosse co' candea, inda q' fosse de dia; o mar q' destas casas seria seria tam largo como o desta cidade à Almadar, E da outra banda se vião cazas e terra.

Chegada pois com o mouro a primeira caza q' hei referido achei a sua mulher de boa estatura e fermoza com hu' menino nos braços e outro de peé E o mouro lhe disse por min, aqui te trago a nossa christaã, dizme o q' te pareçe? E ella lhe respondeo q' folgava de me ver, ainda q' queixoza de min, por eu ter tam grande medo, mas q' os poucos annos me disculpavão. E

(page 5)

me pedio tivesse muito cuidado daquele homen q' era seu marido q' não era para nehu' mal meu, pedindome mais lhe prometesee pela minha Ley de o servir em tudo o q' elle me mandasse, ainda q' tivesse alguã molestia. E eu lhe disse q' assy o faria; E q' ella viera aly so por me ver, aquele dia e q' me mostrava aqueles meninos q' erão seus filhos, dizendome se os queria eu trazer para , ao q' eu lhe respondi q' para a minha terra não podia eu trazer hu's senhores tam grandes como elles mais q' para os servir porq' o pay q' me havia levado me tinha dito q' era muito fidalgo, e q' o tittulo q' tinha na sua terra era como ser duque nesta nossa, E perguntandome mais se me parecia bim ou se na minha terra erão as mulheres mais fermozas? Lhe disse q' ella o era muito; E q' tambem na minha havia alguãs; E com isto me pos a mão pelo rosto e se despidio de min com grandes recommendações do marido; o quel me tornou a trazer me pós em caza de meu pay pelo mesmo caminho por onde fomos.

E dahy por diante me veyo sempre buscar o mesmo marido huãs vezes de noute outras de dia, pelos mesmos termos q' o fez a primeira vez E de cada vez q' eu la hia via mais huã pessoa; ese forão multiplicando [a]the chegarem a numero de trinta e seis; onze mulheres e os demais homens todos hu's e outros vestidos a turquesca E todos iuntos no Ultimo dia em q' me acabarão de {de conhecer,} descubrirme, festejarão muito; e com grande alegria, E ficando en suspenssa de ver tanta gente me disserão q' me não

(page 5v)

enfadasse nem intristicesse q' para min era melhor serem muitos; os nomes dos não direi aqui todos {os nomes de todos nam irei declarar} por se nomearem per Familias; mas os que soube e lhe ouvia chamar erão os seguintes: Fatima, Arlaxa, Gumelia, Zygres, Guazules, Bençarrages, Benamares, Murças: Amet E Dyalees, Villaron, Jazemin, Muleyneque, Dianêa, a Real Zygre q' era a primeira moura ou digo Turqua de nação q' me veyo esperar como os senhores q' hey referido.

E depois disto passado e elles discubertos commerçarão de fazer cada qual varias figuras de bichos como erão serpentes, lagartos, sereas, cavallos marinhos, leões e outras diversidades de (animães e) bichos de q' não tenho conhecimento; e nestas Figuras me apparecião em caza de meu pay, E vinha cada dia huã pessoa destas nas sobredittas figures [a]the que todos acabarão aquella e ella acabada representavão outra com o q' me cauzarão grande temor e chegandosse a min, se transformavão logo na pessoa q' era a qual eu depois logo conheçia; advirtindo q' supposto tomarão (todas) as ditas figuras nunca transformavão os olhos nem os mudarão em forma alguã por sempre E erão os mesmos de criaturas humanas e os propios de cada hum delles e he isto tanto assy q' muitas vezes antes de se me descubrirem conhecia eu muitas vezes a pessoa q' vinha naquela forma somente pelos olhos por nunca ja mais os contrafazerem.

Acabada pois toda esta diversidade e laberintho q' foi grande

(page 6)

E durou por largo tempo me levarão aos corredres de baixo escuros aquelles chamarão Alminas, como atras hei referido, e me fazião cavar a terra donde tiravão muita riqueza como era ouro e prata E pedraria de toda a sorte e isto em grande cantidade fazendo do ouro e prata moeda q' forjarião E batião, e me fazião servir igoalmente com elles em todo o ministerio necessario; alem de lhe hir todas as noutes buscar agoa á Fonte q' esta no iardin; E passados dous annos pouco mais ou menos de continuar neste exerçiçio {(de ir bsucar esta augaa)} me disserão se queria eu ver o seu Rey? E dizendo lhe eu q' sim, me levarão a ultima sala de sima q' era a q' tinha tres mesas, digo sinco mesas, q' atras referi; ao qual achei acompanhado de muita gente demais das 36 pessoas q' me tinhão apareçido; e lhe chamarão Realmurça e a mais gente era toda de authoridade E respeito; assy nos trajes como nas persongens, E este primeiro q' me appareceo a primeira vez se chamava Bencerrage mayor e a mulher a Real Zygre os quaes me apresentarão ao Rey dizendo q' visee sua Realeza a christan q' o servia q' me chamava Maria, e o Rey me festeiou muito dizendo folgava de me ver e perguntandome se me fazião alguma mal e respondi q' não ser diligente {supposto que q' algumas vezes} no q' me mandavão fazer e me occupavão; e me encommenou he não faltasse a couza alguã do q' aquela gente me ordenasse q' elle se obrigava a tudo me ser bem satifeito. = Depois de toda a riqueza

(page 6v)

tirada da terra donde estava mandou o Rey fazer partilhas della pondo em lugar dividido o q' lhe pareçeo dizendo era para min, e depois de tudo isto iunto e posto per ordem, asisti sempre a todo o servicio E trecho {tratdo} daquela gente em todo o q' me mandavão per discurso de quatorze annos.

O exerçiçio desta gente era cantar, iugar, e dançar em seus passatempos E trabalhar quando era necessario no q' tenho dito, vivendo pela maneira seguinte no particular dos mantimentos cujo comer era pão, Carne, vinho pouco, carne de porco e Fructas: os Trajes todos a turquesca E nehu' escrupulo me fez nunca sua vida contra a nossa sancta Fee catolica por que la vy a nossa Senhora, o menino Jesus, são Joseph, e nosso Senhor Cruxificado e a elles ouvia sempre falar em Deos e em couzas suas, dizendo se havião de fazer christãos E perguntando me per alguãs vezes, se vendo os eu na minha terra os conheceria? Lhe respondi q' sy; e nesta conformidade vivi e asisti com esta gente [a] the Mayo de seiscentos e sincoenta annos asistindolhe sempre todas as noutes e muitas vezes de dia sem deixarem de me vir buscar não sendo bastante estar por sua vez sangrada treze vezes porq' assy me levarão E em quanto estava doente me não desacompanharão alguãs daquelas pessoas, q' eu somente via em caza de meu pay mas não outrem alguem de caza, e estas infirmidades e doenças se me cauzavão muitas vezes do grande trab=

(page 7)

Trabalho q' com elles tinha, no serviço q' me mandavão fazer por não ser costumada a elle e assy me dava grandissima penna principalmente nas noutes de inverno de q' vinha tam maltratada q' muitas vezes me não podia bulir tres e quarto diaz sem isto ser bastante para me escuzarem de continuar este trabalho.

Em este tempo q' era em septembro cazei com Feliciano Machao meu marido a vinte sete do dito mez de seiscentos quarenta e nove E por reçear q' elle me poderia achar menos da cama me foi forcozo dar lhe conta do principio deste meu successo, q' athe ty(?) elle o não sabia, porq' me não acontecesse algu' dezastre innocentemente E o mayor tormento q' tive foi o manifestarlho pela incredulidade q' teve sempre neste particular para commigo, sem nunca me dar credito dizendome q' tal couza como esta não podia haver na vida nem o havia ouvido, visto, nem lido, nem somente q' tal disesse e finalmente forão tantas as experiencias q' fez sobre este particular q' a elle me reporto para daqui por diante o poder referir sem testemunho e verdade de tudo o q' hey referido me asiney aqui como tambem na Rellação q' o dito meu marido ao diante faz e do q' passou commigo por tudo assym ser e pasar na verdade, escrevendo o elle somente por lho eu dizer pedindo a nosso Senhor pois foi servido permitirme q' hei

(page 7v)

relatado, oseja tambem para q' o mundo o veja e conhecia para mais seu santo serviço E louvor, e para então me acreditarem minha verdade. Lxa 29 de septembro de seiscentos E sincoenta annos.

Maria de Macedo

Seria superfluidade grande (supposto acção corioza) querer referir por menor o q' Maria de Macedo minha mulher me ha deixado a meu cargo para escrever sobre a particular q' ha representado e de q' ha feito menção para q' o Ceo (confio) a elegeo, mas por não cair na culpa q' os coriozos me podião dar deixando passar por alto material tam grave aos mais doctos e de grande averiguação tomo este piqueno trabalho (inda q' para min penoso pelas rezões q' ao diante mostrarey) em q' darei conta e razão summaria, de minha experiencia e do q' por ella pude alcançar sobre esta material com todo o trabalho e cuidado com que a solicitey; de 27 de 7bro de [1]649 por diante em q' cazei com a dita minha mulher.

Tendo pois cazado de poucos dias me deu conta do q' atras ha escrito, com huã lus tam escura q' a penna dava claridade a nehuã intelligencia, por recear declarasse commigo em cauza de tanto

(page 8)

porte e dificil, como para min pobre de credito; E pela corozidade de saber o q' a dita minha mulher me propunha lhe facilitei tudo o q' me dezia pela animar a não me encubrir nada como fez: E ouvido de min todo o principio de seu successo confesso perante nosso Senhor q' o considerei pelo maior dano e pouca Fortuna minha do mundo todo por huãs vezes o atribui ao inimigo dalma q' a perseguiria e tentaria por este meyo E outras a embuste seu, E em milhares de pensamentos e discursos q' me a tormentarão, não tomava asento em couza alguã, porq' para engano lhe sabia a vida e experimentava o tracto, vendola livre e retirada de todas as converssões q' me podião dar occazião (q[do] as tivesse) a ter differente conceito della e para couza Fantastica e diabolica, lhe não via sinal q' o mostrasse, Finalmente me Rezolvi ao experimentar pelo q' o communicarse com o meu confessor e outras pessoas doctas fingindome sempre alegre e contente, por lhe não dar occaião a me encubrir algu' requizito, se mais tivesse q' me dizer e torno a verificar q' muitas vezes me vy quazi com o iuizo perdido por vez q' de tudo o q' me dezia não achava aprovação para a nossa sancta fee catholica, E parecerem mais suprestições, q' premissão Divina.

E rezoluto huã noute me pus alerta sem dormir (suposto o fingi) e senti q' me apalpavão levemente pelos hombros, e pescoço {levemente}; pareçendo

(page 8v)

pareçendome q' a forca me estavão influindo sono pelos olhos porem eu me não descuidei; e dahy a couza de huã hora se levantou minha mulher da cama, E porq' eu lhe havia dito dantes q' quando a viessem buscar me chamasse, por ver se assy o fazia e ella mo haver prometido vy q' nehu' cazo fez de min nem do q' eu lhe havia encommendado, com o q' logo fiquei mui descontente por considerar q' devia ir fora de seu iuizo, e transportada com tudo sentindo a fora da cama, me pus sentado nella, E ouve clarissimamente Falar, sem ver com quem, nem menos a ella, por estaremos sem lux. E perguntando lhe a pessoa com quem falava; o q' eu fazia, lhe respondeo minha mulher q' eu dormia; E aquela vox q' eu com ella ouvy falar, lhe disse as palavras seguintes nesta forma: non durme, nem durmio, E depois disto estiverão falando couza de meyo de quarto de hora o q' eu não entendi por ser summissa a voçe como tambem, por aquela vox q' eu ouvia ser chacoca meyo castelhano {meyo portuguez} serrado e tosto escuro a maneira de mouro, e vindosee depois a dita minha mulher para a cama lhe fiz queixa por q' me não chamara quando foi, pois eu a tinha advertido para o fazer e me respondeo q' aquela pessoa com quem havia falado era huã moura encantada das trinta e seis pessoas q' ia estão {ficam} referidas E q' ella não quizera consentir q' a dita minha mulher me chamasse, porq' sabia q' eu estave açordado. E na verdade asy era

(page 9)

E desta vez não levou consigo. Na noute seguinte fez o mesmo q' na passada E sentindo q' minha mulher se levantava da cama me pus {outra vez} sentado nella a ver o disignio q' levava e immaginando q' não seria ainda partida me detive por espaço de meya hora e indo me saindo para ver se a achava menos da caza q' era o fin porq' so fazia esta experiencia a senti na caza e perguntandolhe o q' fazia, ou porq' rezão e cauza se levantava da cama, me respondeo, q' fora buscar agoa a sua gente {a huã fonte}; E como não sabia quando partio se eu ficava dormindo ou acordado lhe perguntei; q' tempo gastou em vir buscar depois q' partira o q' me disse q' lhe pareçia haver gastado tres horas. E nisto conheçi quam alhea estava da verdade e q' era falsso porq' quando partio havia da de meya noute e a dita, e as q' fez poderia ao muito ser da meya hora sobre a dita com o q' fiquei mui duvidozo e pouco contente vendo q' me não disseria a preposto nem ao certo do q' havia passado, como desta vez não pude conseguir o q' dezejava q' era saber se a achava menos da caza ou se hia corporeamente ou invizivel ou se se na caza se lhe reprezentava tudo a quillo de q' me dava conta tratei de lhe dizer q' pedisse licença aos seus mouros, para q' huã vez somente me deixassem ir la come ella quando a levassem; ou ao menos me conçedessem podela ver ir, e isto fundado na desconfiancia, q' tinha vendose por este meyo podia alcançar alguã circunstancia, palavra ou obra q' ouvesse, perq' concorresee nisto algu' pacto com ella

(page 9v)

mandarão me responder por ella q' não fosse tam coriozo q' não convinha nem me importava nada o querelo saber am o q' (de novo) me acrescerão mayores desconfianças de minha mulher considerando q' isto era couza Fantastica por me fechar os portos a toda a experiencia q' pretendia fazer. E não me constava certeza alguã mais q' por sua confissão della. E vivendo assy neste desconsolação q' sô Deos nosso senhor deixo o encarecimento de quam grande era por boas palavras e amigavelmente tratei de significar (a dita minha mulher) as duvidas e escrupulo q' isto trazia consigo e se me offerecião Nesta materia inquirindo ha do tempo q' se lembrava ter uzo de razão de vita et moribus dizendolhe para este effeito o q' me pareceo E q' meu juizo pode alcancar por muitas vezes, como se fosse seu confessor, reprezentandolhe a sçiençia e sagacidade do Demonio quam grande era, como a todos os {com seus} meyos por onde a poderia enganar trazendolhe muitos exemplos de seus ardins e velhacarias, todos a fin de nos fazer perder fiando tambem della q' pelas razões q' tinhamos de amizade E bem cazados, excepta a obrigacão do Matrimonio me não encubriria couza alguã nem se queriria perder. E pela rellação q' me fez de palavra de seu tracto e costumez não achei nella couza a alguã q' perjudicasse a nossa digo a sua salvação. Dizendome q' nesta materia se

(page 10)

lhe não haver offerecido couza alguã contra a nossa Sancta Feé Catholica e q' nem confessores lha achavão dezendolhe somente q' isto era immaginação sua, q' se tirasse della.

{8.v.} {Neste meyo tempo estando eu tangendo huã noyte com huã guitarra, me disse minha mulher, quiexe como tangia porq' tinha bom ouvinte; E perguntando lhe eu quem era? Me Respondeo q' aquele Mouro q' primeiro lhe apparecoa a quem ella sempre chamava Rabam; E acabando eu de tanger, sem fazer caso da nova alguã nem lhe dar credito, indo na—erem lá acrayxa aquistanao de bayxo de hum escritorio a huã figura de homen pequena de comprimento de hum corado, a qual se foy me de bayxo de huã escada; deycia se—(como q[do] hua nuvem vai correndo com grande ligeyza pelo ar) à qual figura nam vi o Rosto por me mostrar virão aquelas costas, cuyo vestido}

{9} {tam—a elle melhava comprio e verder escuro; E logo a outro dia me disse minha mulher q' o Mouro lhe dicera q' me quizera apparecer para q' eu me dezenganasse de minha desconfiança; Porem elegeo a sua intenta tam dezacertado meyo, q' cada vez mays m' aumenta mayor incredulidade como ao dinate Referey, com as Resões q' me mos verem para mays poser lhe dar credito verdadeiro nam seguir a opposiam q' muitas pessoas seguiam neste cazo crendo tam verdadeiramente nella nelle, como se Deos nosso Senhor no le deyxandm de fe, com discursos Raseyos e como accao depoys experimentey.}

{Depoys disto a meia noyte (estava com minha mulher na cama) huã luz q' andava pela caza; E a claridade q' dava era como os Rayos de hum diamante grande; E perguntado lhe o q' aquillo era? Me disse se aquella pessoa q' a vinha buscar a qual me disse trazia sempre consigo huã pedra de vilou(?) no peyto q' era donde estava(?) aquella luz, com a qual estam o caminho; por donde hiando; E esta—(?) eu muitas vezes sem fazer caso della pela continuação nem me dar cuidado alguem;—de padecer grandessima desconçolação pelo q' minha mulher me dezia sem lha dar a entender, pos alcanzar o q' esta material dava de sy(?): fazendome e—lição dos 14 annos; q' a ditta minha mulher ha relatado onde—tratado—deste Mouro.}

(Mas como a misericordia divina não falta nunca a quem della se val nem obstante o ser tam grande pecado per Christo nosso senhor por sua imensa bondade, e clemencia q' isto tomasse termo neste meyo tempo do meu mayor dozaescego com q' eu tratei expressamente da a averiguar em deste cazo; multiplicar do se me nelle de feycam as—vidas pelo meyos e modos que as diante direy q' Deos bastaria pela muito obrigaram a escrevello como

{9v} {faço alem de desgraça a fez—e foy desta maneira seguinte.

Sendo este cazo de minha mulher sabido por algumas pessoas desta cidade q' tinham noticia; q' ella tratava com mouros encantados, succedeu em o mez de Mayo de [1]650 vim hum homem por nome Joam Penalvo; dizer a meu sogro q' no bayrro d'Alfama E e era hua muler por nome de D. Maria Lisboa, q' tinha hum netto d' El Rey D. Sebastião. E os Mouros com quem minha mulher ha era continuando todos 14 annos era o mesmo Rey D. Sebastião e sua gente à qual ulhamos(?) nacser encuberto de bayxo de signio de elleiçam e q' elle sabia isto ser certo por ter huã cunhada por nome de D. Luiza de Portugal q' tambem corria com o mesmo Rey e gente, com quem minha mulher o fazia, dizendo q' toda a façiam era—}

{Vendo eu escutindo esta inforem babilonica e laberinto de—me(?) considerem(?) pelo Mays errado Diabolico do mundo, e q' nelle podia Penão(?); E tratey com a dita minha mulher de das muito de tocante ào Santo Officio; fomos a mesa(?) de parecer q' decais(?) em cazo de tanta importancia precless(?) toda a verdadeira experiencia e a certeza q' ser pudesse alem da approvacam de nosso Confessor para com toda a clareza e fundamento se poder Resolver muy facilmente aquella podia ser(?). E fazendo eu diligencia—averiguaçam de tem Razões incognito cazo solicitey todos os meyos para conhecer o dito João Penalvo, D. Luiza de Portugal sua cunhada e D. Maria Loba das quays pessoas nem(?) outro tempo eu nam tinha algum conhecimento nem algum podellas haver para q' tal pudessem dizer, pelas contradições e variedades q' estas couzas cauzam em melhores juizos confessando eu porem deste caydado em estes meyos encontrar ditas pessoas (como todos os—, q' quisserem sabia acharam) as}

{10} {quays claramente me disseram ser verdadeiro o q' eu tinha e sempre tive e tenho por mentira, e embuste e me dizeram q' os Mouros a quem minha Mulher a pistia(?) era gente del Rey D. Seastião E isto diziam tam dezencalmente e com tanta segurança q' era publico por muitas pessoas deste Reino q' o signamentemente(?) consideravam por certo.}

{E tenho eu toda esta maquinar pos illuzão do Demonio, fiz huã experiencia com minha mulher e foy dizerlhe soubete dos seus Mouros e lhes perguntasse se q' diziam os ditos Joam Penalvo, sua cunhada D. Maria Loba, E D. Luiza de Portugal era verdadeiro (por ver se conferia huã couza com outra) ella fez assim, e lhe foy Respondido q' assim eram como diziam as ditas trez pessoas; do q' minha Mulher (me disse) lhes fizera queyxa, porq' cauza e Resam se lhe havia a ella encuberto com o titulo, e nomes de Mouros, se eram couza d' El Rey D. Sebastião? Elles lhe disseram q' senam aggravasse as lhe nam verem descubertos quem eram, porq' convinha assim, e era necessario. Dizendolhe mays q' elles todos de haviam feito christãos; E q' o seu Rey D. Sebastião, depoys de sua perdiçam havia andado sempre athe aquelle tempo era viva penitencia, o qual esta va na Ilha encuberta, e era cazado com à senhora D. Auriana, filha d' El Rey de Dinamarca, a qual tinha consigo dous Irmãos, hum chamado Federico, outro Ricardo; E q' o dito Rey D. Sebastião tinha sinco filhos vivos, trez macebos, e duas femeas, afora huã q' lhe morreo: o filho mays velho se chamava D. Joam, o qual estava jâ cazado com huã prima sua, filha do Senhor Ricardo, de quem tinha huã filha q' se chamava a Senhora D. Joanna; E os segundo filho do Senhor Rey D. Sebastião se chamava D. Fernanado, E terceyro D. Duarte: as filhas se chamvam, a Senhora D. Ignacia, e a Senhora D. Ursula; E a q' morreo se chamava a Senhora D. Catherina, q' estava enterrada}

{10v} {em Santa Maria Mayor, q' he huã das Igrejas Matriz da Ilha, como na narraçam da dita Ilha adiante se declara.

{E vendo eu o q' a dita minha mulher dezia, e como se conformava com as ditas trez pessoas, o comformey ainda por mays subil(?) e ardilozenredo(?) e traza diabolica por muitas Rezões q' ao diante mostrarey. Mas por darmos mays clareza a nossos confessors e ao Santo Officio, lhe ordeney continuar neste negocio, sô a fim de ver no q' passava.}

{Conmendo(?) poys este fadario (q' assim lhe posso chamar por meu castiguo) do dito mez de Mayo e do tempo q' isto se lhe descubrio, a fuy inquirindo todas as noytes por ver o q' obrava e o designio, q'—e termo q' tomava tam fantastica e váa esperança E vendo q' ha a vaneando cada vez mays nas mudanças q' faria de cada noyte, conforme se verá pela Rellaçam q' ao diante faço, fuy escrevendo o q' a dita minha mulher me dezia sobre o descubrimento deste Rey.}

Dizendome mais q' todas aquelas gentes ou Mouros havião tomado nomes de Christãos e se havião de Bautizar {haviam bauptizada} e q' com a vinda daquele Rey havia de haver grandes revoluções e castigos nesta cidade {o qual tinha 323 embarcações, 202 Navios, as demays Galês em q' entravam 14 douradas com bandeiras de satim carnezim, e tolda das de veludo carmezim, as quays estavam preparado do anno de 1651} E q' havia de ser em sua noute em q' havia de Renaser o Sol o q' el Rey e Dom Sebastião havia de tirar de trazer outras leys das quaes o numero havia de ser so sinco escriptas por sua mão e confirmada pelo nosso Senhor Jesus Christo. E que derião falava com nosso senhor {Jesus Christo} 3 dias na semana com erão 2as, 4as e Domingos. E este Rey tinha com sigo em sua companhia hu' frade Francisco seu confessor por nome Angelico {de Christo E seu Chronista Frade Bernardo por nome Fr. Angelo.} E q' tinha o dito Rey comsigo sinco filhos 3 macebos e 2 femeas a saber o mais velho por nome D. João, o segundo D. Fernando E o 30 D. Duarte E as femeas D. Ignacia e D. Ursula.

{11} {E em 27 de mayo a manhã com huã—para de dous Mouros naturales da Ilha, hum chamado Francisco, e outro Pedro, a honde estava o Principe q' lhe disseram se em Alemanha o qual estava em companhia de Rey Artur de Inglaterra havia huns mezes E ao del Rey levara huã das duas cartas E outra as dito Principe do Senhor Rey D. Sebastião na qual continha hum pacto q' lhe estava para que se ajuntar com elle e com el Rey d'Aragam, e qual—ja—do Castello desta cidade de Lisboa, E o dito Rey a chegaram escreveo tambem na caza ao Senhor Rey D. Sebastião na mesma noyte e della se partio para Alemanha, E do q' escreveram hu's aos outros todos trez, Resalvou(?) a juntasse sabado o primeiro de Abril do anno de 1651 na Igreja de nossa Senhora da Pena, adonde ella yeyo em companhia de D. Jayme com o de Aragam huã moça de Oleyres por nome de Maria de Conceyçam a qual ella conhecia—la ver alguãs vezes na Ilha; E com el Rey Artur hum mancebo por nome Jorge Balaguer, veneziano de nação; E tanto q' ella chegou com o Senhor Rey, o estayam jâ as dous mays esperando; e se meteram logo todos na Igreja, ficando no alpendre della os tres criados E o q' hiram foy q' tres Santos Profetas lha deram cada hum sua espada a saber S. João Evangelista ao Senhor Rey D. Sebastião: S. Elias as de. Aragão, E Enoc ao de Inglaterra; as quays tinham por guardas huã unaz(?); dando lhes tambem hum quarto de papel de cada hum; E abensando cada Profeta à seu Rey, se depedirão ficando na Igreja, E os Reys vieram athe o pais adonde erão(?); E depoys disseram a minha mulher q' estes Santos Profetas estavam depuzitados em hum templo que havia de apparecer depoys do descubrimento deste Rey D. Sebastião.}

{E sendo isto prezente ao Padre Fr. Luiz de Madre de Deos Religioso da Ordem de S.

Francisco esta cidad E Revedor de livros, lhe}

{11v} {propos as trez couzas abayxo declaradas a q' lhe deram à ella por Reposta para assim achar ao dito Religioso o seguintes q' ficou atonito(?):

p. 1a Que sea Igreja, sequia a oppiniam de S. João Evangelista ser morto como dize estar vivo?

p. 2a Que se tambem os dous Profetas mays Elias e Enoc estavam guardados e depuzitados para virem pregar a vinda do Antichristo como se descazo(?) q' viessem com el Rey D. Sebastião?

p. 3a E q' se os ditos trez Profetas estavam no Paraiso terreal como estavam na Ilha Encuberta?

r. 1a Que se a Igreja seguia a oppiniam de S. joão Evangelista ser morto como não seria Santo, q' fesensesse se sua Morte q' elle estava vivo, e depuzitado para ir com el Rey D. Sebastião pregar o juizo da Reformação.

r. 2a E q' os outros dous Profetas nam negavam estarem depuzitados no Paraiso terreal para virem pregar a vindo do Antichristo q' elle entam sera o fim do Mundo; mas q' primeiro havia de haver a Reformação delle.

r. 3a Que se duvidaram do Paraiso terreal estar na Ilha Encoberta q' perguntasse a todos os homens assim navegantes e a os mays onde o Paraiso achava, poys era certo etar confinado na Terra e nam no mar?

E q' dia de S. Miguel de [1]619 faziam 32 annos q' Deos encubrira El Rey D. Sebastião no Monte do Camposallo que do hia no fim do Reino a(?) Alemanha para a p.re(?) de Veneza; E isto demays(?) dia para a huã hora, e daquelle parto q' hia fugido d' El Rey de Castella (pelo mandar buscar) com as Senhora Auriana sua mulher com dous Senhores filhos, hum q' a dita Senhora levar em seus braços e outros o Senhor D. Sebastião, se adormeceram de cançado q' hiam Monte, se acharam ne Ilha encuberta, sem saberem como.}

E perguntandolhe do q' constava aquela ilha de q' na sua reposta faz menção me Respondeo que chegada a dita ilha, vio tres igrejas q' estavão nella, da grandeza, não podia dar razão pela não ver todas mais q' sinco Ruas grandes entre as quaes estão as Igrejas referidas cujos nomes são os seguintes a Matriz aonde asisteo o Bispo de o nome Santa Maria Mayor = e a 2a São Estevão = e a 3a São João de q' tambem não dava Razão destes tem

(page 10v)

ve de dentro por não entrar nelles e somente velas por fora. E depois de passar as ditas Ruas

{12} {NARRACAM
de ditta ilha, Relatada por minha mulher

Chegada poys à esta Ilha com o Principe D. João, vi trez Igrejas q' estavam em huã povaçam(?) q' nam podrey das Refias(?) da grandeza pelo nam ver—meyo q' somente 5 ruas grandes entre as aquays estam as tres Igrejas seguintes: a Igreja Matriz Santa Maria Mayor;—de aquella hum Arcebispo, e hu' Bispo, a 2.a São Estevão, a 3,a S. João de q' tambem nam dou resam de dentro destes templos por nam entrar nelles somente velos fora E acabando daquelas as ditas Ruas},

vira a hum Campo Largo a modo de praça com 3 fontes no meyo, que se chama a Praça das fontes. E q' logo dahy seguem os Campos honde se dava os fructos da terra o susteneo daquela gente e q' era para maneira seguintes =

As pessoas daquela Ilha erão grandes de estatura, corpulentas, e não muito brancas, a lingoa Portugueza mas grosera aquella gente selebra todos os officios divinos e guarda a ley de Deos muito melhor q' nos pela mesma forma e maneira da q' a santa Madre Igreja nos ensina. E q' a terra he tam abundante q' todas as couzas q' se podem dezejar daé sem trabalho algu' nem delles ser cultivadas mais q' hir cada hum trazer para sua caza o q' ha mister E a saber, pão, carne, fructos e as demais couzas sendo muito fresca de Florez e aves q' avoam{volatiles}. E q' he tanta esta fertilidade q' todos vivem abundantissimamente sem algue' {ninguem} o administrar nem haver quem o saiba fazer porq' ao trigo vão buscar ao Campo e o trazem para suas Cazas, aonde a debulhão com os peés. E q' para a moereira he em huã de pedra q' com hu' ingenho de Rodademão,o q' lhe he necessario e cada hu's quer. E q' as carnez

(page 11)

como são bois, carneiros, e de aves galinhas, vão ao campo buscar para caza tam mansamente q' nenhuã couza lhes reziste. E as aves tam mansas q' cada qual tomas as q' quer sem lhes fugiam nem nada de ser bravo. E as roupas que vestem são das lans das ovelhas e carneiros da mesma cor dar lan ou brancas ou negras confirme as Deos avia por não haver quem saiba tingelas nem fabricalas en cores. E q' de ordinario tecessem a negra com a branca com—tem {as brancas com as negras}.

E q' nesta Ilha ha muito ouro; e prata pouca, e não muita fina E q' disto se não aprovietava nada nem fazem cazo della por não ser necessario. E q he tanta a abundancia {de ouro} q' pelas fontes q' tem dito {q' atraz declarei} q' estão na praça ven ouro correndo com a mesma agoa em folinhas(?), q' ao depois de ficarem asentadas em hu' tanque as apanhão cada hum leva o q' lhe parece para o ter em caza, E não porq' lhe seja necessario.

E q' esta Ilha lhe disserão ser muito grande porem q' ella a não ir a quais q' o tem referido nesta mostração sequia—{a dita minha mulher e nam vistada mays q' epla Refferido nem lha mostraram he agora; E nam me contam mays couzas della, por nam querer ser molesta: Esta Ilha} E q a dita ilha ficava em meyo de outras 2 mais pequenas, q' dellas deycam ver porem q' ella não entrara nelas (nem la' a levarão.

E não me disse mais da dita Ilha.

<Neste tempo fui logo buscarao Dr. Padre Fr. Sebastião de Payvao Relligiozo

(page 11v)

da *Santissima* Trinidade por ter noticia delle erã homem doctor. E que se elle mais facozmente me poderia explicar este cazo e alivrar me da penna e tormento em que andava e receitando lho todo lhe pedi confessasse a dita minha mulher o q' fez Prometer do me q' se fosse couza diabolica me a segurava de o impedir ao diabo.

E depois de confessada, me disse me disse o Dr. Fr. Sebastião de Payvão q' Eu vivesse de serinissidade e sem cuidadão porq' o q' ella dezia podia ser por agolidade hir vir por Deos lhe mandar Reprezentar em qual Parte ou caza q' aluesse Com o q' não tratar mais deste negocio nem me deu cuidado a Lgo(?) *para* tratar delle.

Feliciano Machado>

NOTES

Introduction

1. Inquisição de Lisboa, Processo 4404, 1:31, Arquivo Nacional da Torre do Tombo, Lisbon (hereafter cited as ANTT). Processo 4404 has two series of folio numbers, and so citations to this source consist of series number, colon, and folio number(s). All translations are the author's own, unless otherwise noted.

2. See Carlo Ginzburg, *The Cheese and the Worms*, trans. John Tedeschi and Anne C. Tedeschi (Baltimore: Johns Hopkins University Press, 1980); Carlo Ginzburg, *The Night Battles*, trans. John Tedeschi and Anne C. Tedeschi (Baltimore: Johns Hopkins University Press, 1983); Emmanuel LeRoy Ladurie, *Montaillou: The Promised Land of Error*, trans. Barbara Bray (New York: Vintage Books, 1986); and Jaime Contreras, *Sotos contra Riquelmes: Regidores, inquisidores y criptojudíos* (Madrid: Anaya & M. Muchnik, 1992).

3. See João Lúcio de Azevedo, *A evolução do sebastianismo* (Lisbon: Livraria Clásica Editora de A. M. Teixeira, 1984), 86; Jacqueline Hermann, *No reino do desejado: A construção do sebastianismo em Portugal séculos XVI e XVII* (São Paulo: Companhia das Letras, 1998), 280–301; and Mark Emerson Cooper, "Messianic Expectation and Collective Myth Formation: Prophecy, Society and Imagination in Early Modern Portugal" (Ph.D. diss., University of California, Santa Barbara, 2004), 180–236.

4. Inquisição de Lisboa, Processo 4404, 2:123, ANTT.

5. There is a considerable literature on the issue of social disciplining during the early modern period. For an important contribution to the issue, see Richard Po-Chia Hsia, *Social Discipline in the Reformation: Central Europe 1550–1750* (London: Routledge, 1989). Though it is only a study of the situation in Germany, its conclusions are of wider application. For the Inquisition's role in social disciplining, see Henry Kamen, *The Spanish Inquisition: A Historical Revision* (London: Weidenfeld and Nicholson, 1997), esp. chap. 12. For the Portuguese case, see António Borges Coelho, *Inquisição de Evora: Dos primórdios a 1668* (Lisbon: Editorial Caminho, 1987), vol. 2. For some important microhistorical studies of the Inquisition's campaign against popular beliefs and customs, see Ginzburg, *Cheese and the Worms*; Ginzburg, *Night Battles*; and Guido Ruggiero, *Binding Passions: Tales of Magic, Marriage, and Power at the End of the Renaissance* (New York: Oxford University Press, 1993). Ginzburg, it should be noted, sees the elite campaign against popular culture as being more closely related to the increased social stratification that took place during the price revolution than to the confessional disputes between Catholics and Protestants. I would only say that those two reasons are not mutually exclusive.

6. See Ginzburg, *Cheese and the Worms*, xxi; Carlo Ginzburg and Carlo Poni, "The Name and the Game: Unequal Exchange and the Historiographic Marketplace," in *Microhistory and the Lost Peoples*

of Europe, ed. Edward Muir and Guido Ruggiero, trans. Eren Branch (Baltimore: Johns Hopkins University Press, 1991), 7; Wolfgang Reinhard, "Disciplinamento sociale, confessionalizzazione modernizzazione: Undiscorso storiografico," trans. Chiara Zanoni Zorzi, in *Disciplina dell'anima, disciplina del corpo e disciplina della società tra medioevo ed età moderna*, ed. Paolo Prodi and Carla Pennuti (Bologna: Società editrice il Mulino, 1994), 123.

7. Edoardo Grendi, "Micro-analisi e storia sociale," *Quaderni Storici* 35 (May–August, 1977): 512, and the discussion of this point in Edward Muir, "Introduction: Observing Trifles," in *Microhistory and the Lost Peoples of Europe*, ed. Edward Muir and Guido Ruggiero, trans. Eren Branch (Baltimore: Johns Hopkins University Press, 1991), xiv–xvi.

8. Muir, "Introduction," and Ginzburg and Poni, "Name and the Game," 7–8.

9. Norman Cohn, *The Pursuit of the Millennium* (Oxford: Oxford University Press, 1970), 90–93, 108–26. Of course, there were similar messianic legends in other parts of western Europe as well. In the late medieval period, many in France believed that Charlemagne was resting, hidden, somewhere below Aachen, to one day be resurrected to conquer the world. And, of course, the legends surrounding King Arthur, who had been hidden twice—once as a child and once after death on the island of Avalon to await the moment of his revelation at the time of England's greatest peril—were almost universally known in early modern Europe.

10. Paul J. Alexander, "The Diffusion of Byzantine Apocalypses in the Medieval West and the Beginnings of Joachimism," in *Prophecy and Millenarianism: Essays in Honor of Marjorie Reeves*, ed. Ann Williams (Harlow, Essex: Longman, 1980), 56–62. See also Cohn, *Pursuit of the Millennium*, 23. It is not wholly clear whether the Arthurian legend was inspired by the Byzantine World Emperor tradition or sprang up independently out of Celtic roots. If its origin was the Roman legend, that influence almost certainly took place before the advent of Islam, and so it is not surprising that a crusade against Islam does not form a part of the earliest traditions about Arthur. The pagan Saxons against whom Arthur supposedly fought play much the same role in the tradition.

11. See Cohn, *Pursuit of the Millennium*, 14–18.

12. See Yves-Marie Bercé, *Le roi caché: Sauveurs et imposteurs. Mythes politiques populaires dans l'Europe moderne* (Paris: Fayard, 1990), 312. Bercé examines the phenomenon of royal pretenders in early modern Europe, the false Sebastians among them. Though he examines pretenders and not messianic figures—he never really addresses the issue of the messianic beliefs about Sebastian before Alcazarquivir, for example—many of his conclusions about the causes of the phenomenon and about the roles lost rulers and pretenders play within society are valid in the case of messianic figures as well.

1. The Millenarian Tradition in Early Modern Portugal

1. Delno C. West and Sandra Zimdars-Swartz, *Joachim of Fiore: A Study in Spiritual Perception and History* (Bloomington: Indiana University Press, 1983), 11–12.

2. Marjorie Reeves, *Joachim of Fiore and the Prophetic Future: A Medieval Study in Historical Thinking* (Stroud, Gloucestershire: Sutton Publishing, 1999), 6–7.

3. Ibid., 32–33.

4. Harold Lee, Marjorie Reeves, and Giulio Silano, *Western Mediterranean Prophecy: The School of Joachim of Fiore and the Fourteenth-Century Breviloquium* (Toronto: Pontifical Institute of Medieval Studies, 1989), 27–39.

5. Manuel J. Gandra, *Joaquim de Fiore, joaquimismo, e a esperança sebástica* (Lisbon: Fundação Lusíada, 1999), 39–104.

6. On advocacy by the Jesuits: Marjorie Reeves, "The Abbot Joachim and the Society of Jesus," in *Joachim of Fiore in Christian Thought: Essays on the Influence of the Calabrian Prophet*, ed. Delno C. West (New York: Burt Frankling and Co., 1975), 209–27.

7. Gandra, *Joaquim de Fiore*, 55–104.

8. Paul J. Alexander, "The Diffusion of Byzantine Apocalypses in the Medieval West and the Beginnings of Joachimism," in *Prophecy and Millenarianism: Essays in Honor of Marjorie Reeves*, ed. Ann Williams (Harlow, Essex: Longman, 1980), 56–62.

9. Vicent J. Vallés Borrás, *La Germanía* (Valencia: Institució Alfons El Magnànim, 2000), 32.

10. Ibid., 36–39. The classic work on the *germanías* is Ricardo García Carcel, *Las Germanías de Valencia* (Barcelona: Ediciones Península, 1975); see pages 132–39.

11. Dom João de Castro, *Discurso da vida do sempre bem vindo et apparecido Rey Dom Sebastião nosso senhor o Encuberto desdo seu naçimento tee o presente* (Paris: Martin Verac, 1602), fols. 131–35. See also João José van den Besselaar, *O sebastianismo: História sumária* (Lisbon: Instituto de Cultura e Lingua Portuguesa, 1987), 72.

12. Luís Filipe Lindley Cintra, *Sobre a formação e evolução da lenda de Ourique (até à Crónica de 1419)* (Lisbon: Imprensa de Coimbra, 1957), 6–27.

13. On the Portuguese against Castile: José Mattoso, *A Primeira tarde portuguesa* (Guimarães: Editora do Minho, 1979), 5–7.

14. See João Lúcio de Azevedo, *A evolução do sebastianismo* (Lisbon: Livraria Clásica Editora de A. M. Teixeira, 1984), 9, and Besselaar, *O sebastianismo*, 49–52.

15. Besselaar, *O sebastianismo*, 49–50.

16. Procesos da Inquisição de Lisboa, 3734 e 16905, "Procesos de Luis Dias," extracts reprinted in Azevedo, *A evolução do sebastianismo*, 174–82. See also Elias Lipiner, *O Sapateiro de Trancoso e o Alfaiate de Setúbal* (Rio de Janeiro: Imago, 1993).

17. Proceso da Inquisição de Lisboa, 7197, "Proceso de Gonçalo Anes," reprinted in Theophilo Braga. *Historia de Camões* (Porto: Imprensa Portugueza, 1873), 1:413–16.

18. Ibid., 415 (emphasis added).

19. Ibid., 415–16.

20. Castro, *Discurso da vida*, fols. 3–4.

21. One recent essay offers a rather startling alternative explanation for Sebastian's well-documented aversion to women. See Harold Johnson, "A Pedophile in the Palace or the Sexual Abuse of King Sebastian of Portugal (1554–1578) and Its Consequences," in *Pelo Vaso Traseiro: Sodomy and Sodomites in Luso-Brazilian History*, ed. Harold Johnson and Francis A. Dutra (Tucson: Fenestra Books, 2007), 195–229.

22. "Rei que por milagre nos foi dado." See Azevedo, *A evolução do sebastianismo*, 27.

23. António Quadros, *Poesia e filosofia do mito sebastianista* (Lisbon: Guimarães & C.ª Editores, 1983), 1:35–39.

24. Gandra, *Joaquim de Fiore*, 122–38.

25. William J. Entwhistle, *The Arthurian Legend in the Literatures of the Spanish Peninsula* (New York: Kraus Reprint Co., 1975), 7–63, 215.

26. Quadros, *Poesia e filosofia*, 1:35–57.

27. Mary Elizabeth Brooks, *A King for Portugal: The Madrigal Conspiracy, 1594–1595* (Madison: University of Wisconsin Press, 1964), 16–23.

2. The Evolution of Sebastianism

1. Mary Elizabeth Brooks, *A King for Portugal: The Madrigal Conspiracy, 1594–1595* (Madison: University of Wisconsin Press, 1964), 36–38.

2. Balthasar Gonçalves's trial is found in Inquisição de Lisboa, Processo 5083, ANTT.

3. Ibid., fols. 6–6v.

4. Ibid., fols. 20–21.

5. Ibid., fol. 25.

6. I explore the nature of Dom João de Castro's influence on Sebastianism in greater detail in my essay "The St. Paul of Sebastianism: Tracing the Millenarian Legacy of Dom João de Castro," *Portuguese Studies Review*, 17 (2009–10): 1–20.

7. The classic study of the false Sebastians is Miguel d'Antas, *Les faux Don Sébastien: Étude sur l'histoire du Portugal* (Paris: A. Durand, 1866). For a good summary in English, see Brooks, *King for Portugal*. See also Yves-Marie Bercé, *Le roi caché: Sauveurs et imposteurs. Mythes politiques populaires dans l'Europe moderne* (Paris: Fayard, 1990), 17–81, and in Portuguese, see António Belard da Fonseca, *Dom Sebastião: Antes e depois de Alcácer-quibir*, vols. 1–2 (Lisbon: Ramos, Afonso & Moita, 1978).

8. Dom João de Castro, *Discurso da vida do sempre bem vindo et apparecido Rey Dom Sebastião nosso senhor o Encuberto desdo seu naçimento tee o presente* (Paris: Martin Verac, 1602), fols. 46–48. In his "Advertimentos ao sempre bem vindo e apparecido Rey D. Sebastião" (1604; Biblioteca Nacional de Lisboa [hereafter cited as BN]), D. João de Castro says that he was actively looking for prophecies that proved Sebastian was alive and that Portugal would be liberated (fol. 67v). See also João Lúcio de Azevedo, *A evolução do sebastianismo* (Lisbon: Livraria Clásica Editora de A. M. Teixeira, 1984), 8–28, and João José van den Besselaar, *O sebastianismo: História sumária* (Lisbon: Instituto de Cultura e Lingua Portuguesa, 1987), 49–50.

9. Castro, *Discurso da vida*, fols. 12, 43, 56.

10. Dom João de Castro, *Paraphrase et concordançia de alguas prophecias de Bandarra, çapateiro de Trancoso* (Paris, 1603), fol. 2v.

11. Ibid., fols. 14–17.

12. Ibid., fol. 77. It is a historical irony that the youngest half-brother of the ultranationalist Dom João de Castro was Dom Francisco de Castro, who became inquisitor general of the Portuguese Inquisition in 1629 and who was later implicated in the plot of August 1641 to return Portugal to Spanish control. While their political loyalties differed, their views of the *converso* problem were much the same.

13. Ibid., fols. 2v, 122v–126.

14. Ibid., fols. 123v–124.

15. Ibid., fols. 69–70v.

16. D. João de Castro first made this claim in the "Aurora" (1604–5; p. 6, BN) a few months after Catizone's execution and maintained it for the rest of his life.

17. Manuel Bocarro Frances, *Anacephalosis da monarchia lusitania, primeira parte* (Lisbon, 1624), 11. See also António Quadros, *Poesia e filosofia do mito sebastianista* (Lisbon: Guimarães & C.ª Editores, 1982), 61–62, and Besselaar, *O sebastianismo*, 90–92.

18. Azevedo, *A evolução do sebastianismo*, 48–52.

19. Manuel Bocarro Frances Rosales, "Luz pequena lunar" (1626), fol. 102, in "Jardim ameno," Manuscrita da Livraria 774, ANTT.

20. Ibid., fols. 107v–110. See also Besselaar, *O sebastianismo*, 90–92.

21. See José Filipe Mendeiros, "O Olivento Sebastião do Couto, Mestre Insigne da Universidade de Évora e Alma das Alterações de 1637," *Anais da Academia Portuguesa da História* 18 (1969): 31, and Gabriel Pereira, *Estudos Eborenses: As Vesperas da Restauração* (Évora, Portugal: Minerva Eborense, 1886–87), 1:5–12. Both are named as supporters of João II of Braganza in António de Sousa de Macedo's *Lusitana liberata, ab injusto castellanorum dominio, restituta legitimo Principe, Serenissimo Joanni IV* (London: Richard Heron, 1645), 743.

22. See Joel Serrão, ed., *Alterações de Évora, 1637* (Lisbon: Portugália Editora, 1967), 147–48.

23. D. Francisco Manuel de Melo, *Epanáfora política primeira*, reprinted in Serrão, *Alterações de Évora, 1637*, 134 (originally published in 1660); D. Francisco Manuel de Melo, *Tácito portugues*, ed. Raul Rêgo (Lisbon: Livraria Sá da Costa, 1995), 62. He wonders how even wise and educated men could be pulled in by such "blindness."

24. Panteleão Rodrigues Pacheco, *Manifesto do reyno de Portugal, presentado a Santidade de Urbano VIII, N.S.* (Lisbon: Domingos Lopes Rola, 1643), 26–29.

25. Almeida, Grégorio de [Fr. João de Vasconcelos], *Restauração de Portugal prodigiosa* (Lisbon: António Alvarez, 1643), 7–12.

26. "Macedo, Doutor António de Sousa de (1606–1682)," *Dicionário de história de Portugal*, vol. 4 (Porto: Livraria Figuerinhas, 2000), 112–13.

27. Sousa de Macedo, *Lusitana liberata*.

28. Joaquim Veríssimo Serrão, *Historia de Portugal*, vol. 5, *A Restauração e a monarchia absoluta (1640–1750)* (Lisbon: Editorial Verbo, 1996), 175–77.

29. Jacqueline Hermann, *No reino do desejado: A construção do sebastianismo em Portugal séculos XVI e XVII* (São Paulo: Companhia das Letras, 1998), 226–28.

30. Padre António Vieira, *Sermão dos Bons Anos*, reprinted in *Obras escolhidas*, vol. 10, ed. Hernâni Cidade (Lisbon: Livraria Sá da Costa, 1953), 153–89; see esp. 166–67.

31. Hermann, *No reino do desejado*, 234–48.

32. See, for example, his "Carta" reprinted in António Borges Coelho, *Inquisiçião de Evora: Dos primórdioa 1668* (Lisbon: Editorial Caminho, 1987), 2:235–54.

33. "Alvara del Rey Dom João o 4°" [of February 6, 1649], reprinted in Coelho, *Inquisiçião de Evora*, 2:255–57.

34. Besselaar, *O sebastianismo*, 116–22.

35. Hermann, *No reino do desejado*, 237–38.

36. Padre António Vieira, "Esperanças de Portugal, quinto império do mundo," in P. António Vieira, *Obras escolhidas*, vol. 6, ed. Hernâni Cidade (Lisbon: Livraria Sá da Costa, 1952), 1.

37. Ibid., 2.

38. Besselaar, *O sebastianismo*, 121–22.

39. Hermann, *No reino do desejado*, 239–40.

40. António Baião, *Episodios dramáticos da Inquisição Portuguesa* (Lisbon: Seara Nova, 1972), 209–28.

41. Hermann, *No reino do desejado*, 244.

42. For a rare example of an *afonsoísta* apology, see António Paes Ferraz, *Discurso astrológico das influencies da mayor conjunçam de Jupiter e Marte, que succedeu neste annom de 1660. 28 de Agosto* (Lisbon: Domingos Carpeiro, 1661).

43. Sebastião de Paiva, "O tratado da quinta monarchia e felicidades de Portugal profetizadas," in MS COD 810, fols. 1–169, BN. For comments on the significance of the work, see Besselaar, *O sebastianismo*, 106–7; Azevedo, *A evolução do sebastianismo*, 74; and Manuel J. Gandra, *Joaquim de Fiore, joaquimismo, e a esperança sebástica* (Lisbon: Fundação Lusíada, 1999), 187–201.

44. See esp. de Paiva, "Tratado da Quinta Monarchia," fols. 80–139v. See also Bryan Givens, "The St. Paul of Sebastianism: Tracing the Millenarian Legacy of Dom João de Castro," *Portuguese Studies Review* 17 (March 2010): 12–13.

45. "Jardim ameno," Manuscrita da Livraria 774, ANTT. These anthologies were not always very carefully compiled, however. The "Jardim ameno," for example, contains some abbreviated versions of the works of Bocarro that are clearly unfavorable to Sebastian.

46. MS CODS 128 and 132, BN.

47. The short treatise "O Reyno de Portugal, sua creação, successos, profezidos pello ceo a Esdras nos capitulos 11–12–13 do seu livro 4°," written by João da Cruz, O.P. (MS COD 810, BN) during the reign of Afonso VI, is a significant work that depended heavily on Castro and cited him by name.

48. Azevedo, *A evolução do sebastianismo*, 83–85; Besselaar, *O sebastianismo*, 140–44.

49. MS COD 400, fols. 73v–103, esp. stanzas 75 and 80, BN.

50. MS COD 132, BN.

3. Maria de Macedo and the Vision in Her Own Words

1. Inquisição de Lisboa, Processo 4404, 2:33–35v, ANTT.

2. Chancelleria de D. Afonso VI, Livro 30, fols. 219v–220, ANTT.

3. Inquisição de Lisboa, Processo 4404, 2:191, ANTT.

4. Ibid., 4.

5. Joel Serrão and A. H. de Oliveira Marques, *Nova história de Portugal*, vol. 5, *Portugal, Do Renascimento à crise dinástica* (Lisbon: Editorial Presença, 1999), 286–89.

6. For some recent work done on manuscript literature in early modern Portugal, see Fernando Bouza, *Corre nanuscrito: Una historia cultural del Siglo de Oro* (Madrid: Marcial Pons, Historia, 2001), 27–83.

7. R. A. Houston, *Literacy in Early Modern Europe: Culture and Education, 1500–1800* (London: Longman, 1988), 181–85. See also Kate van Orden, *Street Songs and Cheap Print during the French Wars of Religion* (Berkeley: Doe Library of the University of California, 1998).

8. Inquisição de Lisboa, Processo 4404, 1:26, 46v, ANTT.

9. The text of the original, shorter version is followed here and is given preference when there are minor differences of word order or vocabulary. Passages found only in the long version are denoted by the use of braces { }; the few sentences found only in the short version are denoted with angle brackets < >. Parentheses ( ) are used when they were used in the original text or when they would be in English usage. Brackets [ ] are used for all editorial additions and comments, with those of a more speculative nature noted by a reference to the translator (myself). Ellipses and illegible words and passages are denoted by a dash—and a question mark in parentheses (?).

4. The Trial of Maria de Macedo

1. The denunciation is found in Inquisição de Lisboa, Processo 4404, 1:2–6v, ANTT.

2. For information about royal administration during the Restoration, see Joachim Veríssimo Serrão, *História de Portugal*, vol. 5, *A Restauração e a monarchia absoluta (1640–1750)* (Lisbon: Editorial Verbo, 1996), 125–27.

3. Inquisição de Lisboa, Processo 4404, 2:107, ANTT.

4. Ibid., 1:78.

5. For the *Regimento de 1640*, see Conselho Geral, Livro 342, ANTT.

6. Inquisição de Lisboa, Processo 4404, 1:1, ANTT.

7. Information on these officials can be found in Inquisição de Lisboa, Livro 106, fols. 8, 109v, and 148 for Barreto, de la Cerda, and Castilho, respectively, ANTT.

8. For the depositions of the first six witnesses, see Inquisição de Lisboa, Processo 4404, 1:4–32, ANTT.

9. I looked diligently for someone named Maria de Conceição in this time period but found nothing. The Inquisition, at least, did not take the claim seriously enough to follow it up. However, if information could be found about this person (if she existed at all), it could have some interesting implications for our understanding of Maria de Macedo's visions.

10. See Inquisição de Lisboa, Processo 4404, 1:33, ANTT.

11. For Maria de Macedo's first depositions, see ibid., 2:1–8v.

12. See ibid., 9–10.

13. For Maria de Macedo's second, third, and fourth depositions, see ibid., 11–28.

14. See ibid., 29–31.

15. For Feliciano Machado's depositions, see ibid., 1:37–41, 46v–54.

16. For the depositions of Manoel Soares de Britto and Isabel de Britto, see ibid., 42–46v, 55–58, respectively.

17. For Maria de Almeida, see ibid., 59–64v.

18. For Maria de Macedo's sixth deposition, see ibid., 2:36–38v.

19. For Maria de Macedo's seventh deposition, see ibid., 41–43v; for the eighth, see ibid., 44–54v.

20. For de Santo's appointment as Maria's defense counsel, see ibid., 64; for his career information, see Inquisição de Lisboa, Livro 106, fol. 52, ANTT.

21. The *contradittas* are found in Inquisição de Lisboa, Processo 4404, 2:75–78v, ANTT.

22. In article 8, she also let slip an interesting observation because she claimed she told Sebastian that the "Padres da Companhia" (i.e., the Jesuits) were very much in favor of him ("lhe erão muito affeiçoados"). Given her circle of listeners, this opinion should not come as a surprise. De Santo makes an interesting comment in this regard as well in his witness list in favor of article 12. "The beliefs common among those vulgarly called *sebastianistas* are notorious in this kingdom as fantastic and without foundation, and which, for legitimate reasons or not, appeal to people of uncertain judgment."

23. See Inquisição de Lisboa, Processo 4404, 2:79–82, ANTT.

24. See ibid., 82v–85.

25. See ibid., 109–12.

26. See ibid., 113–14.

27. Both the questions and answers of the *qualificadores* are found ibid., 116–20v.

28. See Inquisição de Lisboa, Livro 106, fol. 123, ANTT.

29. See ibid., fol. 85v.

30. See Inquisição de Lisboa, Processo 4404, 2:122–24, ANTT.

31. Ibid., 126.

32. For Maria de Macedo's testimony under torture, see ibid., 128–34v.

33. For the confirmation, see ibid., 138–43v.

34. See Inquisição de Lisboa, Livro 8, fol. 127v, and Conselho Geral, Livro 435, fol. 143v, both in ANTT.

35. For all the documents relating to Feliciano's plea, see Inquisição de Lisboa, Processo 4404, 2:158–79, ANTT.

5. *The Element of Time in Maria's Visions*

1. See Inquisição de Lisboa, Processo 4404, 2:138v, ANTT.

6. *A Glimpse of Paradise: Unlocking the Meaning of Maria's Visions*

1. José Pedro Paiva, *Bruxaria e superstição num país sem "caça às bruxas" 1600–1774* (Lisbon: Notícias Editorial, 1997), 159–61.

2. See Francisco Xavier d'Athaide Oliveira, *As Mouras encantadas e os encantamentos no Algarve* (Tavira: Livraria Figuirinhas, 1918), 135.

3. Ibid., 21, 33, 43, 153, 208, 227. For the broader significance of St. John's Day in Portugal, see also Fernando de Castro Pires de Lima, *S. João na alma do povo* (Porto: Portuculense Editora, 1944) 6ff.

4. Athaide Oliveira, *As Mouras encantadas*, 35, 39, 49, 264.

5. Ibid., 190.

6. Inquisição de Lisboa, Processo 4404, 2:11v–12, ANTT.

7. See Athaide Oliveira, *As Mouras encantadas*, 43 (sheep); 48 (goat); 51, 281 (bull); 81, 129, 136, 208, 234 (snake); 136 (lion); 190, 250 (toad); 234 (ram); and 245 (fox) for some examples of the animal forms taken by enchanted Moors.

8. Delmira Maças, *Os Animais na linguagem portuguesa* (Lisbon: Centro de Estudios Filológicos, 1950), 295.

9. Ibid., 296, 306.

10. Ibid., 333.

11. Herman Pleij, *Dreaming of Cockaigne: Medieval Fantasies of the Perfect Life*, trans. Diane Webb (New York: Columbia University Press, 2001), 398.

12. As Peter Burke says, "Saints are well worth the attention of historians because they are cultural indicators. Like other heroes, they reflect the values of the culture which sees them in a heroic light." The same can be said of messianic leaders. See Peter Burke, "How to Be a Counter-Reformation Saint," in *Religion and Society in Early Modern Europe, 1500–1800*, ed. Kaspar von Greyerz (London: George Allen and Unwin, 1984), 45.

13. António de Sousa de Macedo did include a throne for Sebastian, though whether that was part of Maria's original narration to him is unclear. See Inquisição de Lisboa, Processo 4404, 1:4, ANTT.

14. See Inquisição de Lisboa, Processo 4564, ANNT.

15. Inquisição de Lisboa, Processo 557, ANNT.

16. See MS CODS 128 and 400, BN. The text that follows is from the MS COD 128 version, simply for reasons of legibility. For the reference to Madre Leocardia da Conceição in "Resposta de certa pessoa a outra," see MS COD 132, BN.

17. Jacqueline Hermann also notes that the names of his sons—João, Duarte, and Fernando—were probably inspired by João I; his son, D. Duarte, who launched a campaign against Morocco;

and D. Duarte's brother, the Infante D. Fernando, who was captured by the Moors in 1437 and died in prison as a result of his treatment there. Viewed as a martyr, D. Fernando was widely known as the "Infante Santo." See Jacqueline Hermann, *No reino do desejado: A construção do sebastianismo em Portugal séculos XVI e XVII* (São Paulo: Companhia das Letras, 1998), 300.

18. Inquisição de Lisboa, Processo 4404, 1:40v, ANTT.

19. Ibid., 47.

20. Ibid., 2:2v–3.

21. Literally, she said the sun would be reborn ("renascer o sol") when Sebastian returned. Interestingly, this trope also appeared in the legends about the Hohenstaufen emperor Frederick II, who was often compared to the sun reborn. See Ernst Kantorowicz, *Frederick the Second, 1194–1250*, trans. E. O. Lorimer (New York: Frederick Ungar Publishing Co., 1957), 685–89.

22. Inquisição de Lisboa, Processo 4404, 2:53, ANTT.

23. Ibid., 3, 42.

24. For an analysis of the cultural division of the western Mediterranean between Catholics and Muslims, see Andrew C. Hess, *The Forgotten Frontier: A History of the Sixteenth-Century Ibero-African Frontier* (Chicago: University of Chicago Press, 1978). For a description of the hostile attitudes and actions of the Spanish toward Muslims as result of this division, see J. H. Elliott, *Imperial Spain, 1469–1716* (London: Penguin, 1963), 235–41, and Ellen G. Friedman, *Spanish Captives in North Africa in the Early Modern Age* (Madison: University of Wisconsin Press, 1983), esp. xvii–xxvii. While these studies focus on the Spanish, the Portuguese shared a similar attitude toward Muslims, largely as a result of similar Counter-Reformation ideals of Catholic triumphalism and a shared experience as victims of Islamic piracy in the Mediterranean.

25. Inquisição de Lisboa, Processo 4404, 2:3, ANTT.

26. This focus on the small details is largely inspired by the Morellian method discussed by Carlo Ginzburg in the thought-provoking essay "Clues: Roots of an Evidential Paradigm," in *Clues, Myths, and the Historical Method*, trans. John Tedeschi and Anne C. Tedeschi (Baltimore: Johns Hopkins University Press, 1989), 96–125. See also Edward Muir, "Introduction: Observing Trifles," in *Microhistory and the Lost Peoples of Europe*, ed. Edward Muir and Guido Ruggiero, trans. Eren Branch (Baltimore: Johns Hopkins University Press, 1991), vii–xxviii.

27. Dom João de Castro, *Discurso da vida do sempre bem vindo et apparecido Rey Dom Sebastião nosso senhor o Encuberto desdo seu naçimento tee o presente* (Paris: Martin Verac, 1602), fols. 73–73v.

28. Inquisição de Lisboa, Processo 4404, 2:41v–42, ANTT.

29. Ibid., 22.

30. Ibid., 41.

31. "Jardim ameno," Manuscrita da Livraria 774, fols. 8v–10v, ANTT.

32. António Belard da Fonseca, *Dom Sebastião: Antes e depois de Alcácer-quibir*, vols. 1–2 (Lisbon: Ramos, Afonso & Moita, 1978), 96–97.

33. Inquisição de Lisboa, Processo 4404, 1:9v, ANTT.

34. Castro, *Discurso da vida*, fol. 93v; Teixeira's *Aventura admiravel* cited in Belard da Fonseca, *Dom Sebastião*, 47–48. The list of physical signs was also given in the record of Fr. Estevão Sampaio's trial in San Lucar, but it could not have served as a source for this detail for the simple reasons that it did not include the scar above the right eyebrow as a sign and the Spanish never published the record of that trial. See Belard da Fonseca, *Dom Sebastião*, 76–80. A letter from Panteleão Pessoa to Dom Manuel de Portugal, the eldest son of the Prior of Crato, dated December 15, 1600, did include a "scar from a wound above his right eyebrow." See ibid., 106–7. Since it was private correspondence

between two men opposed to the prisoner's claims, it was never published, and I deem it a very unlikely source of Maria's characterization.

35. Inquisição de Lisboa, Processo 4404, 1:9v, ANTT.

36. Castro, *Discurso da vida*, fols. 93–93v.

37. There is a possible objection to this evidence, since Maria, in her own testimony, never gave the physical description of Sebastian recounted by Peixoto. Given his demonstrated predilection to confuse the details of her story, why should we believe she actually said what he claimed? First, though Peixoto often confused details and conflated events that were separate in her narrative, he did not make up any of those details or events out of whole cloth. Second, there is a certain verisimilitude in his testimony in this section that makes me inclined to believe that Maria actually had told him the things he later recounted to the inquisitor. It is plausible to me that her mentioning the detail of the eyebrow would prompt him to later show her a portrait of Sebastian in the hope of obtaining further confirmation of what she had seen. Unfortunately, the inquisitors never asked her about either the eyebrow or the portrait, and thus there is no firsthand testimony from her on the issue. Lacking that, we cannot come to any definitive conclusion about the truth or falsity of Peixoto's statements, though I lean toward the possibility that she did, indeed, say what he said she did for the reasons given above.

38. Inquisição de Lisboa, Processo 4404, 2:40v, ANTT. The names on this list were also mentioned in the testimony of Pedro Peixoto and Manoel da Costa, which only proves that Maria was told a consistent story as far as this detail is concerned.

39. Castro, *Discurso da vida*, fol. 60.

40. See Castro, *Paraphrase*, fols. 69–70v.

41. See de Paiva, MS COD 810, fols. 80–130v, BN.

42. See Bryan Givens, "The St. Paul of Sebastianism: Tracing the Millenarian Legacy of Dom João de Castro," *Portuguese Studies Review* 17 (2009–10): 1–20.

43. Inquisição de Lisboa, Processo 4404, 2:20, ANTT.

44. Ibid., 2v.

45. Ibid., 21v. Since work was unnecessary on the island, one wonders what work they would give up for this Sunday devotion. This is another piece of evidence that Maria's idealized world was cobbled together from disparate elements (i.e., a land of no work, and the pious ideal of giving up work for contemplation's sake) without regard to consistency.

46. Ibid., 1:11.

47. Ibid., 2:12.

48. Ibid.

49. Ibid., 19.

50. Ibid., 41.

51. Ibid., 1:57v.

52. Ibid., 2:20.

53. Ibid., 51.

54. See Frank E. Manuel and Fritzie P. Manuel, *Utopian Thought in the Western World* (Cambridge: Harvard University Press, Belknap Press, 1979), for a good overview of these and other utopian works.

55. For a good examination of this legend and its many variations, see Pleij, *Dreaming of Cockaigne*.

56. Ibid., 100.

57. Hilário Franco Jr., *Cocanha: A história de um país imaginário* (São Paulo: Companhia das Letras, 1998), 5.

58. Ibid., 61–62.

59. See, for example, ibid., 60, and Pleij, *Dreaming of Cockaigne*, 129–36.

60. Inquisição de Lisboa, Processo 4404, 1:9, ANTT.

61. The association between hedonism and popular culture is often made on the basis of Bakhtin, especially in his discussion of the so-called material bodily lower stratum; see Mikhail Bakhtin, *Rabelais and His World*, trans. Hélène Iswolsky (Bloomington: Indiana University Press, 1984), 368ff, although it would be closer to the truth to say that he did not advocate a dichotomous hedonist-popular/ascetic-elite view of early modern culture. Rather, the hedonist/materialist culture of the carnival was open to all, regardless of class. It was opposed not by the sociopolitical elite as a whole but by certain elite institutions like the church. Also, a certain kind of radically egalitarian asceticism manifested itself in movements that were thoroughly popular (and even anti-elite) in nature. See Gábor Klaniczay, "The Carnival Spirit: Bakhtin's Theory on the Culture of Laughter," in *The Uses of Supernatural Power: The Transformation of Popular Religion in Medieval and Early-Modern Europe*, ed. Karen Margolis, trans. Susan Singerman (Cambridge, England: Polity Press, 1990), 15–16.

62. This question is found in the pamphlet and in Inquisição de Lisboa, Processo 4404, 2:3–3v, ANTT.

63. Manuel and Manuel, *Utopian Thought in the Western World*, 49; Pleij, *Dreaming of Cockaigne*, 172.

64. Many of the Cockaigne traditions also placed that land in the West, as opposed to the earthly paradise in the East. See Pleij, *Dreaming of Cockaigne*, 166.

65. In the pamphlet she mentions May 27 as the date when the meeting was arranged, though she does not specify a year. Presumably it would have been the previous year, 1650, around the same time her understanding became explicitly *sebastianista* in nature.

66. See Manuel and Manuel, *Utopian Thought in the Western World*, 61, 183, and Marjorie Reeves, *Joachim of Fiore and the Prophetic Future: A Medieval Study in Historical Thinking* (Stroud, Gloucestershire: Sutton Publishing, 1999), 49.

67. Reeves, *Joachim of Fiore and the Prophetic Future*, 61.

68. Inquisição de Lisboa, Processo 4404, 2:117, ANTT.

69. Reeves, *Joachim of Fiore and the Prophetic Future*, 170.

70. William J. Entwhistle, *The Arthurian Legend in the Literatures of the Spanish Peninsula* (New York: Kraus Reprint Co., 1975), 7–63, 215.

71. Inquisição de Lisboa, Processo 4404, 2:4, ANTT.

72. Ibid., 34 (emphasis added).

73. ("muita amiga de rezar pelas suas contas"), ibid., 75.

74. Ibid., 80v, 82.

75. See Louis Châtellier, *The Europe of the Devout: The Catholic Reformation and the Formation of a New Society*, trans. Jean Birrell (Cambridge: Cambridge University Press, 1989).

76. Inquisição de Lisboa, Processo 4404, 2:13, ANTT.

77. Pleij, *Dreaming of Cockaigne*, 118–27.

78. Susan E. Dinan, "Spheres of Female Religious Expression in Early Modern France," in *Women and Religion in Old and New Worlds*, ed. Susan E. Dinan and Debra Meyers (New York: Routledge, 2001), 72ff. For an example of a group of women who were relatively successful in working outside the most restrictive aspects of this schema, see Susan E. Dinan, "Confraternities as a

Venue for Female Activism during the Catholic Reformation," in *Confraternities and Catholic Reform in Italy, France, and Spain*, ed. John Patrick Donnelly, S.J., and Michael W. Maher, S.J., Sixteenth Century Essays and Studies, vol. 44 (Kirksville, MO: Thomas Jefferson University Press, 1999), 189–214.

79. Andrew Keitt, *Inventing the Sacred: Imposture, Inquisition, and the Boundaries of the Supernatural in Golden Age Spain* (Boston: Brill, 2005), 5.

80. Inquisição de Lisboa, Processo 4404, 2:23, ANTT.

81. Allyson M. Poska and Elizabeth A. Lehfeldt, "Redefining Expectations: Women and the Church in Early Modern Spain," in Dinan and Meyers, *Women and Religion in Old and New Worlds*, 30. Gábor Klaniczay has argued that, in central Europe during the late medieval period, a variety of elite women consciously imitated extant hagiographic legends in order to demonstrate their own piety and religious vocation. See "Legends as Life-Strategies for Aspirant Saints in the Later Middle Ages," in Margolis, *Uses of Supernatural Power*, 95–110. I see no reason, in principle, why a similar process could not have occurred in Maria de Macedo's case, albeit subconsciously and only after her experience had been Christianized. The pattern she imitated, perhaps that of Saint Teresa de Avila, was probably received aurally rather than as a result of reading hagiographic texts, for the reasons already elaborated in regard to her *sebastianista* sources.

82. Inquisição de Lisboa, Processo 4404, 1:9, ANTT.

83. Ibid., 23.

84. Ibid., 12. Direct evidence of this claim is found only in the testimony of Pedro Peixoto, which calls into question its veracity. However, as has been noted, for all his confusions, Peixoto probably did not make up details wholesale. It is also interesting to note that Maria de Macedo was not the only person claiming that Sebastian had somehow intervened in the Battle of Linhas de Elvas: the same claim appears in the description of the vision of Madre Leocardia da Concepção, MS COD 128, fol. 33, BN.

85. This trope is also found in other accounts of lands of paradise. See Pleij, *Dreaming of Cockaigne*, 15.

86. For example, see ibid., 15–18.

7. Utopia's Judges: Understanding Inquisitorial Subculture

1. Inquisição de Lisboa, Processo 4404, 1:33–34, ANTT. Although the *promotor*'s decision is not dated, from its placement in the record we can know that it was written sometime between February 10 and 13, 1665, at least a week before Maria de Macedo's first deposition of February 20, 1665.

2. See the testimonies of Father Pedro Peixoto, Father Manoel da Costa, and Father João Ribeiro for this schema ibid., 13, 24–24v, 28v.

3. See, for example, Inquisição de Lisboa, Processo 4404, 1:5v, 13, 28, 45v, 52, 57, ANTT. João de Deus did mention a "weakness of judgment" as a possibility (though not a likely one) in his *qualificação*, but the inquistors never pursued that suggestion. See ibid., 2:120v. For a similar, though not precisely parallel, discussion of the categories by which female visionaries were understood in early modern England, see Katharine Hodgkin, "Reasoning with Unreason: Visions, Witchcraft, and Madness in Early Modern England," in *Languages of Witchcraft: Narrative, Ideology and Meaning in Early Modern Culture*, ed. Stuart Clark (London: Macmillan, 2001), 217–36.

4. Inquisição de Lisboa, Processo 4404, 2:56, ANTT.

5. Of course, the principal motivating force behind the Inquisition in Portugal was not a generalized fear of heresy but a specific fear of crypto-Judaism. See António Borges Coelho, *Inquisição de Evora: Dos primórdiosa 1668* (Lisbon: Editorial Caminho, 1987), 2:185–87. Francisco Bethencourt states that the Holy Office in Portugal followed a policy of "mild" repression against the deviant practices and beliefs of Old Christians compared with its violent and aggressive policy toward those accused of Judaism. This conclusion is certainly consistent with the outcome in the case of the Old Christian Maria de Macedo. See Francisco Bethencourt, "Portugal: A Scrupulous Inquisition," in *Early Modern European Witchcraft: Centres and Peripheries*, ed. Bengt Ankarloo and Gustav Henningsen (Oxford: Clarendon Press, 1990), 406–8.

6. See, for example, Inquisição de Lisboa, Processo 4404, 2:8, 9, 25v, 53v, 60, ANTT.

7. Ibid., 113–14.

8. Ibid., 115–115v.

9. There were six propositions prepared for qualification by the Conselho Geral, the sixth being concerned with how Maria traveled from the island to other places and how the doors of the churches she visited were opened for her even though no one was seen. Despite the obvious connection to the issue of night flights and supernatural occurrences, we will ignore this proposition, simply because the inquisitors themselves seem to have ignored it. The *qualificador* João Gomes mentioned in passing that it was not contrary to the faith (ibid., 117v.); João de Deus did not mention it at all. Neither did the inquisitors in their subsequent reports, and the Conselho Geral never brought it up again, either. It could be that, on the basis of Feliciano's testimony that he had never seen her leave the house, they believed it was simply another false claim on Maria's part.

10. Ibid., 53v.

11. Ibid., 3v; for another example of a female visionary whose stubbornness did not help her cause before the Inquisition, see Gillian T. W. Ahlgren, "Francisca de los Apóstoles: A Visionary Voice for Reform in Sixteenth-Century Toledo," in *Women in the Inquisition: Spain and the New World*, ed. Mary E. Giles (Baltimore: Johns Hopkins University Press, 1999), 119–33.

12. Inquisição de Lisboa, Processo 4404, 2:117v, ANTT.

13. Ibid., 120v.

14. Ibid., 2v, 27.

15. Frank E. Manuel and Fritzie P. Manuel, *Utopian Thought in the Western World* (Cambridge: Harvard University Press, Belknap Press, 1979), 52–53. There is evidence that Thomas Aquinas specifically disapproved of Joachim of Fiore's works, and the weight of the evidence seems to indicate that the Dominican Order as a whole was suspicious of Joachim. See Marjorie Reeves, *Joachim of Fiore and the Prophetic Future: A Medieval Study in Historical Thinking* (Stroud, Gloucestershire: Sutton Publishing, 1999), 61. Since the Portuguese Inquisition, like its sister institution in Spain, was heavily staffed by Dominicans, this may help explain why the Portuguese inquisitors generally did not look favorably on millennial schemes.

16. Of course, this was also true beyond the boundaries of Roman Catholicism. See Norman Cohn, *The Pursuit of the Millennium* (Oxford: Oxford University Press, 1970), 29–36; Herman Pleij, *Dreaming of Cockaigne: Medieval Fantasies of the Perfect Life*, trans. Diane Webb (New York: Columbia University Press, 2001), 18ff; Manuel and Manuel, *Utopian Thought in the Western World*, 181–83; and Bernard McGinn, "Forms of Catholic Millenarianism: A Brief Overview," in *Millenarianism and Messianism in Early Modern European Culture*, vol. 2, *Catholic Millenarianism, from Savonarola to the Abbé Grégoire*, ed. Karl A Kottman (Dordrecht: Kulwer Academic Publishers, 2001), 1–13.

17. Inquisição de Lisboa, Processo 4404, 2:35–35v, ANTT.

18. Ibid., 123v.

19. Ibid., 134. For a discussion of the essentially conservative nature of official Catholicism after Trent, see Quentin Skinner, *The Foundations of Modern Political Thought*, vol. 2, *The Age of Reformation* (Cambridge: Cambridge University Press, 1978), 144ff, and Michael A. Mullett, *The Catholic Reformation* (London: Routledge, 1999), 39ff.

20. Inquisição de Lisboa, Processo 4404, 2:21–21v, ANTT.

21. Ibid., 19.

22. Ibid., 20–20v.

23. There is also the possibility that de la Cerda's statement was not motivated by a desire for orthodoxy but was, in reality, an attempt to squelch any desire on Maria's part for a more egalitarian socioeconomic system. I doubt that all ideological issues (in the form of points of doctrine, for example) can be reduced to epiphenomena of class structure, but the possibility deserves to be raised.

24. Inquisição de Lisboa, Processo 4404, 1:9, ANTT (emphasis added).

25. Jacqueline Hermann, *No reino do desejado: A construção do sebastianismo em Portugal séculos XVI e XVII* (São Paulo: Companhia das Letras, 1998), 239–40 (emphasis added).

26. Inquisição de Lisboa, Processo 4404, 2:24v, ANTT.

27. For the Spanish case, see esp. Julio Caro Baroja, *The World of the Witches*, trans. Nigel Glendinning (London: Weidenfield and Nicholson, 1964), and Gustav Henningsen, *The Witches' Advocate: Basque Witchcraft and the Spanish Inquisition, 1609–1614* (Reno: University of Nevada Press, 1980). For the Portuguese case, see José Pedro Paiva, *Bruxaria e superstição num país sem "caça às bruxas,"* 1600–1774 (Lisbon: Notícias Editorial, 1997), and Bethencourt, "Portugal," 403–22.

28. For a good discussion of the possibilities, see Brian P. Levack, *The Witch-Hunt in Early Modern Europe*, 3rd ed. (Harlow, Essex: Pearson Longman, 2006).

29. Paiva, *Bruxaria e superstição*, 36–42; Bethencourt, "Portugal," 403.

30. Paiva, *Bruxaria e superstição*, 24f.

31. For another example of inquisitorial skepticism of witchcraft claims based on a desire to follow good (i.e., Roman) criminal procedure, see John Tedeschi, "The Roman Inquisition and Witchcraft: An Early Seventeenth-Century 'Instruction' on Correct Trial Procedure," in *The Prosecution of Heresy: Collected Studies on the Inquisition in Early Modern Italy* (Binghamton, NY: Medieval and Renaissance Texts and Studies, 1991), 205–28.

32. Levack, *Witch-Hunt in Early Modern Europe*, 30–73.

33. See, for example, Inquisição de Lisboa, Processo 4404, 2:7, 26v, 29, 153v, ANTT.

34. Ibid., 29.

35. Ibid., 116v. Gomes specifically cites del Rio here. See Martín del Rio, *Investigations into Magic*, ed. and trans. P. G. Maxwell-Stuart (Manchester: Manchester University Press, 2000), 109–10.

36. Inquisição de Lisboa, Processo 4404, 2:7, ANTT.

37. Ibid., 11v–12. See also del Rio, *Investigations into Magic*, 112.

38. Inquisição de Lisboa, Processo 4404, 2:4v–6, ANTT.

39. Ibid., 1v, 6v. It should be remembered that de la Cerda had already had access to a copy of the long version of the pamphlet by the time he first deposed Maria.

40. Ibid., 13v.

41. Ibid., 7v, 26, 54–54v, 60.

42. Ibid., 23, 26.

43. Ibid., 23–23v.

44. Ibid., 26v–28.

45. Ibid., 27–27 v (emphasis added)

46. Ibid., 29–30.

47. Ibid., 29v–30.

48. The attitude toward evidence shown here by Inquisitor Barreto was not limited to him or to the Portuguese Inquisition but rather was, as the seventeenth century wore on, increasingly a part of conception of the law on the part of canon lawyers throughout Europe. See Tedeschi, "Roman Inquisition and Witchcraft," 205–27. For an important examination of how this attitude toward evidence had real-world results, see Gustav Henningsen's discussion of Inquisitor Alonso de Salazar Frías in *Witches' Advocate*, esp. 175–80 (Salazar's reasons for his first contrary vote) and 366–77 (his recommendations to improve procedures in witch trials).

49. Inquisição de Lisboa, Processo 4404, 2:110–12, ANTT.

50. For the specific reference to standards for a pact, see Conselho Geral, Livro 342, bk. 3, sec. 14, para. 1, ANTT.

51. Inquisição de Lisboa, Processo 4404, 2:122–24, ANTT.

52. See Paiva, *Bruxaria e superstição*, 54–56.

53. See the comments of the *promotor* and Inquisitor Barreto in this regard, Inquisição de Lisboa, Processo 4404, 1:33v, 2:29v–30, ANTT.

54. For more on the options open to religious-inclined women during the Counter-Reformation period, see Susan E. Dinan, "Spheres of Female Religious Expression in Early Modern France," in *Women and Religion in Old and New Worlds*, ed. Susan E. Dinan and Debra Meyers (New York: Routledge, 2001); Elizabeth Rapley, *The Dévotes: Women and Church in Seventeenth-Century France* (Montreal: McGill-Queen's University Press, 1990); Andrew Keitt, *Inventing the Sacred: Imposture, Inquisition, and the Boundaries of the Supernatural in Golden Age Spain* (Boston: Brill, 2005), 5, 106; and Louis Châtellier, *The Europe of the Devout: The Catholic Reformation and the Formation of a New Society*, trans. Jean Birrell (Cambridge: Cambridge University Press, 1989).

55. For a discussion of the often strained relations between *beatas* and the Inquisition, see Mary Elizabeth Perry, "*Beatas* and the Inquisition in Early Modern Seville," in *Inquisition and Society in Early Modern Europe*, ed. and trans. Stephen Haliczer (London: Croom Helm, 1987), 147–68.

56. Inquisição de Lisboa, Processo 4404, 2:4–4v.

57. See Hermann, *No reino do desejado*, 273–79. Inquisição de Lisboa, Processos 4564 (Luzia de Jesus) and 557 (Joana da Cruz), ANTT. Hermann is mistaken here. I never found any evidence that Luzia de Jesus ever mentioned Sebastian; in fact, she refers to the kingly figure as "João" (fol. 23v), and given that the rest of vision is dominated by the war with Castile, the identity of this João seems clear enough. Hermann seems to be using the term *sebastianismo* here as the equivalent of Portuguese messianism, which does not seem justified for the early Restorartion period. Also, Luzia de Jesus was not found guilty because she had a vision but because she claimed to be higher than an angel in God's favor. Joana da Cruz did mention Sebastian briefly, but Sebastianism had nothing to do with her conviction. She was found guilty because she claimed to be equal to the Virgin Mary (fol. 10).

58. Inquisição de Lisboa, Processo 4404, 2:119; João de Deus cites del Rio, *Disquitiones Magicae*, bk. 4, chap. 1, question 3, sec. 2. For an English summary of the section, see del Rio, *Investigations into Magic*, 150. For a broader discussion of the development of the prosecutorial apparatus against women who presumed holiness or special revelations from God, see Anne Jacobson Schutte,

Aspiring Saints: Pretense of Holiness, Inquisition, and Gender in the Republic of Venice, 1618–1750 (Baltimore: Johns Hopkins University Press, 2001), esp. 42–72.

59. Inquisição de Lisboa, Processo 4404, 2:77.

60. Unfortunately, I know of no systematic study of this phenomenon in Portugal, although even a cursory glance of the registers of inquisitorial trial records shows that many more women than men were tried for claiming false visions.

61. Inquisição de Lisboa, Processo 4404, 2:4v, 12.

62. Ibid., 29. The requirement that female visionaries demonstrate an exemplary moral life is also shown by the fact that Maria's defense counsel, Miguel Vieira de Santo, tried to prove that she was very moral "while in her father's house" in subheads 1 and 2 of her *contradittas*. See ibid., 75–78v.

63. Ibid., 111. See 79–85v for the original testimony of the defense witnesses.

64. See, for example, ibid., 26v–28. For the issue of stubborn visionaries, see Schutte, *Aspiring Saints*, 46, where a standard for visionaries from the fifteenth-century Spanish writer Juan de Torquemada is reproduced. Of particular interest is standard 2: "Do the revelations leave the recipient *humble, flexible, and disposed to accept discipline?* [emphasis added]"

65. See Inquisição de Lisboa, Processo 4404, 2:36–38v, ANTT.

66. Peter Burke has argued that many Counter-Reformation saints passed the rigorous tests of canonicity because they fit the best-known stereotypes of sanctity. I would argue the same insight holds true on the opposite end of the scale for the deviant. See Peter Burke, "How to Be a Counter-Reformation Saint," in *Religion and Society in Early Modern Europe 1500–1800*, ed. Kaspar von Greyerz (London: George Allen and Unwin, 1984), 51–52.

67. ("estes pontos e miudezas"), Inquisição de Lisboa, Processo 4404, 2:19, ANTT.

68. Carlo Ginzburg, "The Inquisitor as Anthropologist," in *Clues, Myths, and the Historical Method*, trans. John Tedeschi and Anne C. Tedeschi (Baltimore: Johns Hopkins University Press, 1989), 156–64; Carlo Ginzburg, "Alien Voices: The Dialogic Element in Early Modern Jesuit Historiography," in *History, Rhetoric, and Proof: The Menahem Stern Jerusalem Lectures* (Hanover, NH: University Press of New England, 1999), 71–91.

69. For some insightful comments on the often complicated interaction of oral and written culture in the early modern period, see R. A. Houston, *Literacy in Early Modern Europe: Culture and Education, 1500–1800* (London: Longman, 1988), 218–29. For an important view on the complex relationship between elite and popular culture, see Mikhail Bakhtin, *Rabelais and His World*, trans. Hélène Iswolsky (Bloomington: Indiana University Press, 1984).

70. Adam Fox in his study of oral and literate culture in early modern England concludes that many elements of popular folklore actually had their origin in printed collections of classical stories and fables. See Adam Fox, *Oral and Literate Culture in England, 1500–1700* (Oxford: Clarendon Press, 2000), 9–10.

71. Of course, both the index and activities of examiners of books show that the Inquisition also felt a profound fear of the power of the books they deemed heretical. See Virgilio Pinto Crespo, "Thought Control in Spain," in *Inquisition and Society in Early Modern Europe*, ed. and trans. Stephen Haliczer (London: Croom Helm, 1987), 171–88.

72. Inquisição de Lisboa, Processo 4404, 2:29, ANTT.

73. Ibid., 116–21.

74. See del Rio, *Investigations into Magic*, 6, esp. 209–10, 233–34.

75. Ibid., 150–51.

76. Ibid., 112, 151.
77. Ibid., 98.
78. Ibid., 91.

Conclusion: The Intersection of Two Worlds

1. Harmut Lehmann argues that the pious middle classes formed a "self-reliant and cultural alternative" to both court culture and peasant culture during the Reformation. No comprehensive study is available to answer the question of whether the "pious middle classes" (of whom Maria de Macedo seems to be an example) played an analogous role in Counter-Reformation Portugal, but it would be intriguing to see the results of such a study. Perhaps, in the end, it will become clear that Maria de Macedo was less a passive receptacle, caught between high and low, and more a representative of a "middle synthesis." See Harmut Lehmann, "The Cultural Importance of the Pious Middle Classes in Seventeenth-Century Protestant Society," in *Religion and Society in Early Modern Europe, 1500–1800*, ed. Kaspar von Greyerz (London: George Allen and Unwin, 1984), 33–41.

2. Inquisição de Lisboa, Processo 4404, 2:123, ANTT.

3. Ibid., 1:4v, 16–25.

4. Ibid., 7–13v, 29v–33, 42–46, 59–64.

5. Ibid., 12, 57–57v, 27–29.

6. Ibid., 14–15v; 2:84v–85.

7. Feliciano did mention that, at first, he thought his wife might have "gone out of her mind" (ibid., 1:52), proof that he considered, at least briefly, the fourth option of madness. But, again, the inquisitors did not pursue that option, nor did Feliciano mention it again. It is not completely clear why in either case.

8. José Pedro Paiva, *Bruxaria e superstição num país sem "caça às bruxas" 1600–1774* (Lisbon: Notícias Editorial, 1997), 149–59.

9. See Mikhail Bakhtin, *Rabelais and His World*, trans. Hélène Iswolsky (Bloomington: Indiana University Press, 1984).

10. This is particularly true when speaking of popular religion in the early modern period. For some insightful comments on the problematic aspects involved in the use of the terms "popular" and "elite" religion, and for some ways to avoid the negative consequences of that usage, see Ellen Badone, introduction to *Religious Orthodoxy and Popular Faith in European Society*, ed. Ellen Badone (Princeton: Princeton University Press, 1990), 3–23.

11. The fact that the Inquisition spoke with one voice could be a very good thing. See Gustav Henningsen, *The Witches' Advocate: Basque Witchcraft and the Spanish Inquisition, 1609–1614* (Reno: University of Nevada Press, 1980), particularly 388–89, for an excellent discussion of the witch craze in Navarre that was stopped by the actions (and standards) of a single inquisitor backed up by the Suprema.

12. Inquisição de Lisboa, Processo 4404, 2:77–78, 119, 123, ANTT. Nor should we forget that, even in 1584, the inquisitors of Lisbon let the "first *sebastianista*," Balthasar Gonçalves, go because they viewed his odd claims about Sebastian as the product of madness rather than an example of heresy. See *Inquisição de Lisboa*, Processo 5083, ANTT.

13. The Inquisition attempted to suppress Sebastianism in the 1750s as part of the Marques de Pombal's campaign against the Jesuits, but the political configuration within the kingdom was very,

very different than it had been in the Restoration period. See João José van den Besselaar, *O sebastianismo: História sumária* (Lisbon: Instituto de Cultura e Lingua Portuguesa, 1987), 156–59.

14. See MS COD 402, 106–106v; MS COD 126; and MS COD 128, all in BN.

15. Carlo Ginzburg and Carlo Poni, "The Name and the Game: Unequal Exchange and the Historiographic Marketplace," in *Microhistory and the Lost Peoples of Europe*, ed. Edward Muir and Guido Ruggiero, trans. Eren Branch (Baltimore: Johns Hopkins University Press, 1991), 8 (emphasis added).

BIBLIOGRAPHY

Primary Sources

Manuscripts

ARQUIVO NACIONAL DA TORRE DO TOMBO, LISBON

Chancellaria de D. Afonso VI, Livro 30—Doações.

Conselho Geral, Livro 342—*Regimento de 1640.*

Conselho Geral, Livro 435—Listas dos Autos da Fé.

Inquisição de Lisboa, Livro 8—Lista dos Autos da Fé.

Inquisição de Lisboa, Livro 12—Livro de Certidões, Confisco de bens.

Inquisição de Lisboa, Livro 106—Ministros e oficiais, 1656–1683.

Inquisição de Lisboa, Livro 236—Quaderno do Promotor 37.

Inquisição de Lisboa, Processo 557—Joana da Cruz.

Inquisição de Lisboa, Processo 4404—Maria de Macedo.

Inquisição de Lisboa, Processo 4564—Luzia de Jesus.

Inquisição de Lisboa, Processo 5083—Balthasar Gonçalves.

"Jardim Ameno," Manuscrita da Livraria 774.

BIBLIOTECA NACIONAL DE LISBOA

MS COD 126—"Epítome das esperadas venturas de Portugal."

MS COD 128—Escritos sebastianistas, Eighteenth-Century Collection.

MS COD 132—"Resposta de certa pessoa a outra" e outros escriptos sebastianistas.

MS COD 400—Escritos sebastianistas, Seventeeth-Century Collection.

MS COD 402—Documentos para o estudo de sebastianismo.

MS COD 551—Textos sebastianistas.

MS COD 810—"O tratado da quinta monarchia e felicidades de Portugal profetizadas," by Fr. Sebastião de Paiva; "O Reyno de Portugal, sua creação, successos, profezidos pello Ceo a Esdras nos Capitulos 11–12–13 do seu Livro 4°," by João da Cruz, O.P.

Castro, D. João de. "Advertimentos ao sempre bem vindo e apparecido Rey D. Sebastião," 1604.

———. "Aurora," 1604–5.

———. "Avisos divinos e humanos para os memorandos conquistadores da Terra da Promissão dos nossos tempos, que he todo o universo," 1617.

———. "Da quinta e ultima monarchia futura com muitas outras cousas admiraveis dos nossos tempos," 1597.

———. "Discursi dirigido a El R. D. Sebastião," 1588.

———. "Remonstrança feito de novo aos illustrissimos senhores do Conselho d'Estado E Privado del Rey Christianissimo; em suseitiçam da causa E dos acontecimentos admiraveis do Serenissimo Rey de Portugal, Dom Sebastião, primeiro do nome,"1603.

———. "Renovação do tratado apologético que eu, Dom João de Castro, compus contra hu' livro defamatoria que alguns Portuguezes contra mi fizeram e imprimiram na cidade de Paris," 1620.

———. "Segundo apparecimento del Rei Dom Sebastião do primeiro, e de toda sua vida: Dirigido aos tres estados do Reino de Portugal," undated, probably 1602–3.

———. "Tratado apologético contra hum libello diffametorio que imprimirão em França certos Portuguezes com o titulo que se vê na folha seguinte," undated.

———. "Tratado dos Portuguezes de Veneza, ou ternario, senario, e novenario dos Portuguezes, que em Veneza solicitarão a liberdade del Rey D. Sebastião: com hu'a breve mencão do Snr. D. António," 1622–23.

Printed Sources

Almeida, Grégorio de [Fr. João de Vasconcelos]. *Restauração de Portugal prodigiosa*. Lisbon: António Alvarez, 1643.

Araújo, Dr. Juan Salgado de. *Marte portugues contra emulaciones castellanas; o iustificaciones de las armas del Rey de Portugal contra Castilla*. Lisbon: Lourenço Anberes, 1642.

Bocarro Frances, Manuel. *Anacephaleosis da monarchia lusitania, primeira parte*. Lisbon, 1624.

———. *Anotações sobre o primeiro anaceleosis da monarchia lusitana*. Lisbon, 1624.

Camões, Luís de. *Os Lusíades*. 4ª Edição. Lisbon: Publicações Europa-America, 1997.

Canons and Decrees of the Council of Trent. Translated by Rev. H. J. Schroeder, O.P. St. Louis: B. Herder Book Co., 1960.

Castro, Dom João de. *Discurso da vida do sempre bem vindo et apparecido Rey Dom Sebastião nosso senhor o Encuberto desdo seu naçimento tee o presente*. Paris: Martin Verac, 1602.

———. *Paraphrase et concordançia de alguas prophecias de Bandarra, çapateiro de Trancoso*. Paris, 1603.

Cunha, Euclides da. *Rebellion in the Backlands*. Translated by Samuel Putnam. Chicago: University of Chicago Press, 1957.

del Rio, Martín. *Investigations into Magic*. Edited and translated by P. G. Maxwell-Stuart. Manchester: Manchester University Press, 2000.

Ferraz, António Paes. *Discurso astrológico das influencies da mayor conjunçam de Jupiter e Marte, que succedeu neste annom de 1660. 28 de Agosto.* Lisbon: Domingos Carpeiro, 1661.

Lyra, António Velozo de. *Espelho de lusitanos em o cristal do psalmo quarenta e tres.* Lisbon: Paulo Craesbeeck, 1643.

Melo, D. Francisco Manuel de. *Epanáfora política primeira.* Reprinted in *Alterações de Évora, 1637,* edited by Joel Serrão, 1–139. Lisbon: Portugália Editora, 1967. Originally published in 1660.

———. *Tácito portugues.* Edited by Raul Rêgo. Lisbon: Livraria Sá da Costa, 1995.

Monteiro, Dr. Nicolai. *Vox turturis, portugalia gemens ad Pontificem Summum.* Lisbon: Domingos Lopes Rosa, 1649.

Pacheco, Panteleão Rodrigues. *Manifesto do reyno de Portugal, presentado a Santidade de Urbano VIII, N.S.* Lisbon: Domingos Lopes Rola, 1643.

Proceso da Inquisição de Lisboa, 7197. "Proceso de Gonçalo Anes." Reprinted in Theophilo Braga, *Historia de Camões,* 1:411–16. Porto: Imprensa Portugueza, 1873.

Procesos da Inquisição de Lisboa, 3734 e 16905. "Procesos de Luis Dias." Extracts reprinted in João Lúcio de Azevedo, *A evolução do sebastianismo,* 174–93. Lisbon: Livraria Clásica Editora de A. M. Teixeira, 1984. Originally published in 1918.

Severim de Faria, Manuel. "Relação do que sucedeu em Portugal e nas mais provincias do Ocidente desde 1637 até Março de 1638." Reprinted in *Alterações de Évora, 1637,* edited by Joel Serrão. Lisbon: Portugália Editora, 1967. Original date unknown.

Soùsa de Macedo, António de. *Lusitana liberata, ab injusto castellanorum dominio, restituta legitimo Principe, Serenissimo Joanni IV.* London: Richard Heron, 1645.

———. *Panegyrico sobre o milagrosso successo, com euq Deos livrou a el Rey Nosso Senhor da sacrilega treição dos castelhanos.* Lisbon: Paulo Craesbeeck, 1647.

Veiga, P. Manoel da, S.J. *Vida, virtudes, e doutrina admiravel de Simão Gomes, Portuguez, vulgarmente chamado o Çapateiro Santo.* Lisbon: Joseph Filippe, 1709. Originally published in 1626.

Vieira, Padre António. *Clavis prophetarum.* Reprinted in P. António Vieira, *Obras escolhidas,* vol. 9, edited by Hernâni Cidade and António Sérgio, 173–267. Lisbon: Livraria Sá da Costa, 1953.

———. *Defesa perante o Tribunal do Santo Oficio.* Edited by Hernâni Cidade. Vols. 1–2. Bahía, Brazil: Universidade de Bahía, 1957.

———. *História do futuro.* Reprinted in P. António Vieira, *Obras escolhidas,* vols. 8–9, edited by Hernâni Cidade and António Sérgio. Lisbon: Livraria Sá da Costa, 1953.

———. "Esperanças de Portugal, quinto império do mundo." In P. António Vieira, *Obras escolhidas,* vol. 6, edited by Hernâni Cidade, 1–66. Lisbon: Livraria Sá da Costa, 1952.

———. *Sermão dos Bons Anos.* Reprinted in P. António Vieira, *Obras Escolhidas,* vol. 10, edited by Hernâni Cidade, 153–89. Lisbon: Livraria Sá da Costa, 1953.

Secondary Sources

Ahlgren, Gillian T. W. "Francisca de los Apóstoles: A Visionary Voice for Reform in Sixteenth-Century Toledo." In *Women in the Inquisition: Spain and the New World*, edited by Mary E. Giles, 119–33. Baltimore: Johns Hopkins University Press, 1999.

Alexander, Paul J. "The Diffusion of Byzantine Apocalypses in the Medieval West and the Beginnings of Joachimism." In *Prophecy and Millenarianism: Essays in Honor of Marjorie Reeves*, edited by Ann Williams, 53–106. Harlow, Essex: Longman, 1980.

Almeida, Fortunato de. *História de Portugal*. Vol. 4. Coimbra: Imprensa de Universidade, 1926.

Amaral, Diogo Freitas do. *D. Afonso Henriques: Biografia*. Lisbon: Bertrand Editora, 2000.

Antas, Miguel d'. *Les Faux Don Sébastien: Étude sur l'Histoire du Portugal*. Paris: A. Durand, 1866.

———. *Os Falsos D. Sebastião*. 2nd ed. Translated by Sales Loureiro. Lisbon: Heuris, 1985.

Athaide Oliveira, Francisco Xavier d'. *As Mouras encantadas e os encantamentos no Algarve*. Tavira, Portugal: Livraria Figueirinhas, 1918.

Azevedo, João Lúcio de. *A evolução do sebastianismo*. Lisbon: Livraria Clásica Editora de A. M. Teixeira, 1984. Originally published in 1918.

Badone, Ellen. Introduction to *Religious Orthodoxy and Popular Faith in European Society*, edited by Ellen Badone, 3–23. Princeton: Princeton University Press, 1990.

Baião, António. *Episodios dramaticos da Inquisicão Portuguesa*. Lisbon: Seara Nova, 1972.

Bakhtin, Mikhail. *Rabelais and His World*. Translated by Hélène Iswolsky. Bloomington: Indiana University Press, 1984.

Baroja, Julio Caro. *Inquisición, brujería y criptojudaísmo*. Barcelona: Ediciones Ariel, 1970.

———. "Witchcraft and Catholic Theology." In *Early Modern European Witchcraft: Centres and Peripheries*, edited by Bengt Ankarloo and Gustav Henningsen, 19–43. Oxford: Clarendon Press, 1990.

———. *The World of the Witches*. Translated by Nigel Glendinnig. London: Weidenfeld and Nicolson, 1964.

Belard da Fonseca, António. *Dom Sebastião: Antes e depois de Alcácer-quibir*. Vols. 1–2. Lisbon: Ramos, Afonso & Moita, 1978.

Benjamin, Walter. *Illuminations*. Edited by Hannah Arendt. Translated by Harry Zohn. New York: Schocken Books, 1985.

Bercé, Yves-Marie. *Le roi caché: Sauveurs et imposteurs. Mythes politiques populaires dans l'Europe moderne*. Paris: Fayard, 1990.

Besselaar, João José van den. *O sebastianismo: História sumária*. Lisbon: Instituto de Cultura e Lingua Portuguesa, 1987.

Bethencourt, Francisco. *História das Inquisições: Portugal, Espanha, e Itália*. Lisbon: Temas e Debates, 1996.

———. "Portugal: A Scrupulous Inquisition." In *Early Modern European Witchcraft: Centres and Peripheries*, edited by Bengt Ankarloo and Gustav Henningsen, 403–22. Oxford: Clarendon Press, 1990.

Bilinkoff, Jodi. "Navigating the Waves (of Devotion): Toward a Gendered Analysis of Early Modern Catholicism." In *Crossing Boundaries: Attending to Early Modern Women*, edited by Jane Donawerth and Adele Seeff, 161–72. Newark: University of Delaware Press, 2000.

Bloomfield, Morton W. "Recent Scholarship on Joachim de Fiore and His Influence." In *Prophecy and Millenarianism: Essays in Honor of Marjorie Reeves*, edited by Ann Williams, 21–52. Harlow, Essex: Longman, 1980.

Borrás, Vicent J. Vallés. *La Germanía*. Valencia: Institució Alfons El Magnànim, 2000.

Bouza, Fernando. *Corre manuscrito: Una historia cultural del Siglo de Oro*. Madrid: Marcial Pons, Historia, 2001.

Bovill, E. W. *The Battle of Alcazar: An Account of the Defeat of Don Sebastian at El-Ksar el-Kebir*. London: Batchworth Press, 1952.

Boxer, C. R. *A Great Luso-Brazilian Figure: Padre António Vieira, S.J., 1608–1697*. London: Hispanic and Luso-Brazilian Councils, 1957.

Brooks, Mary Elizabeth. *A King for Portugal: The Madrigal Conspiracy, 1594–1595*. Madison: University of Wisconsin Press, 1964.

Burke, Peter. "How to Be a Counter-Reformation Saint." In *Religion and Society in Early Modern Europe, 1500–1800*, edited by Kaspar von Greyerz, 45–55. London: George Allen and Unwin, 1984.

Carcel, Ricardo García. *Las Germanías de Valencia*. Barcelona: Ediciones Península, 1975.

Châtellier, Louis. *The Europe of the Devout: The Catholic Reformation and the Formation of a New Society*. Translated by Jean Birrell. Cambridge: Cambridge University Press, 1989.

Chaves, Luiz. *Lisboa no folclore*. Lisbon: Impresa Libanio da Silva, 1939.

Cidade, Hernâni. *Padre António Vieira: A Obra e o homem*. Lisbon: Editora Arcádia, 1964.

Cintra, Luís Filipe Lindley. *Sobre a formação e evolução da lenda de Ourique (até à Crónica de 1419)*. Lisbon: Imprensa de Coimbra, 1957.

Coelho, Adolfo. *Contos populares portugueses*. Lisbon: Publicações Dom Quixote, 1985.

Coelho, António Borges. *Inquisiçião de Evora: Dos primórdioa 1668*. Vols. 1–2. Lisbon: Editorial Caminho, 1987.

Cohn, Norman. *The Pursuit of the Millennium*. New York: Oxford University Press, 1970.

Coleman, Stanley Jackson. *Portuguese Legendary Lore*. Douglas, Isle of Man: Folklore Academy, 1954.

Contreras, Jaime. *Sotos contra Riquelmes: Regidores, inquisidores y criptojudíos*. Madrid: Anaya & M. Muchnik, 1992.

Cooper, Mark Emerson. "Messianic Expectation and Collective Myth Formation: Prophecy, Society and Imagination in Early Modern Portugal." Ph.D. diss., University of California, Santa Barbara, 2004.

Crespo, Virgilio Pinto. "Thought Control in Spain." In *Inquisition and Society in Early Modern Europe*, edited and translated by Stephen Haliczer, 171–88. London: Croom Helm, 1987.

Cunha Saraiva, José Mendes da. "Causas do levantamento da Nação em 1640." In *Congresso do Mundo Português*, 7:57–93. Lisbon: Secção de Congressos, 1940.

Davis, Natalie Zemon. *Fiction in the Archives: Pardon Tales and Their Tellers in Sixteenth-Century France*. Stanford: Stanford University Press, 1987.

———. *The Return of Martin Guerre*. Cambridge: Harvard University Press, 1984.

Diaz, Dilia Flores. *Trance, Posesion y Hablas Sagradas: Un studio etnológico de la comunicación*. Maracaibo: Universidad del Zulia, 1988.

Dinan, Susan E. "Confraternities as a Venue for Female Activism during the Catholic Reformation." In *Confraternities and Catholic Reform in Italy, France, and Spain*, edited by John Patrick Donnelly, S.J., and Michael W. Maher, S.J., 189–214. *Sixteenth-Century Essays and Studies*, vol. 44. Kirksville, MO : Thomas Jefferson University Press, 1999.

———. "Spheres of Female Religious Expression in Early Modern France." In *Women and Religion in Old and New Worlds*, edited by Susan E. Dinan and Debra Meyers, 71–92. New York: Routledge, 2001.

Doel, Fran, Geoff Doel, and Terry Lloyd. *Worlds of Arthur: King Arthur in History, Legend and Culture*. Stroud, Gloucestershire: Tempus, 1998.

Domingues, Mário. *D. João IV e a campanha de restauracão*. Lisbon: Romano Torres, 1970.

Elliott, J. H. *The Count-Duke of Olivares: The Statesman in an Age of Decline*. New Haven: Yale University Press, 1986.

———. *Imperial Spain, 1469–1716*. London: Penguin Books, 1963.

———. *The Revolt of the Catalans: A Study in the Decline of Spain (1598–1640)*. Cambridge: Cambridge University Press, 1963.

———. "Revolution and Continuity in Early Modern Europe." In *The General Crisis of the Seventeenth-Century*, edited by Geoffrey Parker and Lesley M. Smith, 108–27. New York: Routledge, 1997.

Entwhistle, William J. *The Arthurian Legend in the Literatures of the Spanish Peninsula*. New York: Kraus Reprint Co., 1975.

Fonseca, Jorge. "Elementos sobre a Revolta Popular de 1637 em Montemor-o-Novo." *Almansor* 3 (1985): 85–99.

Fraker, Charles. "Goncalo Martinez de Medina, the Jeronimos, and the *Devotio Moderna*." In *Joachim of Fiore in Christian Thought: Essays on the Influence of the Calabrian Prophet*, edited by Delno C. West, 611–31. New York: Burt Frankling and Co., 1975.

Franco, Hilário, Jr. *Cocanha: A história de um país imaginário*. São Paulo: Companhia das Letras, 1998.

Franco, José Eduardo, and Paulo de Assunção. *As Metamorfoses de um polvo: Religião e política nos regimentos da Inquisicão Portuguesa (Sec. XVI–XIX)*. Lisbon: Prefácio, 2004.

Friedman, Ellen G. *Spanish Captives in North Africa in the Early Modern Age*. Madison: University of Wisconsin Press, 1983.

Fromm, Erich. *The Forgotten Language: An Introduction to the Understanding of Dreams, Fairy Tales, and Myths*. New York: Grove Press, 1951.

Fox, Adam. *Oral and Literate Culture in England, 1500–1700*. Oxford: Clarendon Press, 2000.

Gandra, Manuel J. *Joaquim de Fiore, joaquimismo, e a esperança sebástica*. Lisbon: Fundação Lusíada, 1999.

Garcia, Pablo Pérez, and Jorge Antonio Catalá Sanz. *Epígonos del encubertismo: Proceso contra los agermandados de 1541*. Valencia: Biblioteca Valenciana, 2000.

Gaskill, Malcolm. *Crime and Mentalities in Early Modern England*. Cambridge: Cambridge University Press, 2000.

Ginzburg, Carlo. "Alien Voices: The Dialogic Element in Early Modern Jesuit Historiography." In *History, Rhetoric, and Proof: The Menahem Stern Jerusalem Lectures*, 71–91. Hanover, NH: University Press of New England, 1999.

———. *The Cheese and the Worms*. Translated by John Tedeschi and Anne C. Tedeschi. Baltimore: Johns Hopkins University Press, 1980.

———. "Clues: Roots of an Evidential Paradigm." In *Clues, Myths, and the Historical Method*, translated by John Tedeschi and Anne C. Tedeschi, 96–125. Baltimore: Johns Hopkins University Press, 1989.

———. "The Inquisitor as Anthropologist." In *Clues, Myths, and the Historical Method*, translated by John Tedeschi and Anne C. Tedeschi, 156–64. Baltimore: Johns Hopkins University Press, 1989.

———. *The Night Battles*. Translated by John Tedeschi and Anne C. Tedeschi. Baltimore: Johns Hopkins University Press, 1983.

Ginzburg, Carlo, and Carlo Poni. "The Name and the Game: Unequal Exchange and the Historiographic Marketplace." In *Microhistory and the Lost Peoples of Europe*, edited by Edward Muir and Guido Ruggiero, translated by Eren Branch, 1–10. Baltimore: Johns Hopkins University Press, 1991.

Givens, Bryan. "Sebastianism in Theory and in Practice in Early Modern Portugal." In *Braudel Revisited: The Mediterranean World, 1600–1800*, edited by Gabriel Piterberg, Teófilo F. Ruiz, and Geoffrey Symcox. Toronto: University of Toronto Press, 2010.

———. "The St. Paul of Sebastianism: Tracing the Millenarian Legacy of Dom João de Castro." *Portuguese Studies Review* 17 (2009–10): 1–20.

Goodman, Felicitas D., Jeanette H. Henney, and Esther Pressel. *Trance, Healing, and Hallucination: Three Field Studies in Religious Experience*. Malabar, FL: Robert E. Krieger Publishing Co., 1982.

Grendi, Edoardo. "Micro-analisi e storia sociale." *Quaderni Storici* 35 (May–August 1977): 512.

Henningsen, Gustav. *The Witches' Advocate: Basque Witchcraft and the Spanish Inquisition, 1609–1614*. Reno: University of Nevada Press, 1980.

Hermann, Jacqueline. *No reino do desejado: A construção do sebastianismo em Portugal séculos XVI e XVII*. São Paulo: Companhia das Letras, 1998.

Hess, Andrew C. *The Forgotten Frontier: A History of the Sixteenth-Century Ibero-African Frontier.* Chicago: University of Chicago Press, 1978.

Hodgkin, Katharine. "Reasoning with Unreason: Visions, Witchcraft, and Madness in Early Modern England." In *Languages of Witchcraft: Narrative, Ideology and Meaning in Early Modern Culture*, edited by Stuart Clark, 217–36. London: Macmillan, 2001.

Houston, R. A. *Literacy in Early Modern Europe: Culture and Education, 1500–1800.* London: Longman, 1988.

Johnson, Harold. "A Pedophile in the Palace or the Sexual Abuse of King Sebastian of Portugal (1554–1578) and Its Consequences." In *Pelo Vaso Traseiro: Sodomy and Sodomites in Luso-Brazilian History*, edited by Harold Johnson and Francis A. Dutra, 195–229. Tucson: Fenestra Books, 2007.

Kagan, Richard L. *Lucrecia's Dreams: Politics and Prophecy in Sixteenth-Century Spain.* Berkeley: University of California Press, 1990.

Kamen, Henry. *The Spanish Inquisition: A Historical Revision.* London: Weidenfeld and Nicholson, 1997.

Kantorowicz, Ernst. *Frederick the Second, 1194–1250.* Translated by E. O. Lorimer. New York: Frederick Ungar Publishing Co., 1957.

Keitt, Andrew. *Inventing the Sacred: Imposture, Inquisition, and the Boundaries of the Supernatural in Golden Age Spain.* Boston: Brill, 2005.

Klaniczay, Gábor. "The Carnival Spirit: Bakhtin's Theory on the Culture of Laughter." In *The Uses of Supernatural Power: The Transformation of Popular Religion in Medieval and Early-Modern Europe*, edited by Karen Margolis, translated by Susan Singerman, 10–27. Cambridge, England: Polity Press, 1990.

———. "Legends as Life-Strategies for Aspirant Saints in the Later Middle Ages." In *The Uses of Supernatural Power: The Transformation of Popular Religion in Medieval and Early-Modern Europe*, edited by Karen Margolis, translated by Susan Singerman, 95–110. Cambridge, England: Polity Press, 1990.

Ladurie, Emmanuel LeRoy. *Montaillou: The Promised Land of Error.* Translated by Barbara Bray. New York: Vintage Books, 1986.

Lee, Harold, Marjorie Reeves, and Giulio Silano. *Western Mediterranean Prophecy: The School of Joachim of Fiore and the Fourteenth-Century Breviloquium.* Toronto: Pontifical Institute of Medieval Studies, 1989.

Lehmann, Harmut. "The Cultural Importance of the Pious Middle Classes in Seventeenth-Century Protestant Society." In *Religion and Society in Early Modern Europe, 1500–1800*, edited by Kaspar von Greyerz, 33–41. London: George Allen and Unwin, 1984.

Levack, Brian P. *The Witch-Hunt in Early Modern Europe.* 3rd ed. Harlow, Essex: Pearson Longman, 2006.

Lima, Fernando de Castro Pires de. *S. João na alma do povo.* Porto: Portucalense Editora, 1944.

Lins, Ivan. *Para conhecer melhor António Vieira.* Rio de Janeiro: Bloch Editores, 1974.

Lipiner, Elias. *O Sapateiro de Trancoso e o Alfaiate de Setúbal.* Rio de Janeiro: Imago, 1993.

Maças, Delmira. *Os Animais na linguagem portuguesa*. Lisbon: Centro de Estudos Filológicos, 1950.

Manuel, Frank E., and Fritzie P. Manuel. *Utopian Thought in the Western World*. Cambridge: Harvard University Press, Belknap Press, 1979.

Mattoso, José. *A Primeira tarde portuguesa*. Guimarães, Portugal: Editora do Minho, 1979.

Mauro, Frédéric. *Le Portugal et L'Atlantique au XVIIe Siècle (1570–1670)*. Paris: S.E.V.P.E.N., 1960.

McGinn, Bernard. "Forms of Catholic Millenarianism: A Brief Overview." In *Millenarianism and Messianism in Early Modern European Culture*, vol. 2, *Catholic Millenarianism, from Savonarola to the Abbé Grégoire*, edited by Karl A Kottman, 1–13. Dordrecht: Kulwer Academic Publishers, 2001.

Mendeiros, José Filipe. "O Olivento Sebastião do Couto, mestre insigne da Universidade de Évora e alma das Alterações de 1637." *Anais da Academia Portuguesa da História* 18 (1969): 19–32.

Muir, Edward. "Introduction: Observing Trifles." In *Microhistory and the Lost Peoples of Europe*, edited by Edward Muir and Guido Ruggiero, translated by Eren Branch, vii–xxviii. Baltimore: Johns Hopkins University Press, 1991.

Mullett, Michael A. *The Catholic Reformation*. London: Routledge, 1999.

Nalle, Sara Tilghman. *Mad for God: Bartolomé Sánchez, the Secret Messiah of Cardenete*. Charlottesville : University Press of Virginia, 2001.

Neves, António da Silva. *Bandarra: O Profeta de Trancoso*. Mem Martins, Portugal: Publicações Europa-América, 1990.

O'Connell, Marvin R. *The Counter Reformation, 1559–1610*. New York: Harper and Row, 1974.

Oliveira, António de. *Poder e oposição política em Portugal no período filipino (1580–1640)*. Lisbon: Difusão Editorial, 1990.

Oliveira Marques, A. H. de. *História de Portugal*. Vol. 2, *Do Renascimento às Revoluções Liberais*. Lisbon: Editorial Presença, 1997.

Orden, Kate van. *Street Songs and Cheap Print during the French Wars of Religion*. Berkeley: Doe Library of the University of California, 1998.

Paiva, José Pedro. *Bruxaria e superstição num país sem "caça às bruxas," 1600–1774*. Lisbon: Notícias Editorial, 1997.

Pereira, Gabriel. *Estudos eborenses: As vespereas da Restauração*. Vols. 1–2. Évora, Portugal: Minerva Eborense, 1886–87.

Pereira, Isaías da Rosa. *Processos de feitiçaria e de bruxaria na Inquisição de Portugal*. Lisbon: Academia Portuguesa da História, 1982.

Perry, Mary Elizabeth. "*Beatas* and the Inquisition in Early Modern Seville." In *Inquisition and Society in Early Modern Europe*, edited and translated by Stephen Haliczer, 147–68. London: Croom Helm, 1987.

Pleij, Herman. *Dreaming of Cockaigne: Medieval Fantasies of the Perfect Life*. Translated by Diane Webb. New York: Columbia University Press, 2001.

Po-Chia Hsia, Richard. *Social Discipline in the Reformation: Central Europe, 1550–1750*. London: Routledge, 1989.

———. *The World of Catholic Renewal, 1540–1770*. Cambridge: Cambridge University Press, 1998.

Poska, Allyson M., and Elizabeth A. Lehfeldt. "Redefining Expectations: Women and the Church in Early Modern Spain." In *Women and Religion in Old and New Worlds*, edited by Susan E. Dinan and Debra Meyers, 21–42. New York: Routledge, 2001.

Quadros, António. *Poesia e filosofia do mito sebastianista*. Vols. 1–2. Lisbon: Guimarães & C.ª Editores, 1983.

Rapley, Elizabeth. *The Dévotes: Women and Church in Seventeenth-Century France*. Montreal: McGill-Queen's University Press, 1990.

Reeves, Marjorie. "The Abbott Joachim and the Society of Jesus." In *Joachim of Fiore in Christian Thought: Essays on the Influence of the Calabrian Prophet*, edited by Delno C. West, 209–27. New York: Burt Frankling and Co., 1975.

———. "Joachimist Influences on the Idea of the Last World Emperor." In *Joachim of Fiore in Christian Thought: Essays on the Influence of the Calabrian Prophet*, edited by Delno C. West, 511–58. New York: Burt Frankling and Co., 1975.

———. *Joachim of Fiore and the Prophetic Future: A Medieval Study in Historical Thinking*. Stroud, Gloucestershire: Sutton Publishing, 1999.

Rêgo, Yvonne Cunha. *Feiticeiros, profetas e visionários: Textos antigos portugueses*. Lisbon: Imprensa Nacional da Casa de Moeda, 1981.

Reinhard, Wolfgang. "Disciplinamento sociale, confessionalizzazione modernizzazione: Un discorso storiografico." Translated by Chiara Zanoni Zorzi. In *Disciplina dell'anima, disciplina del corpo e disciplina della società tra medioevo ed età moderna*, edited by Paolo Prodi and Carla Pennuti, 101–23. Bologna: Società editrice il Mulino, 1994.

Rodrigues, Francisco, S.J. "A Companhia de Jesus e a Restauração de Portugal (1640)." In *Anais da Academia Portuguesa da História*, vol. 6. Lisbon: Academia Portuguesa da História, 1942.

Rodrigues Cavalheiro, António. "Os antecedentes da Restauração a a posição do Duque de Bragança." In *Congresso do Mundo Português*, 7:11–56. Lisbon: Secção de Congressos, 1940.

Ruas, Henrique Barrilaro. *Luís de Camões*. Lisbon: Grifo, 1999.

Ruggiero, Guido. *Binding Passions: Tales of Magic, Marriage, and Power at the End of the Renaissance*. New York: Oxford University Press, 1993.

Santana, Francisco. *Bruxas e curandeiros na Lisboa joanina*. Lisbon: Academia Portuguesa da História, 1996.

Schutte, Anne Jacobson. *Aspiring Saints: Pretense of Holiness, Inquisition, and Gender in the Republic of Venice, 1618–1750*. Baltimore: Johns Hopkins University Press, 2001.

Serrão, Joel, ed. *Alterações de Évora, 1637*. Lisbon: Portugália Editora, 1967.

———, ed. "Macedo, Doutor António de Sousa de (1606–1682)." *Dicionário de história de Portugal*, 4:112–13. Porto: Livraria Figuerinhas, 2000.

Serrão, Joel, and A. H. de Oliveira Marques. *Nova história de Portugal*. Vol. 5, *Portugal, Do Renascimento à crise dinástica*. Lisbon: Editorial Presença, 1999.

Skinner, Quentin. *The Foundations of Modern Political Thought*. Vol. 2, *The Age of Reformation*. Cambridge: Cambridge University Press, 1978.

Tedeschi, John. "Inquisitorial Law and the Witch." In *Early Modern European Witchcraft: Centres and Peripheries*, edited by Bengt Ankarloo and Gustav Henningsen, 83–118. Oxford: Clarendon Press, 1990.

———. "The Roman Inquisition and Witchcraft: An Early Seventeenth-Century 'Instruction' on Correct Trial Procedure." In *The Prosecution of Heresy: Collected Studies on the Inquisition in Early Modern Italy*, 205–27. Binghamton, NY: Medieval and Renaissance Texts and Studies, 1991.

Teixeira Pinto, Pavlo. *Do Direito ao império em D. Sebastião*. Lisbon: Mirandela & Ca., 1985.

Valensi, Lucette. *Fables de la memoire: La glorieuse bataille des trois rois*. Paris: Seuil, 1992.

Valladares, Rafael. *Felipe IV y la restauración de Portugal*. Málaga: Editorial Algazara, 1994.

Veríssimo Serrão, Joachim. *História de Portugal*. Vol. 4, *O Governo dos Reis Espanhóis (1580–1640)*. Lisbon: Editorial Verbo, 1990.

———. *História de Portugal*. Vol. 5, *A Restauração e A Monarchia Absoluta (1640–1750)*. Lisbon: Editorial Verbo, 1996.

———. *O tempo dos Filipes em Portugal e no Brasil (1580–1668)*. Lisbon: Colibri História, 1994.

West, Delno C., and Sandra Zimdars-Swartz. *Joachim of Fiore: A Study in Spiritual Perception and History*. Bloomington: Indiana University Press, 1983.

INDEX

Note: "MM" refers to Maria de Macedo.